A Rabbi and His Dream

Building The Brotherhood Synagogue

A Memoir

Photo: Hal Reiff

A Rabbi and His Dream

Building The Brotherhood Synagogue

A Memoir

Rabbi Irving J. Block

KTAV Publishing House, Inc.
Hoboken, NJ

Library of Congress Cataloging-in-Publication Data

Block, Irving J.
    A rabbi and his dream : building the Brotherhood Synagogue : a
memoir / Irving J. Block.
        p.   cm.
ISBN 0-88125-657-9
1. Block, Irving J. 2. Brotherhood Synagogue (New York, N.Y.)
3. Rabbis--New York (State) --New York --Biography. 4. Judaism-
-Relations--Christianity--1945- 5. Christianity and other religions--
--Judaism --1945 I. Title.
BM755.B594A3 1999
296'.09747 ' 1--dc21

                                                              99-18025
                                                                  CIP

Manufactured in the United States of America

Dedication

To
My dear wife
Phyllis Susan Block
whose life personifies the idea
of religious brotherhood.
תנו לה מפרי ידיה, ויהללוה בשערים מעשיה
"Give her of the fruit of her hands,
And let her own works praise her in the gates."

PROVERBS 31:31

Table of Contents

Preface   ix

Introduction   xi

Foreword by Rabbi Block   xv

Acknowledgements   xix

1. Jerusalem 1947-1948   1

2. A Connecticut Yankee   19

3. Studying for the Rabbinate   35

4. Founding The Brotherhood Synagogue   55

5. Building a Congregation   87

6. Rabbi and Minister: Telling Our Story   109

7. Dr. Stitt Retires, New Minister Spurns Covenant   135

8. In Search of a New Home   161

9. Conflict and Crisis   187

10. A Decade of Achievement   207

11. "The People's Synagogue"   229

12. Black Jewish Communities   259

13. Christian-Jewish Relations: A Personal Perspective   279

14. A Lifetime of Service   301

15. Israel as I See It   325

16. Summing Up   345

Addendum   361

Preface

At the Kiddush following my first visit to The Brotherhood Synagogue, I remember being impressed with the dignity of the Shabbat service, the comfort level of the Bar Mitzvah boy, and the friendliness of the congregation. Rabbi Block then greeted me warmly and asked if I could help him with an important task back in the Sanctuary. There we went up and down all the aisles straightening the Bibles and prayer books in their racks.

Over the years as an assistant and associate to Rabbi Irving J. Block, I learned much from my mentor. And my education began with the straightening of those books. In the words of the Hasidic figure, Leib son of Sarah: "I came to my teacher, the great Maggid of Mezeritch, not to listen to discourses, nor to learn from his wisdom; I came to watch him tie his shoelaces."

The import of this declaration is that the religious dimension is to be found in even the smallest details, that how we perform the everyday, seemingly mundane tasks of life can raise us to a higher spiritual level. Religious ritual is the basis of our particularity, and ethical behavior often depends more on learned habits than on principle.

That we should be concerned with the feelings of our shoes (which one gets put on first, which one gets tied first) extends our compassion to inanimate objects. If we should not offend our shoelaces, if we should straighten a book containing God's name, then how much more so we should be sensitive to our fellow human beings created in God's image. Rabbi Block, in his life-long dedication to the idea of brotherhood, exemplifies my Seminary teaching that one kind act will teach more about the love of God than a thousand sermons. It was in The Brotherhood Synagogue that I truly learned the beauty of holiness.

When Rabbi Block elected to retire and I was named his successor, I heard the constant refrain of what "big shoes they were to fill." But what always impressed me was not the size of his shoes but the many miles they travelled in so many trailblazing directions. Rabbi Block's memoirs are a fascinating record of that journey. I pray that the congregation will continue to strive toward the lofty ideals of The Brotherhood Synagogue that he established. May we always be concerned where our feet take us, for where we show up is often the greatest indication of our priorities and values.

January 1999   Rabbi Daniel Alder

Introduction

I first met Rabbi Irving Block in 1959 when he came to speak in the synagogue in which I was then serving in New Jersey. He was joined by his colleague and friend, the Rev. Dr. Jesse W. Stitt, a Presbyterian minister, and the two described for an enthralled audience their unique and unprecedented experiment in brotherhood: the two served congregations occupying one building in Greenwich Village. They shared facilities; they exchanged pulpits; they even covered for each other on occasion. The Brotherhood Synagogue, which Rabbi Block had founded in 1954, had entered into a remarkable Covenant with its Presbyterian partners, whose building hosted the two congregations. It was a partnership that was to last magnificently for over seventeen years until the untimely death of Dr. Stitt. His successor, alas, shared none of the minister's grand vision and love of the Jewish people to such a point that the Synagogue congregation felt compelled to seek its own quarters, which it did on historic Gramercy Park in a former Quaker Meeting House. The partnership may have been dissolved but the dream continued in a new venue.

This is the story of that uniquely inspiring experiment. It was an experiment based on Rabbi Block's commitment to the ideal that "brotherhood is still the hope of the world." And The Brotherhood Synagogue never swerved from that path. Yes, there were times when some of the laity of The Brotherhood Synagogue assailed Rabbi Block for spending too much time on interfaith matters with non-Jews. But to my astonishment, the normally gentle and genial Rabbi Irving Block tilted swords with his detractors and prevailed. He prevailed because his cause was just and his methods were beneficent.

The Brotherhood Synagogue did not just confine its work to interfaith matters. Indeed, it served as an exemplar to other synagogues and pioneered (as I learned for the first time) in a variety of diverse areas. It was the first synagogue to develop religious education for the retarded. It showed the way for other houses of worship to design their structures for the disabled by adding ramps and an elevator. It followed Rabbi Block's lead (despite some objections) to welcome the community at large to worship on the High Holydays without tickets or membership status, thereby fulfilling Isaiah's dream that God's house would be a house of worship for all the people. It opened the first synagogue shelter for the homeless in 1983. It created a charming biblical garden and a memorial garden and launched the first synagogue-sponsored coffee house to bring together young people in a Jewish environment. The Brotherhood Synagogue also pioneered in bringing interns from the neighboring General Theological Seminary, a Protestant (Episcopal) school, to the Synagogue to work with Rabbi Block and learn about Judaism first hand.

Irving Block never seemed to lack both ingenuity and chutzpah. He and Dr. Stitt went to merchants, banks and the Parks Department cajoling them into erecting Menorot at Chanukah time. He was one of the very first in the Jewish community to reach out to Black Jews, welcoming them into the bosom of the synagogue and Jewish life. Nor should we forget his role in dramatizing the plight of Ethiopian Jewry at a time when few in this country or in Israel for that matter, really cared about that exotic body of Jews. Naturally, Israel has occupied a crucial role in Rabbi Block's life and loyalties as the book amply documents. But who could expect less from a rabbi who had gone to study at the Hebrew University only to end up a soldier in the Haganah in Israel's desperate struggle for independence?

All through the richly productive years of his rabbinate until his retirement in 1994, Rabbi Irving Block eschewed party labels and championed a Synagogue that would serve the needs of all Jews; that would be at once traditional and liberal; that would revere Jewish tradition, yet would not be bound to ironclad rules. Rabbi Block sums up his philosophy in a succinct paragraph:

"It requires tremendous efforts to build bonds of mutual respect; sadly, it sometimes takes but a misguided act by a single individual to tear them apart. Our task is to teach each generation that there are many points of view and that we are all the children of God."

This is a beautiful book because it is by and about a beautiful man who has found favor and pleasure in the eyes of God and humanity.

January 1999   Rabbi Gilbert S. Rosenthal
                                Executive Vice President,
                                The New York Board of Rabbis

Foreword by Rabbi Block

It has been said that a man should accomplish three goals in his lifetime: develop his skills so that he may be gainfully employed, raise a family, and write a book. I have achieved two of the goals, and now the third.

On numerous occasions when I have described the philosophy and history of The Brotherhood Synagogue, people have said to me, "Yours is a story waiting to be told." Interestingly, the sages believe that one of the reasons why God made man is because God loves good stories!

The year of my retirement in 1994 marked four decades since my ordination as a rabbi. The number 40 is frequently referred to in biblical texts: the 40 days Moses spent on Mount Sinai; the 40 years the Israelites wandered from Egypt to the Land of Promise; and, as recorded in the Book of Judges, the 40-year periods in which the land had peace.

At a special program marking my retirement, the congregation gave me a gift of a "monogrammed" computer. The committee called my attention to the three letters IBM affixed to the monitor and explained that they stood for "Irving **B**lock's **M**emoirs."

I had long hoped to write a history of our Synagogue and now I would have the time to do so; but it has taken much longer than I had anticipated because there was such a rich lode of material to review. As I was reviewing old files, bulletins, journals, and newspaper clippings, and reminiscing with our members, even I was amazed at how much we as a congregation have achieved in so many areas of Jewish life and community service. I am so proud of our fine reputation.

As I wrote and rewrote each chapter, I was mindful of a compelling verse in the Midrash: "God revised the Torah four times before giving it to Israel." I asked myself, shall I, being a mere mortal *(basar va'dam)*, do anything less?

Yet another reason why the research and writing moved along slowly is that Parkinson's Disease has taken a toll on my physical strength. I am grateful to my physicians for their excellent care, which has enabled me to manage reasonably well.

I wanted to write this book because ecumenism has been one of the hallmarks of The Brotherhood Synagogue. I believe a more traditionally oriented synagogue is in a better position to develop a brotherhood program with a congregation not of our faith. It is essential, however, that the minister be a friend of Israel and the Jewish people; otherwise, don't even think of starting.

It is also my hope that this book will encourage Jews who are unaffiliated to seek out a synagogue — regardless of the branch of Judaism — a spiritual environment where they can feel "at home" and at the same time be counted among the household of Israel.

Perhaps some of my experiences can be instructive to my younger rabbinic colleagues and guide them in their relationships with congregational leaders and the community. I would urge them to evaluate their efforts from the viewpoint of heaven — how does their work appear in the sight of God? — and to recognize that what some people might consider failures may become opportunities for even greater achievements.

The first eleven chapters of the book, except for Chapter 1, are in chronological order. I made the decision to begin my memoir with a flashback to the turbulent months I spent in Eretz Yisrael in 1947 and 1948, before I entered rabbinical school, because that year preceding statehood defined and profoundly affected the course of my career, indeed my entire life.

In the following chapters I review my childhood years, my Hebrew and secular education, rabbinical school training, the founding of our Synagogue, our unique partnership with a congregation of another faith, the dissolution of this partnership, the challenges we faced, how we came to Gramercy Park, a major crisis from within, our determination to overcome these conflicts, and our many pioneering and innovative programs and activities. In the concluding sections I discuss my thoughts on the Black Jewish community, Jewish-Christian relations, my years of community service, and the State of Israel. The final chapter sums up the beliefs and aspirations that have guided me through life.

As I was writing, I endeavored to be mindful of the requirement of giving credit where credit is due *(B'sham Omru)*. "Whoever learns from another," says the Talmud *(Ethics of the Fathers)*, "even a single letter, ought to pay honor to that person." I tried carefully not to overlook anyone.

In God's House the element of love must ever be present. I hope I have succeeded in conveying the deep feelings of love that have emanated from the members of The Brotherhood Synagogue since its inception, and, in the words of the Talmud, I fervently pray that these sentiments will flourish for many more years to come.

> *May the Almighty who has caused His name to dwell*
> *in this house*
> *cause to dwell among you*
> *love and brotherhood*
> *and peace and friendship.*

Acknowledgements

This project would not have been possible without the encouragement and love of family, members and friends of my congregation. I want to acknowledge my heartfelt gratitude to those who have assisted in so many ways.

There are two people in particular who have brought to this task professional editing skills: one is Inge Dobelis, a past President of our Synagogue, who read through all the early drafts, an assignment she volunteered to assume, and whose suggestions for organizing and presenting the material improved the text enormously. The other is my wife, Phyllis, who edited all the drafts and gave totally of her time, talent, and strength and whose devoted support enabled me to complete this book.

I express my gratitude to Malcolm Davis, President of our congregation, the Synagogue officers and members of our Board of Trustees for their enthusiasm and encouragement, as well as to all who contributed so generously to the Rabbi's Writing Fund. At my request, all proceeds from the sale of this book will benefit The Brotherhood Synagogue.

The initial funds required to begin work on this book were provided by a very generous benefactor, Bertram Teich, who steadfastly believes in a vision of a world of brotherhood. All of us are extremely grateful to him.

I appreciate the gracious remarks in the Preface and Introduction by Rabbi Daniel Alder, my highly regarded successor, and by my esteemed colleague and friend, Rabbi Gilbert S. Rosenthal.

Facts were not always at my fingertips and I thank those whose research spared me a great deal of time and effort: my son,

Herbert, used his computer to prepare a birthday gift for me —
references to The Brotherhood Synagogue and his father in daily
New York City newspapers from November 1970 through January
1993, and whose college term paper on the history of our building was an important resource.   Suzanne Goldberg efficiently
organized forty years of Synagogue bulletins, and Robert Halpern
classified my files, which facilitated my research.   Lucie Benedikt
and Elizabeth Hendricks shared their remembrances of the activities of the Quakers in the Meeting House during the post World
War II years. Eli N. Evans's description of our congregation
became the title of Chapter 11, and Jeffrey Friedman used his
computer skills to research a Talmudic verse.

I appreciate the interest of others who were kind enough to
read parts or all of the text and whose insightful comments were
very helpful: Herbert Block; James D. Dougherty, past president
of the Gramercy Neighborhood Associates; Vertella Gadsden, past
President of our Synagogue, who discussed with me the Black
Jews of America; The Rev. Stephen Garmey, Vicar of Calvary
Church, author of *Gramercy Park—An Illustrated History of a New
York Neighborhood* (Balsam Press, 1984), an important historical
resource; Lois B. Grayck, administrator of the Center for Jewish-
Christian Relations and Studies at the General Theological
Seminary; Moshe Kagan, a member of the Jewish Agency; Rabbi
Leon Klenicki, Director of the Department of Interfaith Affairs of
the Anti-Defamation League of B'nai B'rith; Rabbi Hailu Paris, for
his in-depth review of the chapter on Black Jewish communities;
the noted author Ralph Martin; Elizabeth Moger, Keeper of the
Records of the New York Meeting of the Religious Society of
Friends; Edna Rosenman of the New York Association for New
Americans; Phillip Rothman, Executive Director and Education

Director of The Brotherhood Synagogue; and our members Wally
Dobelis, who supervises our homeless shelter; Roslyn Statsinger,
who chaired our art shows for a number of years; and Martin
Warmbrand, who has long been involved with the Black Jewish
community.

I also want to convey my gratitude to Arthur J. Greenbaum, a
Trustee and past Chairman of our Board, for his friendship over
the years and his wise counsel in the preparation of this book; to
Comm. I. Joseph Harris, a past Trustee whom I have known since
my days as a rabbinical student and who talked with me for hours
about the book and its approach even before I began writing, and
who read the entire text; and to Hon. Robert J. Ward, also a
Trustee, whose family has been part of the congregation since our
first year. His suggestions and guidance reflected his deep understanding of the law and of human nature.

A number of longtime members of the congregation reminisced
with me and recorded "oral histories": Dr. Robert and Marion
Brown; May Lipton Cummins; Selma Frishling, our first Synagogue
secretary; Minna Michael; Annette Siepser Rosner; Diane and
Allan Shafer; Dr. Nathan and Ruth Schutz; Lillian Zucker; and my
brother and former Associate, Rabbi A. Allen Block.

How were books written before word processing? I was fortunate to have had the assistance of some very skilled computer
specialists in the congregation: David Cohen and Wally Dobelis,
who selected and set up the computer, and Devick Sellam, who
patiently taught us how to use it and managed the files.

The formidable task of entering the text into the computer and
making the revisions was carried out by a team of dedicated,
skilled word processors, especially our member Naomi Jones,
who worked on the book from beginning to end for over three

years, and Cynthia Bell, who typed the final revisions. I express my thanks to them and to Otto Berk, Sharon Brown, Judith Chaitow, Cynthia Dorner, Susan Einarson, Jenifer Kari Gold, Peggy Keilus, Molly Riemer, Grace Rubin, and to three students from Yeshiva College and Stern College, Luba Nakhutina, Ricky Novick, and Rachel Tawil. Marti Wagner carefully reviewed page proof.

The Synagogue staff was always helpful. Phillip Rothman, our Executive Director, assisted in countless ways, tangible and intangible, and I appreciate the interest in this project on the part of the office staff: Judi Golden, Nori Goldsmith, and Peggy Keilus.

Florence Reiff, a member of our congregation, graciously presented me with photographs of our Gramercy Park building and activities, as well as portraits, taken by her late husband, the eminent photographer Hal Reiff, and I greatly appreciate this priceless gift to the Synagogue.

Some of the photographs were taken especially for this book by our members Arthur Kantor and Ben Saltzman, and I am grateful to them for sharing their time and talents with us.

I express my gratitude to the New York Times and to all the photographers who gave me permission to use their work in this book. I regret that in a few cases I was unable to contact some of them personally, but I have indicated their names in the photo credits.

I also want to thank the staff of Kanter Press, stationers, and Dependable Printing, copying services, for their many courtesies.

Bernard Scharfstein of KTAV Publishing House encouraged me to move forward with my desire to tell the history of our congregation. I appreciate his confidence in the project from the outset.

In the course of the years I have been influenced by distinguished rabbis and lay leaders in the field of interreligious affairs whose writings and activities have helped shape my own thinking. I express my abiding thanks to them and to all my clergy colleagues.

I wish I could have mentioned everyone in my beloved congregation and in the Village Presbyterian Church with whom I worked so closely, particularly in the early years, and whose efforts and faith helped me achieve my dream — building The Brotherhood Synagogue.

To all, I say *Todah Rabah* — my abiding thanks.

January 1999   I.J.B.
Shevat 5759

1

Jerusalem 1947–1948

"The personal contribution made by each one of you...
as well as the personal sacrifices were all part of
the great endeavor made at the time to build
a new State of Israel... and you should all be
proud of the role you played."

YITZHAK RABIN, MINISTER OF DEFENSE 1988,
AT THE 40TH WORLD MAHAL REUNION IN ISRAEL

It has been said that the stones in the Land of Israel are heavier than in other lands. When you lie stretched out on one of the hills of Jerusalem at night with a grenade in one hand and a pistol in the other, the stones pressing against your rib cage not only feel heavy but are exceedingly hard.

In the final days of 1947 a unit of the Haganah, assigned to a Palmach[1] command, lay absolutely quiet and prostrate on one of the hills of Jerusalem in the darkness of the night. I was part of that unit. With reports of armed bands of Arabs seen in the vicinity of the Katamon neighborhood for several nights, the Haganah commanders decided to clear the area. Our unit, formed for the most part of American students who had come to Jerusalem to

---

1. The Palmach was the fighting unit of the Haganah, the defense forces of the Jewish people in the days prior to the birth of the State of Israel.

study at the Hebrew University, was selected for this assignment. Now we were bound together in combat as we were in study.

That night, before leaving the base of operation, we were carefully checked over to be certain that our clothing was dark and that we were wearing sneakers or rubber-soled shoes to muffle our steps. As the officers doled out weapons from a cardboard box, it became obvious that no two guns were alike. I was handed a grenade and I asked myself, Why me? Was it because in the training sessions a few days earlier the ability of my left arm to hurl objects had made an impression? When I requested a pistol or a revolver as well, the only weapon left in the box was a semiautomatic pistol whose wooden handles had fallen off. "How in the world do you fire this?" I asked. The officer acknowledged that it was a very dangerous weapon because the exposed coiled springs could slice your hands into pieces when the weapon was fired. Spotting a small piece of cardboard and a rubber band, I wrapped them around the gun's metal frame as a shield, figuring that this would be better than nothing.

As we waited for the action to begin, each passing moment seemed like an eternity. The night winds carried echoes from afar so that it became difficult to tell whether the Arab voices we heard came from over the hill or whether the enemy was closer. The cold stones on the ground gave no comfort. Fortunately I had taken along my leather jacket and a woolen scarf, and I managed to pull them down quietly to cover my thighs.

Now and then I felt the grenade to make certain that the pin was in a secure position, and my fingers would touch the letters *USA* etched into the metal. During our training session I had asked the instructor whether that inscription meant these weapons came from the United States of America. With a wry smile, he replied, "USA stands for the Yiddish words *Undzer*

Szelbshtendike Arbet—the product of our own handiwork." I cannot recall all the thoughts that entered my mind at the time, but I must have often asked myself, How did I get into this situation?

I felt like our forefather Jacob on the first night of his journey from Beersheba to Haran. In an area very close to where my Haganah unit was stationed that evening, he had interrupted his journey to gather rocks to build a protective wall around himself and to find a secure place in which to sleep. That was a night of dreams, of angels ascending and descending a ladder. And when he awoke he said, "How full of wonderment is this place! This is none other than the House of God and this is the gate of heaven." Jacob prayed to God that if he were ever returned to his family in safety, he would erect a sanctuary on that spot. I too made a pledge on the hills of Jerusalem, that if God would take care of me, I would endeavor to make God's world a better place to live in. After a while the Arab voices faded away and the operation was called off. We returned to our base.

FIRST WEEKS IN PALESTINE

I had come to Palestine during the summer following graduation from the University of Connecticut, where I had received the degree of Bachelor of Science in Business Administration. I was now eager to broaden my knowledge with studies in humanities, leading to ordination in the rabbinate. I had heard that the Hebrew University in Jerusalem was accepting applications from abroad and that I would be eligible to study under the GI Bill of Rights for World War II veterans. Since all costs would be basically covered, I could fulfill my hope and dream to study in that historic city so dear to the hearts of Jewish people. I applied and was accepted.

In July 1947 I boarded the SS *Marine Carp*, sailing from New York to Haifa. The ship was one of many vessels hastily constructed during World War II that plied the seas transporting soldiers and equipment and, like all troop ships, totally lacked passenger conveniences and amenities.

The two-week voyage took us across the Atlantic, through the Strait of Gibraltar, and into the blue waters of the Mediterranean. Time went by quickly. We were fully aware that we were coming to this ancient land during turbulent times. Great Britain had long ago reneged on its promise, affirmed by the Balfour Declaration of November 2, 1917, that it would look with favor upon the establishment in Palestine of a national home for the Jewish people. The League of Nations had authorized Great Britain to establish such a homeland of 40,000 square miles, but by the time of the San Remo Conference in 1920, the British government had reduced that area to 10,000 square miles. Now even this sliver of land was in jeopardy.

As the hills of Mount Carmel and Haifa came into view, we gathered at the railing and sang songs of the *chalutzim* (pioneers of Israel), expressing exaltation over the rebuilding of the land and redemption of the Jewish people.

Aboard ship there had been little else to do but converse with other passengers and hear their reasons for going to Palestine. One person I met was Eva Altman. She was traveling to visit her niece and nephew, who lived in Jerusalem and whose last name was Bloch. Naturally we began to discuss whether there was any relationship between her family and mine, but we could only conclude that all Jews were related to one another. Through that conversation, however, I met a wonderful family.

Since I was also going to Jerusalem but had not arranged for a place to stay, Mrs. Altman offered the assistance of her nephew, who was going to meet her in Haifa. Heinrich Bloch proved ready and willing to help. He was a broad-shouldered young man in his forties, serious-minded and intelligent. "Do as I do and follow me," he advised, and together we managed to get through the customs procedures with the usual tumult and aggravation that occur in every port. I paused to recite the benediction of *Shehecheyanu*: "Thank God for keeping me alive, sustaining me, and bringing me to this moment when I can put my feet upon the ancestral soil."

As I sat in the bus that was taking us to Jerusalem, my eyes darted about everywhere. What a beautiful land, compact and varied—coastal plains, a mountain range, sloping valleys, plateaus, farmland, and clusters of villages in the hills. When the bus shifted gears, climbing the slope of the Judean hills and going over the crest into Jerusalem, stone houses glowed in the setting sun; I understood then why it was called a City of Gold.

We arrived at the Egged bus station in the center of town just minutes before the 7:00 P.M. curfew imposed by the British. Everyone was in a state of frenzy. Fortunately, we found a taxi and convinced the driver to take us the two short blocks to Beit Aboulafia, an apartment house at 20 Ben Yehuda Street. Within moments we rushed into the building and up the stairs to the third-floor apartment where other members of the family were eagerly waiting for Mrs. Altman. There was no time for formalities. Hurriedly, the steel shutters of the windows were closed as the sirens wailed their curfew. Anyone seen on the street after that hour could be detained, arrested, or even shot.

"And now, who is this young man?" asked Eve Altman's niece Maryla, Heinrich's wife, a woman with a gentle manner and beautiful speech. Aunt Eva explained that we had met aboard ship and discovered the similarity of our names, that I planned to study at the Hebrew University, and that with the curfew approaching there had been no time for me to find lodging for the night.

The Blochs, a warm, friendly family with a three-year-old son, Binyamin, invited me to stay overnight. Also joining them for the night was Maryla's brother, Ezri Atzmon. As we sat at the dinner table, we heard an explosion at some distance from our building. I gazed at Ezri, wondering aloud what the reaction to that incident would be. Briefly he replied, "You have just come. Wait and you'll soon find out." Within a minute or two there was heavy machine-gun fire just outside the building. Quickly we crouched down on the floor and scampered to the water closet (bathroom). I can still hear the voice of little Binyamin ringing in my ears, crying out through his tears: "Why do they shoot in the streets of Jerusalem? Why don't they shoot in the streets of London?" Not even 24 hours had passed since my coming to the land of Palestine and already I was held captive by the struggle.

How strange life is! I remained in touch with the family, and seventeen years later, when Ezri Atzmon was Associate Professor in the Department of History and Philosophy of Education at New York University, he was a speaker at The Brotherhood Synagogue.

The next day I made arrangements with the Office of the Department of Youth to spend the first Shabbat weekend at Kfar Etzion, a religious kibbutz not too far from Jerusalem: I also made plans for a tour of major sites of interest. When I inquired whether any other students from the United States had arrived, I was told that there was one, Samuel Klausner, who was living in the Talpiot section of Jerusalem. Sam was very gracious, warm, and friendly—just what I needed at that time. After we talked a bit, he explained that he was in the midst of studies but suggested that I take a stroll with another guest whom he was expecting any moment, a young Frenchman who had served in the *maquis*, the wartime French resistance movement.

As this young man and I were rambling along the road leading to the Government House of the British High Commissioner, conversing as best we could in Hebrew, English, French, and Spanish, we heard an explosion. Turning toward the city, I could see frenzied activity—vehicles racing about in one of the nearby British camps. I beckoned to my new acquaintance to step out of view, as I was certain that the road we were on would be under surveillance. Indeed, in moments a British truck came roaring up the road in the direction of the Government House.

As soon as the truck was out of sight, I suggested that we turn around and walk back leisurely to avoid any suspicion. But hardly had we reached the road again when the same vehicle came bearing quickly down on us and stopped abruptly at our side. Six or seven British soldiers pointed their rifles at us and ordered us to keep our hands up. We were searched and asked for identification. I took my passport out of my jacket and announced, "Irving Block, Sergeant, United States Army." (I had merely left out the word "former.") My papers seemed to be in order, but when the officers spoke to the young Frenchman, who might have come to Palestine illegally, they could not find a common language in which to converse, despite my efforts to help. One of the officers beckoned to him, "Come along." I asked if I could accompany him, but the officer retorted, "No need to do that, he'll be back very shortly."

Sam Klausner berated me. "You shouldn't have let him go by himself. He'll be in prison a week to ten days." On the other hand, had I accompanied the young man during his interrogation, I could visualize the headlines in my hometown, Bridgeport,

Connecticut, blaring: "Local student in Palestine detained as suspected terrorist." And I could hear my father lamenting, "I told him to keep out of trouble." I learned that the young man was eventually released after two weeks, but I never saw him again. Samuel Klausner and I became friends. Later he became an eminent sociologist at the University of Pennsylvania.

Every rabbinic student ought to have a Hebrew Bible, a Tanach, and it was one of the first purchases I made in Jerusalem, in a store at the intersection of Jaffa and King David Roads. That blue-covered leather pocket Bible is still with me and I use it daily. But I was reluctant to make my next purchase, a small pocket knife that I thought would come in handy. My hesitancy was apparent to the storekeeper, and I explained that I just felt the incongruity of buying a book of God's word and a knife, a steel implement that could be used to commit an act of violence. The merchant then shared a Midrash (legend) with me, that the Book and the sword came down from heaven together. Our task in life is to choose between the spiritual and the material. Either we are going to follow the precepts of the Book and peace will prevail, or the sword will dominate and there will be only destruction. I reflected on his words and bought the little knife.

SUMMER ON A KIBBUTZ

The weeks between my arrival and the beginning of my classes at the Hebrew University gave me the wonderful opportunity to work in two kibbutzim. The first, called Maalé ha-Hamisha, was perched on a hill about eight miles from Jerusalem. The air was so clear there that at night we could see the lights of Tel Aviv. My assignment was to pick up rocks, place them in a basket, and carry them over to the slope of a hill that was to be terraced for planting vines. That task, called *sikul,* left me with an aching back but helped me to understand the beauty of the words of the Prophet Amos, "The mountains drip sweet wine and all the hills shall melt."

Then I spent a month on Kibbutz Dafna in the far north, not too far from where the River Dan receives its waters from Mount Hermon and begins its flow southward. Here my task was to pick apples, as well as to help prepare pools of water for breeding fish.

CAPTIVATED BY JERUSALEM

Just before Rosh Hashanah I returned to Jerusalem. I was fortunate to be able to spend the second day of the holiday at the Kotel Ha-Ma'aravi, the Western Wall (then referred to as the Wailing Wall), because someone in our group had obtained permission to do so and arranged for a guide to take us there. I shall never forget the sight of those massive stones out of which clusters of grass were growing from between the cracks. The area in front of the Wall was very small because the Arabs had over time constructed houses both to the right and the left of the Wall. Nonetheless, with my JWB abridged prayer book in hand—given to Jewish members of the U.S. armed forces by the Jewish Welfare Board—I felt many emotions surging within me as I stood in prayer before this glorious remnant of Jewish history.

In the weeks that followed I would often sit on the back steps of the university on Mount Scopus gazing endlessly at the Old City, which was highlighted by the glistening golden Dome of the Rock, the site from which Muslims believe Muhammad ascended to heaven. It adjoins the Western Wall, occupying an area known as the Temple Mount, where King Solomon had built his great House unto the Lord. On the other side of the university was an amphitheater from which one could see the mountains of Moab in the distant desert. I loved to walk through sections of Jerusalem, fascinated by the blending of the old and the new, and feeling that I had been there before. The city is one of such amazing beauty that it's no wonder it captured the hearts of the prophets and so enthralled them that they were inspired to teach their imperishable message of righteousness and social justice. From the crowns of the hilltops and into the valleys one can see how the rays of the sun strike the stone houses, throwing off a spectacular spectrum of colors.

All during 1947 Palestine had been at the center of the world's attention. The United Nations Special Commission on Palestine had filed a report indicating that the land could or should be divided between the Jewish and the Arab peoples. The decision to approve or reject the report came on Saturday evening, November 29, 1947, in New York City—midnight in Jerusalem. The commission recommended, and the United Nations General Assembly approved, that the land be partitioned into two states, one Jewish and one Arab.

I knew that the United Nations vote would be a great and historic occasion for our people, and I surely did not want to miss any celebration in Jerusalem. I had asked some friends in my dormitory, Pension Pax, to knock loudly on my door and inform me of the decision whenever it came. Shortly after midnight, I heard the knock; I dressed hastily and joined the hundreds of others who were pouring into the streets. What an extraordinary scene! On top of a British tank, young Jewish boys and girls, and even the tank crew, were waving blue and white flags. It seemed to foretell a Messianic moment when the lion and lamb might be sitting down together in peace.

The whole city was in a state of jubilation, one perhaps unparalleled in Jewish history for the past 2,000 years. People hardly took time to dress properly before coming out of their homes—some walked into the street wearing pajamas and robes. They came from the four corners of the city, pressing themselves toward its center around the Jewish Agency building. Almost every Jewish community was represented there that night—Ashkenazim from Europe, Sephardic Jews from Spain and North Africa, Yemenites and Kurds from Arabia—Jews from every country in the world. There were youngsters dressed in khaki shorts and short-sleeved shirts, and Hasidim wearing their black broad-brimmed *shtreimels* (fur hats). Although the Hasidim have strict codes against looking at women, the mood of the celebration was so joyful and overpowering that some even found themselves dancing with women.

For hours the large throng was caught up in dancing, and there in the circular driveway of the Jewish Agency building I too danced, I sang, I cried. I thought of my parents, whose efforts for the cause of Zionism helped make this moment possible. It was they who encouraged me to carry around the blue and white Jewish National Fund *pushka* (charity box) and collect funds for the restoration of the land that would someday be ours—the land that the Bible describes as flowing with milk and honey. I reflected on the words of Theodor Herzl, the father of modern Zionism, who, at the time of the first World Zionist Congress in Basel, Switzerland in 1897, wrote: "At Basel I founded the Jewish State. If I said this aloud today I would be answered by universal laughter. Perhaps in five years, certainly in fifty, everyone will agree."

Our joy was short-lived, for several days later columns of smoke were rising above the business section of the city. Arab bands were running amok, attacking Jewish businesses and setting them on fire. The outlook for peace now seemed bleak.

JOINING THE HAGANAH

Not long after these attacks, I was summoned to a dormitory room and asked by several of the students if I, like them, would join the Haganah fighters. The situation had become so volatile that every person was desperately needed. I paused for a moment and then replied, "My father urged me to avoid any involvement and trouble, but if he were here at this very moment he would surely want me to say yes."

Under the very noses of the British, American students at the Hebrew University were invited to a social evening of singing and dancing that, in reality, was an opportunity for Haganah officers to gather information about our military experience. To this day I carry in my wallet an identification card that was issued to me under the heading of "*Sherut Ha-Am*"—"for the service of the people." The officers in charge wanted to know what weapons we were familiar with, and I indicated the standard army rifle, the Colt 45 semiautomatic pistol, and the Thompson submachine gun (which was manufactured in my hometown of Bridgeport). Years later I learned that it was most likely General Uzi Narkiss, one of the 1967 liberators of Jerusalem, who conceived the idea of mobilizing American students at the Hebrew University, realizing that a number of us were World War II veterans with military training.

Our first Haganah training session was in the basement of the university's Teachers' Seminary. Young children were posted outside, ostensibly playing games, but really watching for any British vehicle coming to search the area. For more intensive training we went to a small village outside of Jerusalem, focusing on how to assemble and disassemble the sten gun. Since no two weapons were alike, we had to become familiar with many types of weapons manufactured in different countries. Our training sessions concluded with an instructor lobbing a hand grenade into the valley, and I reflected upon a verse from Psalms: "Yea, though I walk through the valley of the shadow of death, I will fear no evil."

I found that the *sabra* (native-born) sons and daughters were very clever in battle strategy and military ingenuity. I still smile when I recall an order passed through the ranks that we go to see movies depicting war scenes, especially films produced with the guidance of American and British military experts, and to observe the military tactics and maneuvers.

Events moved quickly. Each day brought new experiences. In 1947 the first night of Chanukah fell on December 7, and our unit was told to gather at the Bukharian Synagogue. We went up an outdoor flight of steps that led to the second-floor synagogue sanctuary, where we lit the first Chanukah candle and sang *Maoz Tzur*, "Rock of Ages." As we gazed upon the flickering candlelight, there was a knock on the door. The *shamas*, or sexton, of the synagogue went to the door and let in several pretty young women, their blouses and skirts revealing some rather buxom shapes. The young women followed the *shamas* to the Holy Ark and, as he took out the cloth bags in which prayer shawls and *tefillin* (phylacteries) were kept, they opened their blouses and brought out pistols, grenades, and parts of the sten gun. What a sight! So reminiscent of the indomitable spirit of the Maccabees! But that's how weapons were transported, and the young women were fully aware that if they were caught by the British, they would be arrested and the weapons confiscated.

Each day was a battle for Jewish survival, with murderous attacks by Arab bands requiring us to patrol the streets. One house was our military post, not too far from the landmark Montefiore windmill. We hid our revolvers there in an empty water tank high above the toilet bowl. We figured that the British would not poke their noses around such an unlikely hiding place.

Then, in January 1948, I was assigned to a team of two men to serve as backup to protect others who were conducting a night-time operation to stop and search cars entering Jerusalem. My partner, Moshe Perlstein, was a young man from Brooklyn whom I had met aboard ship on my way to Palestine. Moshe had been a yeshiva student and had no American military experience. Hidden and out of view, we talked in hushed tones as the night hours ticked by. He told me that he had joined a Hebrew-speaking unit of the Haganah to improve his language skills. At daybreak we returned to the site where we had procured our weapons and said good-bye.

Just one day later Moshe Perlstein and 34 other young men, many of them students at the Hebrew University, were ambushed on the way to relieve the military pressure on the Kfar Etzion bloc and to bring in needed supplies and aid. All 35 lost their lives, and their bodies were mutilated. When they were discovered, some of these brave young soldiers were still clutching the rocks they had grabbed when their ammunition was spent. When I learned the tragic news from one of the officers, I was so over-wrought that I literally seized his lapels screaming, "Tell me it's not so, tell me it's not so!!" giving him such a shaking that he almost fell backward.

Moshe Perlstein became the first American to lose his life in the battle. Several thousand other men and women from the United States and Canada, as well as from all over the world, volunteered their skills and services to participate in Israel's War of Independence, and over a hundred of them, Jews and Christians, gave their lives so that the State of Israel could come into being. They have earned the eternal gratitude of the Jewish people.

A CALL FROM AMERICA

One day I received a telephone call from Connecticut from my sister Lillian, who, at the insistence of our family physician, reported that our mother's health had greatly deteriorated. She was very weak, and I was urged to return home. The call stunned me and I paced the floor for hours, pondering what to do. I knew that the military situation was perilous and that every individual was desperately needed in the battle for Jewish survival. When I finally made the decision to return, I comforted myself with the thought that I would be able to continue my efforts on behalf of Israel by doing some vital work in the United States, such as speaking to groups about the situation in Palestine and helping recruit experienced military personnel. It was a difficult but correct decision, for my mother passed away not long after.

On Sunday, February 22, 1948, I boarded an early morning bus for Tel Aviv, the first leg of a sad journey back to the United States. About five or ten minutes after six o'clock the driver was going through the aisles to collect tickets and make sure all bags were properly secured, when suddenly there was a tremendous explosion, which seemed to throw our bus into the air. I can hear the driver's voice: "Do not panic, do not panic!" He ran to his seat, slammed the door of the bus shut, roared the engines, and swiftly drove out of the bus station. All we could see behind us were clouds of dust and flying debris. Later we learned that it was Ben Yehuda Street that had been blown up, just two short blocks from the bus station—and across the street from the building where I had spent my first night in Jerusalem. More than 50 people were reported killed and over 120 wounded, an enormous tragedy perpetrated by Arab and British collaborators.

En route to Tel Aviv, the bus stopped just once, flagged down by a Haganah unit to warn us about possible danger on the highway, and so we alighted from the bus to gather rocks and stones as our weapons of defense. When we finally arrived in Tel Aviv, the passengers exclaimed in almost one voice to the driver: "Thank you, thank you so much." He replied, "Do not thank me, thank God that we are here."

On May 14, 1948, the State of Israel officially came into existence. I was in Champaign-Urbana speaking at the University of Illinois at the invitation of Rabbi Sanford Saperstein, Hillel director of the university, who had learned about my service in Palestine. In my remarks I revealed Israel's secret weapon: *ein breira* (there is no alternative), the determination of the Jewish people to create a Jewish state.

On occasion, I have been asked whether, during my service in the Haganah, I ever shot or wounded anyone. I came close, but, thank goodness, no. It would have weighed too heavily on my mind to have taken a life, even in self-defense, and possibly would have made me feel unworthy of the career that lay ahead of me.

Many are the times since those days that I have thought of the Psalmist's injunction, "If I forget thee O, Jerusalem, let my right hand forget its cunning, let my tongue cleave to my mouth if I remember thee not, if I set not Jerusalem above my chiefest joy."

O, Jerusalem, how can I ever forget thee!

RETURN TO PENSION PAX

In the summer of 1988 I visited Israel, this time as a member of the American Veterans of Israel, a group known as MAHAL, the American volunteers who came from outside Israel to participate in the War of Independence.

I was particularly interested in visiting an organization known as Keren-Or, a home in Israel that provides life, love, and laughter to one of Israel's most painful populations—her blind children who also suffer other handicaps. These children ordinarily would be relegated to the back room of homes where their parents would struggle to care for them.

As we drove toward the neighborhood where Keren-Or's former facility was located, I found myself saying: "This area is familiar to me. I lived here when I was in Jerusalem in 1947 as a student at the Hebrew University."

When we got out of the car, I reminisced: "It was in just such a setting where 40 years ago I lived in a house something like this. It was called Pension Pax.

"Pension Pax!" exclaimed Emil Dere, a Board member of Keren-Or who escorted me. "That's the home of Keren-Or."

The next thing I knew I was revisiting the very room where I had dormed in those tremendously exciting days during the birth pangs of Israel.

"Children," said the teacher, "this is a rabbi who has come from America to meet you. He lived here 40 years ago." At that point a little hand reached out to hold mine and the face of a blind child was raised upward, and these words fell from his lips: "Ani mevarech otcha, I welcome you, I bless you."

I shall never forget that moment, I shall never forget that voice. Blessed is the work of Keren-Or.

2

A Connecticut Yankee

"Train a child in the way to go,
and when he is old,
he will not depart from it."

Proverbs 22:6

I doubt that my mother of sainted memory realized that it was
Saint Patrick's Day when she gave birth to me at home on March
17, 1923. That we were an ecumenical family is further demonstrated by the fact that my younger brother, Allen, also a rabbi,
was born on All Saints' Day, and my son, Herbert, was born on
Easter Sunday at the beginning of the third day of Passover.

I was born on Hough Avenue on the east side of Bridgeport,
Connecticut. When I was an infant, my family moved to Taft
Avenue on the North End of the city where avenues were named
for presidents, such as Madison, Lincoln, Jackson, Cleveland,
McKinley, Garfield. The streets were lined with three-story wood
frame houses and the families were mainly Italian, Polish,
German, and Jewish. The city had already acquired the reputation
of being the industrial capital of New England. With a Jewish population of about 14,000 in a city of 158,000, it was a community
that could also boast that it had given to the Jewish world a number of rabbinic families, educators, and communal and Zionist
leaders.

MY FAMILY BACKGROUND

My parents were European-born. My mother, Mae Lena Slotnick Block, affectionately known as Mamie, came to New York with her mother, Sarah Rivie, and her younger brothers about 1912 from the small village of Svislovitz in the Province of Grodno, Poland, which was also the childhood home of such great scholars as Rabbi Ahron Kotler, who headed a prominent yeshiva in Lakewood, New Jersey, and Rabbi Samuel Belkin, later president of Yeshiva University in New York. My maternal grandfather, Eliezer Slotnick, had preceded his wife here several years earlier but passed away while Grandma and her children were on the ship en route to New York. To support her family, Grandma opened a fruit and vegetable stand on Suffolk Street on Manhattan's Lower East Side.

My father, Philip, was born in Tavrig, Lithuania, on the eastern border of Germany. With his parents, Abraham and Sadie, he and his brother and sisters entered the United States in 1904 through the port of Boston and several years later moved to Rockland, Maine. After a few years Grandfather acquired land in the village of Thomaston, seven miles south of Rockland and the site of the Maine state prison, and there he continued the family tradition of dairy farming. In the dining room of my apartment there is a framed, tinted photograph of my father as a young man, in overalls and straw hat, standing and holding a bottle of milk alongside his father's horse-drawn buggy, which is decorated with the emblem of a cow's head. They would often ship metal containers of milk on the early train to Boston, and they also provided the state prison with dairy products and produce from their farm.

The Blocks were the only Jewish family in Thomaston but were actively involved in the synagogue, Adas Yoshuron, which my grandparents had helped found in Rockland in 1912. The congregation purchased the charming building, which is still in use, from the Advent Christian Church for $1,800; the church members sold it because they were convinced that the apocalypse was at hand. Among the other founders was the Berliowsky family, whose daughter was the renowned sculptor Louise Nevelson. (When I *davened* [prayed] in the synagogue as a youngster, someone predicted that I would become a rabbi. Years later I returned with my family to officiate at the Bar Mitzvah of a cousin, a great-grandson of Abraham and Sadie Block, and my son read Torah at the Shabbat service commemorating the seventy-fifth anniversary of the founding of the congregation.)

According to some family stories, my father left the farm as a young man and became a dancing teacher, which may account for the fact that I love to dance. After he married my mother, whom he met when she came to Rockland to visit a cousin, my parents moved to Bridgeport and my dad set himself up as an independent contractor, specializing in housepainting and paperhanging. Each morning before going to work he davened at home with *tallis* (prayer shawl) and *tefillin* (phylacteries), and on every Shabbat and holiday he was in synagogue.

He handled the brush with dexterity and was a master craftsman of great integrity. I can still tell at once by the way a person holds a brush whether that individual is a skilled painter or a *schmirer* (slapdash worker). We used to say at home, with a twinkle in the eye, that my father's special claim to fame was that he painted the Bridgeport home of Clara Stern, sister of former Prime Minister Golda Meir of Israel.

Then there was the annual routine of my mother reminding my father of the very large kitchen closet which contained all of our dishware, pots, and pans and which had to be painted before

Passover. After much debate, my father would finally consent, asking, "What color should I paint it?" And my mother's stock answer was, "Just paint it—clean!"

Bridgeport was where the Blocks, Gordons, Slotnicks—my aunts, uncles, and cousins from New York, Pennsylvania, Maine, and Massachusetts—came to spend Passover. Some stayed with us and others stayed with our cousins the Cohens, on Capitol Avenue. Where did we put everybody? The adults had the bedrooms and the children slept on blankets on the living room carpet. We had a great time all week playing our favorite game, Monopoly, and just having fun together. I remember one of my uncles coming with his family and bringing a large fish, which he kept alive in water in our bathtub until it was time to transform it into gefilte fish for the Seder.

My mother, who devoted all her time to running a busy household of four children —my older sister, Lillian; myself; my sister Evelyn; and my younger brother, Allen—was a highly respected woman in the community. She maintained a kosher home and was very involved in the Pioneer Women's Organization, which was dedicated to rebuilding the Land of Israel, and in the Women's Auxiliary of the Grand Street Synagogue. Her deep feeling for others and good common sense led many ladies in our neighborhood to seek her advice. So sensitive was she that, although she would often wash clothes on Sunday, she never hung the laundry out on the line until the next day because *nit zu farshteren*, she didn't want to "show disrespect" for her non-Jewish neighbors on their Sabbath. And when I asked whether the Christian community would reciprocate by not hanging its wash on the Jewish Sabbath, her reply was, "Who knows? Maybe in time they will."

So beloved was my mother that upon her passing in 1948 at the young age of 55, it seemed that the entire community was present to mourn at the funeral of a true *Eshes Chayil* (a woman of valor). I found strength and comfort in the sight of more than a hundred cars in the cortege to the cemetery in Fairfield, grateful that I had returned home to be with her. Her last months were filled with pride, witnessing the establishment of the State of Israel and knowing that I had made the decision to become a rabbi.

My two sisters, who were five years apart, were quite popular and had many friends. Our telephone rang incessantly, sometimes to the point of distraction, prompting us kids to announce, as we picked up the receiver, "Hello? Grand Central Station!" or, "Beardsley Park Zoo!" Following our parents' example, all of us were active in Jewish causes. Lillian devoted herself to Hadassah, Evelyn spent a year in Israel on a study program, and Allen became a rabbi and eventually my associate at The Brotherhood Synagogue.

My father was a member of the religious school committee of the North End Talmud Torah, a program of the Charles Street Synagogue, where I attended afternoon Hebrew classes Mondays through Thursdays at the end of the public school day, and two hours on Sundays mornings, and where I had my Bar Mitzvah (I delivered my speech in Yiddish). We were blessed with a marvelous teacher, Rebbe Israel Bowman, a kind and gentle man, even though he carried a wooden ruler as he walked around the classroom. Happily, he used it primarily to point out to students their place in the book when he found their minds wandering; on rare occasions he gave a child a loving tap on the hand to wake him up. He was born in Lithuania but had resided for a number of years in England, a fact that accounted for his Oxonian accent. He spoke with refinement of speech and perfect grammatical structure and was obviously well educated in both Jewish law and secular subjects. Never once did I hear from his lips any derogatory remark or even a hint or an allusion that would in any way denigrate any culture, race, or religion. Rebbe Bowman taught us to be steadfast in our faith and in our religious tradition while still being a universalist in the sight of God and man, carrying out the biblical dictum, "Love thy neighbor as thyself." His teachings and my parents' example have influenced me throughout my life.

During my early childhood a playmate who lived across the street made a remark that had a painful and profound effect upon me. One day as we played together, he interjected the deicide charge: "The Jews killed my God!"—a statement he attributed to something he learned in church. I countered that I had nothing to do with it; in fact, I didn't even know what he meant. But that accusation was so deeply embedded in my mind and heart and made such an impact on me that, as I grew up, I resolved that someday I would do everything possible to eradicate all such cruel statements and false, malicious allegations. I can still visualize the exact spot on the driveway alongside his house where those words were hurled at me. Once, when my wife and I were visiting Bridgeport, I pointed out the driveway to her and reflected that it might have been that very incident that impelled me to found The Brotherhood Synagogue and devote my life to interreligious relationships.

There was a church across the street from one of the synagogues I attended. I usually avoided walking on that side of the street, because I had a feeling that churches showed little respect for people of other faiths. As I listened to Father Charles Coughlin on the radio in the 1930s, I wondered why his church failed to censure him.

Even now, though I have many acquaintances and good friends who are religious leaders of all denominations and for whom I have the highest respect, I nevertheless still feel something of an inner pang from the accusations of that youngster. It demonstrates how powerful words and stereotypes can be in shaping the lives and thoughts of all of us.

GROWING UP

As I grew up, I had the privilege of singing during the High Holydays in the men's and boys' choir of the Grand Street Synagogue. The Cantor had invited me to audition, and my high-pitched tenor voice seemed quite acceptable. We studied long and conscientiously to prepare for the many services—Selichot, Rosh Hashanah, the Sabbath of Repentance, and the great and awesome day of Yom Kippur. The first year I sang I received a gift of three dollars. The second year the officers of the synagogue graciously increased my stipend to five dollars. By the third year, I was bold enough to ask on my own for an increase. We argued and I settled for seven dollars… and received my walking papers.

I think there was another reason for the end of my singing career. My dear mother had encouraged me to ask the Cantor for a solo selection. Others sang solo. Why not her son? I could see from the look on the Cantor's face that he was not happy with her request. At the next service, and completely unexpectedly, he pointed to me and said, "Block, sing *Ahavas Olam* (With Everlasting Love)!" I was not prepared for this and was totally off key, so the Cantor had to hastily direct the other members of the choir to sing along with me. Still I do have to thank the Cantor for introducing me to the beautiful melodies of the High Holydays and for teaching me that song is essential to life. According to Jewish tradition, the Messiah will not only be a powerful preacher and teacher but, like King David, also a gifted singer of praises to the Lord.

At home all the children helped mother with the household chores. I had two assignments: ironing towels, which I liked to do because it produced results quickly, and taking chickens to a *schochet* (ritual slaughterer). We had live chickens and brown eggs delivered regularly from a local farmer; the Cantor was also the *schochet,* and my mother preferred fresh eggs and freshly slaughtered chickens. As I carried a chicken in a burlap bag slumped over my back, it would peck constantly at my buttocks, while I hummed "Yankee Doodle Dandy" to divert my mind. When the *schochet* finished his work, he grabbed the chicken by its legs and placed the limp bird back into my bag for the trip home, and I paid him ten cents. Sometimes I helped my mother pluck the feathers and prepare the chicken for kashering (soaking and salting).

As a young child I attended Sheldon Elementary School, just a hop, skip, and jump from the house of the famous midget Tom Thumb. Bridgeport was the home of Mr. Thumb's boss, P. T. Barnum, founder of the Barnum and Bailey Circus and once mayor of the city.

When I was 12 years old I joined the Boy Scouts and became a member of Troop 53, sponsored by the North End Talmud Torah. I went through the ranks to First Class and Star, and then, just as I began a concerted effort to work toward additional merit badges, I was invited to transfer to a newly formed Sea Scout Ship, No. 100, called *Nodidaw*, which in Hebrew means "wanderer." I have always had the highest regard for scouting, for its emphasis on learning, mastery of one's emotions, character development, love of nature, and respect for the rights and feelings of others. Long after my own scouting days, my involvement continued as a rabbi. I served as a merit badge counselor, and one summer a member of my congregation arranged for me to be the Jewish chaplain at an international Girl Scout roundup in Vermont, an unusual and delightful experience.

At Central High School, from which I graduated in 1940, I joined the track team as a half-miler and was also a member of the chess team. We were proud of Central's four state championships that year in baseball, basketball, football, and track, a rare achievement indeed. Years later the high school, which had been located a good two miles from my home, was converted into the City Hall, and a new high school was built—just diagonally across the street from where I had lived.

During my high school and college years I held a variety of jobs, not only to earn money, but also to learn and to meet people. I was a stock boy in a women's shoe store, a parking lot attendant, and a painter in a factory. During winter vacations I worked in the post office, clerked in a store selling Christmas tree ornaments, and took inventory in a silverware factory. In my senior year of high school my father bought me a 1929 Chrysler for $25—a two-door coupe with a rumble seat—that could accommodate six to seven passengers, depending on their size. Gas cost $12\frac{1}{2}$ cents a gallon and I estimated that I could get 10 to 11 miles per gallon. That summer I offered to drive people to the beach at Seaside Park, on Long Island Sound, a trip of $2\frac{1}{2}$ miles from my neighborhood. At 10 cents per passenger, it was less expensive than the bus fare, and a bargain for a family. We all gained: they had a pleasant, comfortable ride, and I made a little extra money to buy a few more gallons of gas to use for my own personal enjoyment. I would head toward the Merritt Parkway, open up the throttle, depress the gas pedal, and watch the speedometer climb to 40 mph.

A PIVOTAL ENCOUNTER

I was about 16 years old when I entered a church for the first time. The great preacher Rabbi Stephen Samuel Wise was coming to Bridgeport to address the community on a Sunday afternoon at the large United Congregational Church on State Street and Park Avenue, and I was eager to hear him. As I walked up the steps, I felt very self-conscious and wondered how to respond if questioned as to why a Jewish boy was visiting the church. I did not have to be afraid. No one ever asked. (Long after, I learned that I shared the same birthday with Dr. Wise; I was somewhat disappointed that I would not be the first rabbi born on St. Patrick's Day. In the spirit of the day, I always wear a green skullcap and a green tie that has a small shamrock next to a Star of David.)

The sanctuary was filled to capacity, all awaiting the arrival of Dr. Wise. When he entered and began to speak, he relaxed the group by explaining the reason for his delay, saying that he had to fight his way through the crowd in order to hear himself talk. Stephen Wise was one of the country's most articulate, powerful, and sought-after speakers. He talked that afternoon about Judaism and Christianity, about the world in which we lived, and about the animosities and estrangements that have for centuries pitted people against people, religion against religion, nation against nation. It was 1939. Dr. Wise elaborated on the tragic events unfolding in Europe and discussed the rise of Nazism, with all its implications for the world and for the Jewish people.

During the question-and-answer period someone asked,"Dr. Wise, you know the adage, where there's smoke, there's fire. Don't you think that your people may be responsible for some of the things that are happening to them?" Dr. Wise replied with candor and courage, conceding that where there is smoke, there may be fire, but that the smoke and fire had for almost two thousand years regrettably been Christian insensitivity, inhumanity, and anti-Semitism. No one could challenge or reprove Rabbi Wise for that response, because he had earned a reputation as a man of great feeling for all religions and for all humanity. He fervently believed that the teachings of Jesus were Jewish teachings, and he would often say that Christians should either follow them or give them back to the Jewish people. Dr. Wise's remarks and his concept of Christian–Jewish relations opened up a whole new approach for me so that, nine years later when I decided to study for the rabbinate, I chose the Jewish Institute of Religion, which Dr. Wise had established in New York City.

COLLEGE AND DECISIONS

Choosing a profession or occupation was a major task for me as for so many high school students. The choices fluctuated between two professions: Should I study to become a rabbi, or should I major in business administration? To complicate my decision, a young rabbinic student who came to Bridgeport to be considered for the position of rabbi of the Charles Street Synagogue demonstrated such an extensive knowledge of Talmud and an equally impressive understanding of philosophy that I remember asking myself, "How can I ever be able to acquire all that knowledge?" In effect, his coming became both a concern and a challenge. Could I fulfill the academic requirements of rabbinic studies? At one point I inquired of Yeshiva College whether there was a program combining religious studies and business administration, to give me a little more time to make my decision. When the answer came back that there was only one course in economics, I applied to the school that seemed most likely to offer courses in both humanities and business, the University of Connecticut in Storrs, where tuition was only $125 a year. It proved to be a good choice.

My mother had given her approval to my joining a college fraternity, Tau Epsilon Phi, which she saw as an opportunity for me to develop social skills. As for the track team, there were students from all over the state who were far better runners. I couldn't compete with them. I chose to become a cheerleader and, over 50 years later, I occasionally entertain my family with the old rousing cheers when we watch UConn games on television. At UConn I became friendly with the scholarly Rabbi Maurice Zigmond, director of the Hillel Foundation, and remained in touch with him over the years. He encouraged me to lead Sabbath services, to participate in the Hillel choir, and to serve as one of the speakers who traveled with him around the state urging people to support Hillel. Later I chaired the first United Jewish Appeal campaign on our campus; we surpassed the goal that we had set for ourselves, with gifts not only from the Jewish student body but from non-Jewish students as well as from the faculty and administration.

ARMY DAYS

Since UConn was a state university, male students were obligated to join the ROTC, the Reserve Officers Training Corps. The moment I heard about the bombing of Pearl Harbor, I knew that

America would soon be at war, and I began to pay closer attention to the military instruction. In November 1942 I enlisted in the Army. I was called to active duty in March 1943, just a few days before my twentieth birthday, and was ordered to report to Fort Devens, Massachusetts. I was in the second semester of my junior year at college.

I'll always remember that first day. The recruits, including other college students, were greeted by the barking commands of a noncommissioned officer that went something like this: "All right, line up!" and, holding his left hand high, he ordered, "Place your f——— right hand over your f——— right heart!" Well, Block, I thought, you're in the Army now. As an enlisted soldier, I was transferred to Fort Benjamin Harrison in Indiana and, since I had majored in business administration, I was assigned to the Finance Department. I took 13 weeks of basic military training and additional specialized instruction in the preparation of contracts and payroll computations.

Then came a furlough, followed by orders to report to the port of embarkation at New Orleans, where a convoy, escorted by destroyers, was leaving for the Caribbean. After one day out at sea our ship was forced to break away from the convoy because of a fire in the engine room. We donned life jackets and prepared to abandon ship. Fortunately, the crew was able to extinguish the blaze, but we had to change our course and head for Key West, Florida, for repairs. Several days later we ran the German submarine gauntlet alone and arrived in the Canal Zone, where my orders were to report to Fort Gulick on the Atlantic side of the isthmus. We were part of the Caribbean command responsible for safeguarding the Panama Canal, so crucial to the success of the war effort.

In Cristobal-Colón, not far from my base, I met a number of Jewish families, many of whom had fled Nazi Europe in the 1930s and were living in Panama until they could emigrate to the United States. While the Jewish Welfare Board provided two Passover Seders at the Hotel Washington, I preferred to accept invitations to celebrate the holidays at family dinner tables. I kept up a friendship with some of these families long afterwards. One of them, the Loebs, even came to my college graduation.

I wrote to my parents regularly but, because of military censorship, I couldn't indicate where I was stationed, and they wrote to me at an APO address. They first learned where I was from the December 15, 1943 edition of the Yiddish *Forward*, which printed in its rotogravure section a photograph of military personnel at a USO–JWB function in the Canal Zone; they recognized me in the far left corner.

Life in the barracks could get very boring at times. I kept myself occupied by assisting the military chaplain, taking classes in Spanish at the Canal Zone Junior College, serving as assistant scoutmaster of Canal Zone Troop 6, and playing catcher on our office softball team.

I spent three years in Panama, taking discharge at Fort Gulick in December 1945. I decided to remain on for another six months as a civilian employee of the War Department because this was a good opportunity finally to make a major decision: Did I want accounting, or did I want the rabbinate? The commanding officer had written that my work was outstanding, but I had come to realize that, rather than "pushing a pencil," I was much more interested in people-to-people relationships.

I returned to the University of Connecticut in the fall of 1946. At the suggestion of Rabbi Edward E. Klein, Associate Rabbi of Dr. Wise's congregation, the Free Synagogue, I completed my requirements in accounting so as not to lose a year or two by changing majors. He also approved of my decision to spend a year at the Hebrew University to obtain a good academic foundation for my rabbinic studies.

I was able to graduate college within a year after I returned from Panama because I had accumulated enough credits before reporting to the Army. (I finished my last term paper the night before I left.) Those credits, plus the ones I earned in my senior year, including credit for military service and courses at the Canal Zone Junior College, enabled me to graduate in June 1947.

A few weeks later I was on my way to Jerusalem.

A PATIENT'S GRATITUDE

I was a celiac baby at birth, constantly crying because of abdominal pain. My dear mother physically exhausted herself going from doctor to doctor, until she finally located a pediatrician in New York City who diagnosed my condition and recommended a diet of bananas, the browner the better. Thirty years later I located the doctor, I. H. Goldberger, whose office was still on the Grand Concourse, in the Bronx, and invited him to attend my ordination. I had a difficult time trying to explain to his secretary on the phone why I wanted an appointment, that I was not a father of a child, but that as an infant I had been one of Dr. Goldberger's patients. I simply wanted to thank him personally for enabling me to overcome a very difficult childhood illness.

Laden with an armful of neckties as an expression of my gratitude, I was ushered into the doctor's office, with my Uncle Jack, who had often accompanied my mother on the long subway ride from his home on the Lower East Side to the Bronx. As I reached out a hand to introduce myself, the doctor said, "Irving, I recognized you when you walked in. I won't be able to attend the ordination, but I certainly appreciate your invitation. I wish more of my patients would keep me informed about what they're doing."

3

Studying for the Rabbinate

*"Rabbinical seminaries must prepare men for service
in the rabbinate, for contributing to Jewish
learning, and for community service...
intellectually and spiritually free in
accordance with undogmatic liberalism, which
is at the heart of the genius of Judaism."*

RABBI STEPHEN SAMUEL WISE

FOLLOWING RABBI WISE

The year of my birth, 1923, coincided with the first school year of
a newly founded seminary, the Jewish Institute of Religion, for
educating and training rabbis in New York City. It was located on
West 68th Street, near Central Park, in the same building where,
15 years earlier, Rabbi Stephen Samuel Wise had established the
Free Synagogue. His goal was to develop a school where students
could follow any branch of Judaism, be it Orthodox, Conservative,
Reform, or what we today call Reconstructionist. He did not want
to have students think alike. To the contrary. When he spoke with
young people on college campuses about pursuing the rabbinate
as a profession, he realized that in their search for a sustaining
philosophy of life, they often had changes of heart: the Reform-
oriented became traditionalists and traditionalists became

Reform. Rather than favor one approach over another, Dr. Wise stressed the unity of the Jewish people. Born in Hungary, he had been raised in a traditional home, and in the early years of his rabbinate he served in a Conservative congregation, B'nai Jeshurun, in New York City. Later he closely identified with the liberal movement.

Early in 1949, a year after my return from Israel, I applied, again under the GI Bill of Rights, to matriculate at the Jewish Institute of Religion. This was just the time that Dr. Wise was merging his school with the Hebrew Union College in Cincinnati, founded by a distinguished scholar who coincidentally bore the name Wise as well. The dreams of both Rabbi Isaac Mayer Wise and Rabbi Stephen Samuel Wise seemed to coalesce: to train a cadre of rabbis for the ever-growing American Jewish community. After 25 years, the constant fund-raising required of all heads of institutions became too physically taxing for Rabbi Wise. He realized that to ensure the continuity of his school, he should join it with another institution. Both schools projected a plan to maintain two separate campuses under a single administration. That merger took effect before Dr. Wise's death in April 1949.

When I first came to New York, I had very limited resources, so I was fortunate to be able to make my home with an aunt and uncle, Bess and Jacob Slotnick, and their daughter, Renee, active members of the Free Synagogue. I was especially close to them because Aunt Bess was my father's sister and Uncle Jack was my mother's brother. Their apartment became my home away from home.

Since I had applied to rabbinical school in the middle of the academic year, Dean Henry Slonimsky suggested that in the interim I enroll in several evening courses at the Hebrew Union School of Jewish Education and register for university classes in the humanities. (I had planned to do this at the Hebrew University, but instead I became involved in the Haganah.) I accepted his recommendations and found myself enjoying the poetry courses I took at Columbia University with the great Irish poet Padriac Colum and his wife, Mary. These efforts on my part satisfied the faculty and gave me confidence that I could cope with the class work. In the fall of 1949 I formally matriculated in the Hebrew Union College–Jewish Institute of Religion.

The studies were more arduous than I anticipated. Once, during a scheduled test on Bible, my teacher, Dr. Harry Orlinsky, noticed me pacing in the hall and asked why I was not in class. I had to admit that I just couldn't seem to focus on my studies, but he reassured me that this was a common complaint among students who had returned to school after their military service. Even with such reassurances, my confidence waivered. Each day I came up with another idea: perhaps I should become involved in Zionist youth activities, or return to Israel where there was a possibility of obtaining a position with the Central Bureau of Statistics. Today I can identify with the inner turmoil of so many young people regarding their future. When I talk with them, I often explain that struggle is part of everyone's growth and development. Indeed, we are called the Children of Israel because Jacob, our patriarch, wrestled all night with an angel, and God gave Jacob the name "Israel," which means to wrestle and prevail with God. While struggle may be painful, it is not necessarily harmful; it may even prove to be a blessing.

By the end of the fall semester I had written to Dean Slonimsky of my decision to withdraw, but an incident occurred that entirely changed my perspective. A fellow student, Gerald Raiskin, who throughout my years at the College–Institute was a quiet source of inspiration, suggested that instead of going out for lunch that day we could enjoy a delicious deli sandwich at the school for just a dollar. Students had been invited to attend an all-day *Kallah* (study-conference) of faculty and alumni of the two rabbinic schools, and lunch would be served.

The seminars and discussions focused on an examination of biblical text and the problems facing the new State of Israel. I listened intently to the inspiring midrashic tales. However, when the topic dealt with the future of the State of Israel, I kept repeating to myself that I didn't share the rabbis' conclusions. Since I had recently been in Eretz Israel, my perspective was different from theirs. It was then that I became aware that the rabbinate offered me the best opportunity to express my own views on Israel and Jewish life in general. I looked around the room, spotted Dean Slonimsky, and asked permission to withdraw my resignation. That reversal would be acceptable, he said, provided I write another letter requesting reinstatement. That evening, when I went home to my aunt and uncle for dinner, they would not serve me until I had not only written that letter but delivered it to the Dean's office. I returned, exhausted but exhilarated, and they were naturally relieved, since they had long been convinced that the rabbinate was the right profession for me.

A DISTINGUISHED FACULTY

In the words of the Talmud, "from all my teachers I have gotten understanding." The Talmudic tractate *Pirkei Avot*, the Ethics of the Fathers, instructs us to honor those from whom we learn a single chapter, a single rule, a single verse, a single expression, or even a single letter. If I were even to attempt to highlight what I learned at HUC–JIR, I would not be able to do justice to the stimulating lectures by a faculty of eminent scholars whose eloquent teaching of the concepts, principles, and traditions of Judaism had an enormous influence on me and on the direction of my work for the next 40 years.[1]

From a Midrash I gleaned great meaning from the verse "God created man" (Genesis, 1:27). God took sands of different colors from all over the world and mixed the sands with the waters of all the oceans, lakes, and rivers, thus fashioning Adam as multicolored so that no one should ever be able to say, 'My ancestor is superior to yours. My race preceded yours.'"

In my class on Hasidism I was inspired by a mystical tale about the formation of the world and how God contracted the universe to a singular point of light from which emanated rays as multiple as the rays of the sun. There followed a cataclysmic explosion, and sparks of light from the rays flew off into the vast universe, each spark clothed with a shell of nothingness, yet alighting on all things. The Hasidim say that the challenge in life is to bring these sparks together and make the divine rays whole again. War, jealousy, strife, and hatred repel the sparks; conversely, peace, love, friendship, and joy act as magnets that attract these sparks and reunite them.

My teachers impressed upon me that the history of our people has to be studied intensely and in depth and transmitted with integrity under the guidance of rabbis and scholars.

---

1. So high is my regard for them that I want to list their names as they appear on my Smicha, the certificate of ordination: the President, Dr. Nelson Glueck, Dean Henry Slonimsky, Drs. Harry M. Orlinsky, John J. Tepfer, I. Edward Kiev, Abraham W. Binder, Abraham N. Franzblau, Aaron Giat; Rabbis Bernard Heller, Samuel Atlas, Ezra Spicehandler, Emanuel Green, Sidney E. Goldstein, and Michael Alper. In addition, there were other teachers who were influential: Rabbis Julius Mark, Samuel Wolk; Drs. Theodore Gaster, Philip Jaffe, Guido Kisch, and Mr. Windsor P. Daggett.

But rabbis must also be able to assume multiple roles: priest and prophet, educator and administrator, counselor, and, especially, interpreter of God's word. They must be fully conversant with all the traditions and rituals of Jewish life-cycle events, mindful of the admonition of the sage Rabbi Moses Luzzato that each ceremony must have two components: it must be significant, and it must be beautiful. Each service of worship should be conducted with dignity, formality, and even a touch of the dramatic; rabbis should develop the ability to speak, read aloud, and write well. A rabbi's articles and sermons must be carefully crafted in order to convey the message clearly. Writing a column in the synagogue bulletin is an avenue rabbis can take to communicate with their congregations and communities and, at the same time, to reflect the rabbi's direction and philosophy.

One of the professors with whom I developed a warm relationship was Dr. Harry Orlinsky, eminent biblical scholar, who guided me in the research for my Master's thesis on "The Book of Proverbs in the Light of the Wisdom Literature of the Ancient Near East." He taught us that even in a serious discussion, humor has a rightful place. He also admonished us that research, whether in Bible or in other subjects, must be pursued objectively rather than to prove a preconceived viewpoint.

From the viewpoint of Rabbi Sidney E. Goldstein of the Free Synagogue, the role of a rabbi is to interpret the events of the day in the light of our historic past. On one occasion, when he wished to substantiate a point by citing a biblical verse, he asked a student to go to the library and bring back a Bible. As the student reached the door, Rabbi Goldstein raised his voice and said, "Make it a Bible we can all understand!" When the student returned with a Bible in English, he exclaimed, "I told you to get me a Bible that we could all understand! Now go back and get us the Bible in Hebrew."

Rabbi Goldstein also urged students to undertake internships. We would not entrust our bodies and our physical well-being to inexperienced medical students, he argued; why should we expect people to entrust their spiritual health to inexperienced seminary students?

Not least important, I learned that music is the soul, the sublime experience of prayer, and that rabbis need to prepare themselves vocally to lead and to chant portions of a service as well as the Torah readings.

It was with Rabbi Edward E. Klein, successor to Dr. Wise at the Free Synagogue, that I began an internship during the High Holydays in my first two years as a student. I admired his brilliant mind, great ability as a preacher, warm heart, and friendly manner—a winning combination in the rabbinate. Rabbi Klein also invited me to accompany him at life-cycle events, enabling me to observe and learn from a master. Over the years our families became very close—he knew not only my aunt and uncle but my wife and her parents—and he officiated at my wedding as well as on many family and synagogue occasions.

Dr. Nelson Glueck, internationally renowned biblical archeologist, was the President of the College–Institute at the time of my ordination. Placing his hands upon my shoulders at the ordination ceremonies, as he did with each graduate, he quietly challenged me: "Irving, Yisroel, go out and change the world to make it a better place for all." I hope that I have not failed him.

STUDENT DAYS

While I was at the College–Institute, I met Cantor Leo Mirkovic, whose brilliant career as an opera singer had been interrupted by World War II. Often called the Richard Tucker of Europe, he had sung leading roles in the major opera houses of the Continent. In

1944 he was among the thousand refugees who were admitted to the United States by President Franklin D. Roosevelt and given temporary haven in a camp in Oswego, New York. After obtaining permission to remain in this country, Leo Mirkovic applied to the Hebrew Union School of Sacred Music and was one of the school's first graduates.

I had heard that Cantor Mirkovic was giving voice lessons to rabbinic students and I decided that it would be advantageous for me to learn the proper melodies of such prayers as the *Kiddush* (sanctification over wine), the *El Maleh Rahamim* (prayer for the departed), and the wedding benedictions. Cantor Mirkovic had a great sense of humor but a formidable and stern manner as a teacher; however, no one ever forgot his lessons. One day I jokingly forewarned him that "Some day, I may be the rabbi of a congregation, and you may be the cantor, and then I'll fix you!"

Summer breaks at the College–Institute provided a good opportunity for me to widen my horizons. The first summer I was the staff rabbi at Camp Marlin in Connecticut, where I tutored children who were to have a Bar or Bat Mitzvah in the fall, conducted services, and organized elaborate pageants based on contemporary Jewish events.

The following summer I enrolled in a pioneering clinical internship program at Bellevue Hospital, under the tutelage of Rabbi I. Fred Hollander of the New York Board of Rabbis. For 12 weeks four students, representing Yeshiva University, Jewish Theological Seminary, Hebrew Union College, and the Jewish Institute of Religion, learned from professors of medicine, psychiatry, and social work the important role of clergy in the healing process. One eminent surgeon declared succinctly, "Both a doctor and a chaplain help to cure the sick, but in the matter of therapy, a chaplain has a distinct advantage. He has God on his side."

The next year I spent time with Judge Anna Moskowitz Kross at the Home Term Court, now the Family Court, and in Civil Court in the Bronx with Judge Joseph Levine, President of the Free Synagogue.

During my student years I also served as a religious-school teacher. I feel blessed to have known Rabbi Hugo Hahn, who had fled Germany with many of his congregants and founded Congregation Habonim in New York, as well as Rabbi Ben Zion Steindel of Queens and Rabbi Albert Martin of the Park Avenue Temple in my hometown of Bridgeport. After I preached, Rabbi Martin graciously wrote me that I did "grandly."

As far back as I could remember, I had always felt that inasmuch as clergy of all denominations serve the same one Almighty God, they should be friends with one another. The time to get to know each other was *now*, while we were students; we should not postpone until tomorrow what ought to be accomplished today. With these thoughts in mind, I helped organize an interseminary conference of theological students in New York City. Participants were invited from Union Theological Seminary, the College–Institute, the Jewish Theological Seminary, and Yeshiva University, and we reached out as well to other Protestant institutions such as General Theological, Biblical Theological, and New York Theological Seminaries. Of the Jewish schools only Yeshiva University did not respond. Nor was there any response from the Catholic seminaries to which I had written at the suggestion of an acquaintance, Father Walter Abbot, then editor of the Catholic periodical *America*. As the students talked together, we realized how similar were our goals, hopes, and aspirations. This gathering was a forerunner of similar interdenominational meetings of seminary students, but it would be decades before such programs would be accepted and encouraged by seminary authorities.

As secretary of the College–Institute student body, I did not hesitate to be assertive and invite to the school outstanding scholars, such as the illustrious historian Cecil Roth and the distinguished writer Israel Cohen, both from England. Surely, I thought, these men, when visiting the United States, would be willing to address an eager audience of rabbinical students. The invitations initially raised some eyebrows among the faculty—they were both surprised and pleased that such distinguished scholars would accept an invitation from students—but, after the lectures, the comments were very positive.

Many of the students at the College–Institute were married with families. Some of the single men lived in a brownstone dormitory a few doors away from the Free Synagogue. Sometimes when we wanted a break in our studies, we would walk over to the synagogue on a Sunday evening when the young adult club, the Cardozo Society, often held a social program. That is where I met my wife, Phyllis. One night I saw a very charming, dark-haired young lady talking with a friend of mine at the refreshment table. I wended my way over to position myself for an introduction. My friend, it turned out, was a college friend of the young lady and she introduced us. This was the first time in many months that Phyllis had attended one of these programs; it was *bashert* (destiny). As we danced and talked, I learned that she and her parents, Herman and Belle Robinove, were active members of the Free Synagogue, that they knew my Aunt Bess and Uncle Jack, and that she was a graduate student at Columbia University and served on several synagogue committees. I was impressed by her parents' and her own involvement in congregational affairs, and by Phyllis's academic achievements. Thus began a casual friendship which in time blossomed into courtship and led to our marriage. I proposed on the first day of Chanukah 1963. She accepted and we were married a few months later, in February 1964, at The Brotherhood Synagogue. Our wedding reception was at the Stephen Wise Free Synagogue, in the room where we had first met. I have always been thankful that I went over to that table for coffee. It was the best cup of coffee I ever had.

The College–Institute required us to serve for a period of time in a student pulpit before ordination. Although we did not have to undertake this assignment early in our studies, many students were anxious to do so both for the stipends and for the experience. I chose a different path, however, reasoning that for me it would be more beneficial to accept as many speaking engagements as I could manage, offered mostly through the school, on a wide variety of topics, so that I could improve my oral skills. In a college course on public speaking, the professor had suggested that when we were asked to address an audience, we should always accept, schedule permitting, and then research the topic in the library so as to be able to speak with confidence, knowledge, and enthusiasm. Through friends I had an opportunity to be on the radio, delivering a series of five sermonettes on the program "Faith in Our Time," sponsored by the Mutual Broadcasting System in cooperation with the Synagogue Council of America.

It was also during my student days that I began to be an advocate on behalf of the Black Jewish community in the United States as well as in Ethiopia. (See Chapter 12.)

MY FIRST PULPIT

Whenever the school's placement office received a request for a student rabbi, it would come to me first since the other members of my class already had positions. Therefore, despite a busy extracurricular schedule, I seriously considered the invitation that came from a temple in Greenwich Village. Since it was a Manhattan congregation, I would not have to trek to the suburbs; but even more important to me, the congregation was sharing the facilities of the Village Presbyterian Church on West 13th Street. Here was a ready-made opportunity to further my ideas about men and women of different faiths getting to know one another. However, the position proved to be far more of a challenge than I had anticipated.

The Village Temple, founded in 1948, was initially led by Rabbi Julian Fleg. Sabbath services were held at the Brevoort Hotel, then located on lower Fifth Avenue near Washington Square. Prior to that time the only synagogue in Greenwich Village was an Orthodox congregation, Darech Amuno, at Charles and West 4th Streets. Hardly had the Temple begun to function when the hotel management indicated that it could no longer provide the space. As the Temple's officers searched for new quarters, they also explored the possibility of moving temporarily to another house of worship in the area. A local minister suggested the Village Presbyterian Church on West 13th Street, between Sixth and Seventh Avenues, led by the Reverend Dr. Jesse William Stitt. He telephoned Dr. Stitt and asked if he would like to meet with a rabbi who had a problem. The Minister replied, "I didn't know rabbis had problems, I thought only ministers had them."

Dr. Stitt often related the story of his first meeting with Rabbi Fleg. He pointed out to the Rabbi that the Church did not have a room in the community house large enough to accommodate the Temple, and the auditorium below the sanctuary was being used by the Lemonade Opera Company. "The only thing I could suggest is that you could use the sanctuary," he offered. He also explained that he did not know how his Board of Trustees and the Church's Elders would feel about a congregation of a different faith using their facilities for worship. Nonetheless, he suggested that Rabbi Fleg take up the matter with his officers and promised that he would also discuss it with his leadership. The Minister requested that the Rabbi detail the Temple's needs in a letter that would present all the points necessary for a full and objective discussion by the Church Board.

After the Minister read aloud the Temple's request to use the Church's facilities for six months, there was a considerable debate. Then, as Dr. Stitt described it, an elderly European lady, a truly beautiful soul, short and stout, began to move forward in her seat on the sofa. "I thought to myself," said the Minister, "'Here it comes!' When she sits on the sofa and listens, her feet don't even touch the ground. She never says much, but you can always tell when she is going to say something. She starts to edge forward on the seat, and when she finally gets her feet on the ground, she gets up and starts to speak." Dr. Stitt reminisced, "I never know whether she is going to be on my side or against me. However, I do know one thing about her—whatever she has made up her mind about, it is a very sincere conviction and she will be reckoned with and listened to."

As she stood up to express her opinion that evening she said, "Gentlemen, this has been a very interesting discussion. I would like to say one thing, and that is this: If by taking the Cross and the candlesticks and placing them in the vestry room on Friday night, we are going to violate the Cross in any way, we cannot do it. But it seems to me that if we take the Cross and candlesticks and place them in the vestry room, and allow the Jewish congregation and the Rabbi to have the traditional symbolism of Judaism for their evening service, we will not be violating the

Cross in one instance. We will be fulfilling the real message and spirit of the Cross, because we will be extending the right hand of fellowship to our fellowmen."

"That was all there was to it," Dr. Stitt recalled later. "It would take a theologian a whole book to explain that. It took a simple Christian woman about two paragraphs."

Shortly thereafter the Village Presbyterian Church made an arrangement with The Village Temple to utilize the Church's facilities for a minimal rent, and the congregation held its first worship service there on the first Friday night of January 1949.

After moving to West 13th Street, the members of The Village Temple planned a bazaar to raise funds and proposed conducting it jointly with the Church. Initially, the Church Board was concerned that the Temple was planning something on a much larger scale than the Church could handle. When the Minister mentioned this concern to the Rabbi, he responded, "Look, all we want is a bazaar together... [to demonstrate] that we understand each other and are working together toward the one goal of brotherhood." The two clergymen summoned members of their congregations to form a committee; but when they walked into the room at the very first meeting, they found all the Presbyterians on one side and the Jewish people on the other. By the second meeting, however, subcommittees were formed comprising an equal number from each of the two congregations. On the basis of that activity as well as other programs, word got around in the community, and eventually in local and national publications, about an unusual arrangement on 13th Street—so much so that when the renowned pianist Vladimir Horowitz was asked if he would give a benefit concert for the two congregations, he enthusiastically accepted.

Rabbi Block's parents, Mae Lena Slotnick Block and Philip Block.

Rabbi Block as a Bar Mitzvah and as a soldier in the Army of the United States.

The joint sanctuary of The Brotherhood Synagogue and the Village Presbyterian Church in New York City, Greenwich Village. Photo: Ben Saltzman

Rabbi Block and his colleague The Rev. Dr. Jesse William Stitt in front of their joint sanctuary. Photo: Ben Ross

*Rabbi Block delivering the invocation at a rally celebrating Israel's 8th Anniversary of Independence in New York City in 1956 (*left to right: *Rev. Dr. Stitt, Senator John F. Kennedy, Rabbi Block, Mayor Robert F. Wagner.* Not visible: *Governor W. Averell Harriman)*

Rabbi Block and guest Cantor Otto Brown of the Black Jewish community in New York City, Congregation Mt. Horeb. Photo: Emerich C. Gross

An Ethiopian Jewish leader (Kes) *holding the Torah sent by The Brotherhood Synagogue.* Photo: Joan Roth

Rabbi Block and Cantor Leib Mirkovic leading the procession of Torahs out of our Greenwich Village building on March 19, 1974. Photo: Paul Hosefros/NYT Permissions

The former Friends Meeting House on Gramercy Park, acquired in November 1974 as the new home of The Brotherhood Synagogue. Photo: The New-York Historical Society

Interior of the Gramercy Park sanctuary of The Brotherhood Synagogue.
Photo: Arthur Kantor

Burning the synagogue mortgage, November 1986 (left to right: officers of the congregation—M. Milton Glass, Prof. Julius Marke, Arthur J. Greenbaum, Gerald J. Friedman, M.D., Comm. Gene Norman, behind Rabbi Block, The Rev. Dr. Thomas F. Pike, and Jeannette DiLorenzo of the United Federation of Teachers). Photo: Herbert Block

Rabbi Block teaching a Religious School class.

Dramatizing the story of Chanukah at a school assembly.

At the Western Wall in Jerusalem.
Photo: Goldring

An evening at our homeless shelter. Photo: Arthur Kantor

Russian Jewish immigrants learn about their heritage at a workshop in our sanctuary sponsored by the New York Association for New Americans. Photo: Jerry Soalt

Rabbi Block with his wife, Phyllis, and their son, Herbert. Photo: Hal Reiff

Herbert Block and his bride, Judith Greenberg, June 1996. Photo: Phyllis Block

The first time I had the pleasure of meeting Dr. Stitt was in 1952, shortly after The Village Temple had called our school's placement office. Rabbi Fleg and later Rabbi Sidney Strome had each served for two years as full-time religious leaders, but now the Temple could no longer afford a full-time rabbi. I was excited about two congregations sharing a sanctuary and was interested in applying for this position, but first I was anxious to meet the Minister and see the 13th Street building.

One Sunday morning I went to Greenwich Village with Uncle Jack and listened to a sermon by Dr. Stitt. He was a tall, handsome man with a fine speaking voice, and I congratulated him on his meaningful and very beautiful remarks. My uncle and I left with the very strong impression that it would be possible to work amicably with such a personable minister. Later Dr. Stitt revealed to me that he instinctively knew there was a purpose in our attending that Sunday morning service.

By the summer of 1952 I met with the rabbinic search committee of The Village Temple, and my name was presented to the membership for the position. I began to serve the congregation in October 1952.

As I soon learned, there is a vast difference between a classroom setting and a congregational atmosphere. In the classroom, students discuss their differences frankly but amicably, whereas in a congregation, some people's comments and actions often so irritate those with contrary viewpoints that tempers flare. It did not take me long to realize there were serious conflicts within The Village Temple. It had now been four years since the first contact with the Church, and the arrangement, which was to have been "temporary," had continued. By the time I arrived, Temple members, although initially grateful for the Church's hospitality, were anxious to acquire a building of their own. The Temple treasury was low, its membership was down, and many no longer approved of the original arrangement between the two congregations. Some officers disapproved of my association with the Minister, even for the purpose of raising funds jointly, and they cautioned me not to identify myself too closely nor become too friendly with him. There seemed to be a fear that the relationship with a church might prove a stumbling block for prospective members.

I did not share their concerns, nor could I accept or abide by the demands of the Temple's leadership that I should have little if anything to do with the Minister. Although it was normal for the congregation to want its own building, I felt that as long as we were sharing the facilities of the Church, it was a basic precept of Jewish life to be a "good neighbor," a *shachen tov*, and to be friendly and cordial.

Tensions were high. The Temple's Board of Trustees instructed me to submit my sermonic remarks to them for approval; the result was an open dispute between the Board and me over this fundamental principle of freedom of the pulpit. I was asked to meet with the president of the congregation, who conveyed the sentiment of the Board that it had the power to tell me what topic I might or might not speak on, and with whom I could or could not associate. My proposal to bring the dispute before a special meeting of the congregation was rejected; the trustees contended that their rules regarding the pulpit were final and not subject to discussion.

In addition, I was being chastised for wearing a yarmulke, for emphasizing the regulations of the Sabbath, for pointing out the value of the dietary laws, and for having a relationship with leaders of the Black Jewish community.

I had been educated and imbued with the philosophy of Rabbi Stephen Samuel Wise, who, facing a similar situation early in his own career, had declared that "No self-respecting minister of religion... could consider a call to a pulpit which... shall always be subject to, and under the control of the board of trustees." To me the trustees' attempt to stifle my freedom of the pulpit violated not only the spirit of Judaism but basic tenets of American democracy.

On June 9, 1953, I was ordained. I shared this sacred and joyful occasion with my father, my sisters, my brother, Aunt Bess and Uncle Jack, as well as with members of The Village Temple. The moment I had long envisioned had finally come. I had a sense of peace, inner strength, and confidence.

DIFFICULT DECISIONS

After ordination I continued to serve The Village Temple but, unfortunately, the disputes regarding freedom of the pulpit and future relationships with the Village Presbyterian Church continued.

My opposition to the Temple Board's position on these matters engendered intense discussion among the Temple members, a number of whom agreed with my position and expressed their views openly. Louis H. Solomon, then president of the Greenwich Village Chamber of Commerce, wrote:

Some years ago when I was asked to vote on the subject of holding services in the Presbyterian church, I opposed the move. Since that time I've had full opportunity to reappraise my judgment. I have come to the conclusion that when an opportunity comes to a congregation to influence the thinking of men throughout the nation toward improved relations, better understanding, and a dissemination of the fundamental principles of universal brotherhood, that congregation has a responsibility far greater than the responsibility for the limited service confined to its own congregation for spiritual well-being. It must seize that other responsibility.

Inevitably, we came to a parting of the ways. I left The Village Temple, The Village Temple left West 13th Street, and the Village Presbyterian Church was left with shattered hopes and dreams.[2]

I was now confronted with the wrenching question, "Where do I go from here to carry on my dream of religious brotherhood?"

2. The Village Temple soon acquired its own building on East 12th Street and has been an active Reform congregation in Greenwich Village, with many community-oriented programs.

THE TORAH AND THE FIRST LADY

One day when I was chatting with volunteers in The Village Temple office, I learned that they also volunteered for a United Nations-related organization and were working closely with Eleanor Roosevelt, widow of President Franklin D. Roosevelt. When I inquired about the possibility of having Mrs. Roosevelt speak at a Friday night service, they were not encouraging.

"It would be highly unlikely," they commented.

To which I replied, "Let's try. All she can do is say no." But she said "yes."

It was March 12, 1954. Over a thousand worshippers filled the sanctuary, and Dr. Stitt was with me on the altar. We had been at a loss as to what gift we should present to her. Because we wanted something of a spiritual nature, we decided on an attractive small Torah scroll which contained the complete text of the Five Books of Moses in Hebrew. Embroidered on the mantle were her name and the occasion of her visit. In making the presentation, I did not use the word "Torah," because I was not sure that she was familiar with the Hebrew word. I handed the scroll to Mrs. Roosevelt with a kiss on the mantle. She received it graciously and thanked me for this honor, adding, "What a memorable gift of the Torah you have given me!"

This Torah is now part of the collection in the Franklin D. Roosevelt Library at Hyde Park, and some years ago, on a visit to the Library, I was able to see and hold it once again.

4

Founding The Brotherhood Synagogue

"Two roads diverged in a wood, and I—
I took the one less traveled by,
and that has made all the difference."

ROBERT FROST

Major decisions lay ahead in 1954. Should I found a new congregation, based on my vision of what a synagogue should be, well aware that I would be starting this venture on a shoestring? Or should I accept a pulpit with an already established congregation? I was determined that any synagogue I might lead would be guided by the philosophy of the seventeenth-century Rabbi Jonathan Eibeschutz, an advocate for the poor, who stressed social interdependence and who considered the promotion of good will between Jews and non-Jews as a major individual and communal obligation.

I had already worked with Rev. Dr. Jesse William Stitt, whom I considered to be a sincere friend. A Christian Zionist and a man who had made an abiding commitment to the concept of religious brotherhood, he understood the pain I carried in my heart from the time I was a little boy and taunted as a "Christ-killer." His spirit, his love for all humanity, and his encouragement reinforced my desire to found a synagogue committed to brotherhood in action.

When I speak of a synagogue dedicated to brotherhood, I have in mind reaching out to the non-Jewish world as well as to the Jewish community. It becomes exceedingly difficult to build bridges and establish good relations with non-Jews if there is no unity among our own people. Indeed, I envisioned that some day there would be a parliament of religions peacefully coexisting and led by spiritual leaders who would instill respect for each other's traditions. After all, do we not worship the same one and eternal God? The Psalmist understood this: "How good and how pleasant it is for brethren to dwell together in unity." "No human institution in our long and continuous history has done more for the uplifting of the human race than the synagogue," wrote the non-Jewish historian H. T. Herford. What if, therefore, a synagogue were to spearhead new concepts and ideas to restore God's house to an eminent position as the rightful spiritual citadel around which all must rally?

I often reflected on the nature of an ideal synagogue. It should be:

- a warm and friendly place, because it is God's house;
- a sanctuary open to all, a haven where one can find respite, inspiration, and inner strength;
- a congregation with an open heart and an open door;
- a family whose members reach out to help one another and to assist all people in its community;
- a community where preachers and teachers truly exemplify the qualities of a religious person—one who does justly, loves mercy, and walks humbly with the Lord;
- a center for the arts and culture;
- an institution that fulfills its threefold purpose: to be a house of study, a house of prayer, and a house of assembly *(beit midrash, beit tefilah, beit k'nesset).*

I turned to senior colleagues whom I knew and respected to help me resolve my dilemma. I shared my anxiety with my mentors Rabbi Edward E. Klein of the Stephen Wise Free Synagogue, and Rabbi William F. Rosenblum of Temple Israel in Manhattan, both of whom had gained widespread recognition for their efforts to reach out to the non-Jewish world. They listened and encouraged me to go ahead on my own, but I was still not ready to make a final decision.

Then came a chance meeting with Rabbi George B. Lieberman of the Central Synagogue of Nassau County at a Free Synagogue function. I seized the opportunity to share with him my hopes and my inner struggle. "Irving," he counseled, "whatever you do will be right. But you're a young man, and if you don't try now, you will always regret it. If it doesn't succeed, you will have given up only a few years. But if the idea of brotherhood does succeed, you will be a very happy and contented man." That was exactly what I needed to hear.

FOUNDING A SYNAGOGUE

New York State law requires a minimum of nine individuals to form a religious corporation. I already had some prospective members, including my Aunt Bess and Uncle Jack, my Aunt Sarah Block, a cousin, Mamie Epstein, some friends, and a few people from my former congregation. Being mystically inclined, I chose 23 as the number of charter members because 1954 marked the 300th anniversary of the arrival of the first Jews in New Amsterdam, and that group numbered 23.

Some of our early discussions took place in the waiting room of a local optometrist, Dr. Nathan Schutz, on West 12th Street. He and his wife, Ruth, have been members of the congregation ever since. As we were reminiscing not long ago about those early days, he commented: "It was the concept of brotherhood which interested me. I always felt that this was an important step for the future of our society." Mrs. Schutz, who had been a high school teacher on the Lower East Side, recalled how she had assigned her students to make posters on the theme of brotherhood.

Yet there was one matter I still had to clarify. I did not want my Synagogue to function in the position of a subordinate, as I feared might happen if we had merely a landlord–tenant relationship with the Village Presbyterian Church. I wanted to be able to say unhesitatingly that ours was a *joint* sanctuary, because such an arrangement and sharing would give greater credibility to our work together.

Resolving this issue was crucial. I made an appointment to take it up with the Minister. As I sat in his study, waiting anxiously to find the right moment to broach the problem, Dr. Stitt spoke first.

"Irving," he said, "we had a meeting of the Board of Elders and Trustees last night, and they have been thinking about a kind of relationship other than that of landlord and tenant. We want to discuss the possibility of sharing our facilities as partners. What do you think?"

I jumped from my seat and exclaimed; "Jesse, Jesse! I'm sitting here waiting impatiently to introduce the very same subject! Yes! Yes! It's wonderful!"

I would often reflect on this magnanimous gesture of the Church people. They understood what was in my heart before I expressed it. I rejoiced, knowing that God was surely watching over us.

The term "partnership" would mean that all decisions regarding the maintenance of our buildings would be arrived at jointly. We would share the expenses of maintaining the premises. As time passed, it became abundantly clear how gracious the Church was in being willing to forego unilateral rights to the property.

The first meeting of The Brotherhood Synagogue took place on Wednesday, May 12, 1954, at 8:15 P.M., at 139 West 13th Street, in Dr. Stitt's office in the Village House, the four-story building that adjoined the main sanctuary and housed offices, auxiliary rooms, and an apartment for the sexton and his family. I had the privilege of presiding. Twenty-five men and women attended in addition to myself. Not everyone would remain with the congregation. Some came only to the initial meeting, curious to know what our direction would be. I explained that we would endeavor to meet the needs of modern American Jewry, avoiding uncompromising extremes and emphasizing the significance of the rich traditions of Judaism, and that we would be an independent congregation.

Jack Slotnick indicated that, with my assistance, he had written a letter officially notifying Dr. Stitt and the Elders and Trustees of the Church that a new synagogue was being formed based on five cardinal principles: a free pulpit, free pews, social service, community service, and an active and innovative program of brotherhood with the Village Presbyterian Church.

What is a *free pulpit*? It means the freedom of the rabbi to interpret the events of the present in light of God's teachings, speaking the truth as he or she sees it, without censorship or restrictions from any source except one's own judgment. The rabbi speaks to, and not for the congregation.

Free pews means that we do not own the pews in which we usually sit *(makom kavuah)*. It is the right of every Jew to worship in a synagogue at all times, especially on the High Holydays, without being required to purchase a "ticket."

Social service is our obligation to put forth a conscious effort to help others whenever and wherever necessary, limited only by the resources at our disposal. The synagogue not only should be a sanctuary for prayer, but also should assist its members and their families with problems or direct them to community resources.

Community service enjoins us to become involved in the affairs of the neighborhood in which we are located and to bring to bear the wisdom and insight of our Jewish heritage.

The initial question on everyone's mind was when to conduct our first Shabbat service. Only 48 hours remained before the next Sabbath. Could we possibly reach people in the community to announce our inaugural worship service as a congregation? A wise and generous octogenarian lady, Ruth Lichenstine, proposed, "Why not call the Fifth Avenue Hotel and inquire if a suitable room would be available for this coming Friday night, May 14?" I did so at once and minutes later returned to report that we could use the Jade Suite on the second floor. We took a vote. The decision was unanimous to hold our first service that Friday. Temple Israel, Rabbi Rosenblum's congregation, had offered to lend us prayer books and we would all look through drawers at home to find skullcaps. I would buy one of the small paper Torahs with a white mantle as used in summer camps, and the box in which it came could serve as our *Aron Kodesh* (Holy Ark). Mrs. Lichenstine offered to defray the expenses of the hotel and to provide the Oneg Shabbat (refreshments after the service).

Joseph Lipshie, whom we later affectionately called the "prince" of the Synagogue, took a $50 bill from his pocket, put it on the desk, and urged: "Now, let's get started. There's a great deal of work to be done."

Another supporter, Ida Brill, who worked for an office and stationery supply company, offered to provide whatever supplies we needed. We also approved placing a two-inch ad for two weeks in a local newspaper, *The Villager*. Temporary officers were appointed and interim members of the Board of Trustees were selected. The Rabbi of the congregation would be an ex officio member of the Board and of all committees.

We had not yet chosen an official name for our congregation. In fact, Rabbi Rosenblum had recently posed that very question. Naturally, I had been thinking about it for a long time and proposed "The Brotherhood Synagogue," with the Hebrew name "Congregation Beit Achim" (House of Brothers). Everyone agreed that it would be a splendid and accurate description of our aims. On that note we concluded our first meeting with the singing of "Hatikvah" and "The Star-Spangled Banner" and adjourned with feelings of pride, promise, and hope.

As I walked back to my apartment in Greenwich Village on that night when The Brotherhood Synagogue was founded, my heart and mind were filled with excitement and dreams of the future. I sat at my desk and rapidly jotted down thoughts that rushed across my mind:

Today we have created something which can have a wide, almost universal effect on the contemporary scene. I use the word "created" advisedly, for our achievements have not yet begun in the realm of human relations, though the ideal of religious brotherhood is as ancient as the Bible. What we are aiming for is the realization of these values in the daily lives of men and women.

Central to the moral laws of the Bible is the concept "love thy neighbor as thyself." The nobility of the ideal has made it complex. It is our firm belief that the genius of this cardinal principle is revealed to us in the application of friendship and fellowship to all whom we have occasion to meet.

Will we have success? Only God can know, but we are firmly convinced that we make this attempt for the glorification of God's name here on earth. The theme of our Synagogue is love, its message is brotherhood, its tool is the Bible, its aim is peace, its program is fellowship. Its success will depend on the spirit with which we work together.

Thirty-one people attended our first worship service, including a family who had come to ask God's blessings upon their newborn daughter.

Standing at the lectern that the hotel had furnished, I looked out at *my* first congregation. The small room seemed full and everyone was quietly patient as I made last-minute arrangements for the candle blessing and spoke to the woman who had volunteered to provide a musical background. Naturally I was somewhat tense, but I reminded myself that this was not the first time I had conducted a service, that I was familiar with the Sabbath evening liturgy, and I cautioned myself not to rush. Words from the Talmud were reassuring and gave me confidence: "Do God's will as if it were your will, so that God may do your will as if it were His will." Our first Shabbat service went exceedingly well.

At our second Board meeting, on May 19, the name of our congregation was formally adopted. We were to be incorporated as The Brotherhood Synagogue Congregation Beth Achim of Greenwich Village, to be known in the community as The Brotherhood Synagogue.

At that meeting the Board also discussed forming committees to implement joint activities of the Synagogue and Church, and it reiterated and emphasized that nothing would be done to prejudice the spiritual and religious practices of either congregation. Ours would be a synagogue traditional in our approach and with a liberal attitude toward social issues. The Village Church, like any other church, was very positive in its traditions. But we would work together, not compete, befriend one another and not be rivals.

The Minister kept his office, facing the street, and mine was just down the hall so we could consult with each other easily and often. The Village House next door had two signs at the entrance, the one on the left read "Office of the Minister" and the one on the right, "Office of the Rabbi."

The proposed budget for the first fiscal year, June 1, 1954, to May 31, 1955, was $24,000, including administrative costs, advertising, printing, a $15 petty cash fund, religious articles, an Ark, education, salaries for the Rabbi ($5,000) and the Cantor ($2,500), religious school supplies and salaries, as well as miscellaneous items. We allocated $1,800 for our initial share of the cost of maintaining the two buildings, although this sum was only a small portion of what our contribution should have been. The Village Presbyterian Church, recognizing that we were a new congregation, agreed to accept whatever we could afford at the time.

The Board met again on June 9, 1954, which coincidentally was the first anniversary of my ordination. Being at a meeting in my own congregation would have been unimaginable the year before. It was all like a dream.

We determined that Synagogue dues would be $25 per adult, plus an additional $10 for a spouse, with the children in a family automatically included; and the Board agreed to accept any arrangement made by the Rabbi with those unable to afford full dues. No one would be excluded. The Board also asked the Rabbi to be the one to recommend members to serve as Trustees. The minutes of that meeting further record that the "Rabbi reported a contribution of $15 for a wedding he performed, which will purchase another 10 prayer books. Louis Solomon donated $100 for additional prayer books and hymnals, requesting Rabbi Block to autograph one of these for his personal use." It was also announced that Joseph Lipshie and Fred Greenberg had each donated a Torah to the Synagogue and that Mr. Greenberg would chair the effort to raise funds for a Holy Ark. We were on our way.

Even as The Brotherhood Synagogue became a reality, I nevertheless wanted to reconfirm for myself that sharing a sanctuary on a permanent basis with a congregation of a different faith was acceptable according to *Halakhah* (Jewish law). Some rabbis, who did not favor a close relationship with any other religious bodies, held that Judaism does not permit sharing religious property on a permanent basis. They felt uncomfortable with our arrangement. On the other hand, some equally respected, traditional rabbis had affirmed that our congregation was not violating Jewish law inasmuch as the Church's religious symbols were not displayed during Jewish worship services.

During the next few weeks our congregation received other gifts: funds for an additional 60 prayer books and 50 hymnals, $100 for a pulpit Bible, cash contributions, as well as 16 reams of mimeograph paper, which we shared with the Church. The Board considered an estimate of $100 for painting the Rabbi's study too high and proposed that someone volunteer to paint the room with the sexton. Eventually, the job was completed.

The Synagogue had no staff—we couldn't afford to pay any salaries at this point—so I became the general factotum: I was the secretary, the bookkeeper, the typist, the fund-raiser, while at the same time fulfilling my rabbinical duties. I couldn't have managed without the assistance of a number of our members who volunteered in the office. Others, like Mel Ringler, later Chairman of our Board, used to drive me on Sundays to unveilings and other functions. Thank goodness I didn't have to worry about the sanctuary or building maintenance. Dr. Stitt handled those matters willingly and very efficiently. The summer of 1954 was hectic and overwhelming, but exhilarating and exciting.

Two very important matters were set down in the minutes of our June 30 Board meeting: the names of the founding members of our congregation and a discussion of the steps to be taken to incorporate our Synagogue under the Religious Corporations Law of New York State.

Founding Members

Rabbi Irving J. Block,
Founding Rabbi

David Applebaum	Joseph Lipshie
Sidney Axelrod	Marian Lipshie
Sarah Block	Mary Nathan
Ida Brill	Florence Newfield
Mamie Epstein	Ruth Rosenthal
Nicholas Grant	Bess Block Slotnick
Fred Greenberg	Jacob L. Slotnick
Bess Greene	Louis H. Solomon
William Greene	Vivien C. Speyer
Samuel Herzlinger	Rebecca Palter Swinden
Irving Kurzman	William Weiner
Ruth Lichenstine	

The Brotherhood Synagogue formally adopted the Articles of Incorporation on July 15, 1954, about an hour before the

Sabbath. The following day a leading newspaper in New York City reported, "The Jewish congregation is the only one in the city and possibly the only one in the country that shares the edifice of the Presbyterian Church on a permanent basis."

GETTING STARTED

One of the first topics Dr. Stitt and I discussed was the formation of a Brotherhood Council to manage our joint programs and affairs.

The Minister inquired, "How many people are required for public worship within Judaism?"

"Ten," I replied.

"And what is this called?"

"A *minyan*."

"All right then," he proposed, "let us set up a *minyan* of our two congregations, five from the Church and five from the Synagogue. This will probably be the first mixed *minyan* in the country! You and I will be the eleventh and twelfth members and we can represent the twelve tribes of Israel, or the twelve Apostles." And so it was.

Dr. Stitt and I alternated as chairmen of our Brotherhood Council meetings, which discussed subjects such as building repairs and maintenance, new carpeting for the sanctuary, joint community activities, holiday observances, and fund-raising. We often explained, tongue-in-cheek, that we had three separate Boards—Church, Synagogue, and Council—and three separate treasuries and budgets—Church, Synagogue, and Council—and we usually had three deficits as well.

At one point we had a sexton named Angel, a delightful coincidence that was reported by a columnist in one of the city's daily papers. Whenever we needed him, we would call out "Angel, Angel!" I thought of the legend that in heaven there are angels formed half in fire and half in ice. The fire did not melt the ice and the ice did not extinguish the fire; the sole purpose of these angelic creatures was to prove that even opposites can coexist if only they have the desire to do so.

Dr. Stitt and I considered it very important to write down our principles and goals. We drew up a document we called "Our Covenant of Brotherhood," a statement, we believed, unique in the annals of church and synagogue relations. I had the privilege of writing the first section, which reflects on God's creativity and beneficence and mankind's rejection of the spiritual contract with our Maker. The second portion, written by Dr. Stitt, set forth our purpose and commitment. The complete text is as follows:

We believe that God created man and God blessed man and provided all that is necessary for his sustenance. God exhorted man to live in peace and harmony with his neighbor and together to enjoy these blessings. Man learned the skills needed to till the soil and to develop its natural resources. Through nature and through his daily experiences, man increasingly discovered God and worshipped Him with hymns of praise and deeds of loving-kindness. This is recorded in the Bible and in the other chronicles of world literature.

But verily, these same accounts show that man forsook God and spurned Him; that man was often concerned only with his own wants; that he mistreated his neighbor and wrought implements of violence; that he enlisted others to opinions of unrighteousness; that tribe fought against tribe, people against people, and nation against nation, so that there never has been an age which could not speak of man's inhumanity to man, nor a country which could not cry out that its earth has been stained with human blood. They who claimed to be leaders of religion decried beliefs which differed from theirs and put to the sword those who worshipped God according to their conscience rather than to a regulated mode. Even unto this day man has forsaken the plain truth that there is but One Father and we are all His children, that to do His will is our duty and to love Him and our fellowman is the soul's greatest joy.

Therefore, having been led, as we believe, by the spirit of God, as two religious congregations representing The Brotherhood Synagogue (Congregation Beth Achim of Greenwich Village) and The Village Presbyterian Church, and believing in the Fatherhood of God and the Brotherhood of Man, we most solemnly and joyfully enter into covenant with one another.

We consecrate ourselves to a program of brotherhood.

We commit ourselves to a joint service for the community of man.

We engage ourselves to do whatsoever the hand findeth to do for human welfare, without preference for or prejudice to race, creed, or color.

We undertake this endeavor before God to the end that the truth of universal brotherhood may be established in full measure upon the earth, and man's responsibility to man be accepted as the mandate of God.

We moreover pledge that all our activities and programs jointly sponsored and implemented are to be undertaken without compromise to the religious conscience or the established traditions of our respective congregations.

We believe in this, Our Covenant of Brotherhood, and we invoke God's blessings upon our endeavors that peace and good will may obtain among all the inhabitants of our world and that religion may spread its blessings among us all.

THE HISTORY OF THE BUILDING

The Village Presbyterian Church dated back to 1846, when it was built on land once owned by Congregation Shearith Israel, the Spanish and Portuguese Synagogue. On May 1, 1846, the Reverend Samuel D. Burchard was installed as the first minister of the newly formed 13th Street Presbyterian Church, a congregation of 184 members who had left the parent church on Houston Street because they wanted to take an open stand against slavery. James Polk was President of The United States at the time, our country was embroiled in the Mexican War, and it faced the problems of westward expansion to the Pacific.

In 1884 Rev. Burchard was invited to speak on the same platform with James A. Blaine, Republican candidate for President, who was running against Grover Cleveland. The minister excoriated the Democratic party as one of "Rum, Romanism and Rebellion," which infuriated many voters and may have cost Blaine the election.

Built in Greek Revival style, with six Doric columns, the Church building had a handsome, colonial 800-seat sanctuary with mahogany-trimmed white wood pews with doors at the entrance to each row. Fruits and flowers of the Bible formed the decorative motif of the two-story-high stained glass windows along the sides of the sanctuary.

One of the immediate responsibilities of The Brotherhood Council was to plan for redesigning the altar of the sanctuary to serve the religious needs of both congregations in keeping with the injunction from Isaiah 56:7, "My house shall be called a house of prayer for all peoples." The Church had a lectern in the center of the altar where Dr. Stitt would deliver his sermon and read the Scriptures. I favored a pulpit on one side from which the Rabbi could offer his sermon plus a lectern on the other side for the Cantor. This arrangement was acceptable to Dr. Stitt. We also replaced the side steps leading to the altar with graceful, sweeping, semicircular stairs in the center.

The *Aron Kodesh* (Holy Ark) housing the Torahs contained wood from four continents to convey the universality of God's presence. Designed by the award-winning architect Edgar Tafel, a Greenwich Village resident and former student of Frank Lloyd Wright, the Ark was recessed into the wall of the altar in the main sanctuary.

On a large circular valance above the Ark was the command: "Love Thy Neighbor As Thyself" in English and Hebrew and visible at all times. A maroon velvet curtain hung from beneath the valance and enclosed the Holy Ark. When the Church held its services, a Cross was brought in and placed on the altar table. During Synagogue services, a drape was drawn across the one window that depicted a scene from the New Testament.

The Menorah, a portable seven-branched candelabra, was the work of Emanuel Milstein, a well-known Jewish artist and sculptor, who also designed the beautiful gold letters of the *Sh'ma*, the Jewish Declaration of Faith, surmounting the Holy Ark, as well as a stand for the pulpit Bible, and the panels for the base of the altar table. Since the Church preferred a less ornamental table at its services, the artist made the panels removable. The Menorah and the white custom-designed altar furniture—lecterns, chairs, and table—are still in use in our Gramercy Park sanctuary, and the original Ark stands in the large auditorium below the main sanctuary and holds the Torahs at summer and community High Holyday services.

One of the questions people would frequently ask Dr. Stitt and me was, "What happens when Christian and Jewish religious holidays coincide?" Fortunately for us, the Almighty had already resolved that problem, for centuries ago the rabbis planned the religious calendar so that the observance of Yom Kippur can never fall on a Friday or a Sunday. On the other festivals and holidays, the Synagogue would simply begin its worship service a little earlier, when necessary, and the Church a little later; and we always managed quite well.

I selected the Union Prayer Book (Reform) for our Sabbath evening services, because I thought its English text might be more meaningful to those not fully familiar with synagogue worship. In addition it had an elegant, poetic English translation, and was easy to follow. Two years later, when we introduced Saturday morning services, we chose the Silverman (Conservative) Siddur, which lent itself to more congregational participation. From the very first year we decided to use the (Silverman) *Machzor* (High Holyday prayer book), because we recognized that on those solemn days people seemed to yearn for a more traditional service. (Twenty years later the congregation adopted the Silverman prayer book for Friday nights as well.)

OUR FIRST HIGH HOLYDAYS

As the summer of 1954 went by, it became imperative to engage a cantor without further delay, but I kept postponing initiating a telephone call to the Hebrew Union School of Sacred Music; something seemed to be holding me back. When I finally did reach Cantor Wolf Hecker, administrator of the cantorial school, I explained, hastily and apologetically, that, yes, I realized I may have waited too long before requesting a cantor for the upcoming High Holydays; I was hurrying to an appointment and asked if

I could call him again later in the day, saying that I just wanted to take a moment now to explain our needs to him.

Cantor Hecker replied, "Rabbi Block, how would you like to have Cantor Leo Mirkovic as your *chazan*?"

I countered, "He's in Washington, D.C., with one of the major congregations in the country."

"How would you like to have Leo Mirkovic as your cantor?" he repeated.

Again I said, "Wolf, I beg of you, I'm rushed."

For a third time he insisted, "How would you like to have Leo Mirkovic as your cantor?"

This time I retorted impatiently, "You don't understand. I'm late, the holidays are almost here, I'm in no mood for jokes."

"One moment," he said.

And then a familiar and unforgettable voice with an inimitable accent came on. "Hello, Oiving? This is Leo!"

"Leo! What are you doing in New York?" I shouted.

"I'm staying here. I left the congregation in Washington and I'm looking for another synagogue position."

I immediately responded, "Leo, you must be with us. But," I told him, "a cantor in New York City has to use his Hebrew name." So began twenty years of magnificent music with Cantor *Leib* Mirkovic.

The Cantor was born in Yugoslavia, where, as a child, he was on the bridge in Sarajevo at the time Archduke Francis Ferdinand was assassinated on June 28, 1914—an assault that led to World War I. During the Nazi regime in World War II Leo Mirkovic was imprisoned in a concentration camp, escaped, and joined the Italian underground.

He always sang with passion and intensity, reflecting the pain he bore, the pain of the Jewish people, as well as the joy of worshipping the Almighty. His tones were rich and mellifluous, enhancing each service so that it became a true religious experience. Assisting him was a professional four-voice choir, and we availed ourselves of the magnificent pipe organ installed by the Church many years earlier. Every year he and I would deliver a "Sermon in Jewish Music" together, but, with a twinkle in our eyes, we agreed that I would not sing and he would not preach. Together with the choir we also made a recording of selections from the liturgy. (It was recently reissued on cassette.)

No one who worshipped with us in those years has ever forgotten Cantor Mirkovic's chanting. During one of his trips to Yugoslavia to visit a brother, he was offered the position of head of the Yugoslavian State Opera. But so great had been his suffering during World War II that he declined the offer and chose to remain in America. Former Bar and Bat Mitzvah students still fondly remember his strict, but affectionate, coaching and training. He had no relatives in this country and so my family and the congregation became his extended family.

After his retirement in 1974, and until he passed away in Florida in 1990, the Cantor often returned to sing on the High Holydays—his voice still soaring—and on special occasions such as our son's Bar Mitzvah and the 25th anniversary of my ordination. Leib Mirkovic was a devoted friend and an inspiration to us all.

In 1992, after I had announced my plans to retire, I received a letter from Glenna Parker Wood, a longtime member of the choir:

[I] treasured the many memories of the years I was associated through music and friendship with The Brotherhood Synagogue.... I feel that in some small way...the quartet and the organists provided the necessary musical harmony with the Cantor to support you...as you went about organizing a new synagogue which would welcome all those who would come and believe.... One can only dream what the world would be like if all the nations of the world practiced brotherhood.

As the High Holyday season approached, I reflected on how to make our first New Year as a congregation significant in Jewish life, while also enriching the community at large. What if church carillons were to play Jewish holiday melodies during the days between Rosh Hashanah and Yom Kippur? What if congregants were to hear the *Kol Nidre* played as they went to synagogue on the eve of the Day of Atonement? I shared my thoughts with Dr. Stitt, who wholeheartedly concurred and proposed the idea to the Protestant Council of Churches in New York. The Manhattan division passed a resolution to that effect, observing that 1954 marked the 300th anniversary of the first Jewish settlement in New York. A number of churches agreed to participate and filled the air with the plaintive *Kol Nidre* melody, which the Jewish newspaper *The American Hebrew* heralded in a banner headline: "Churches Make History, Chimes Heard on Yom Kippur."

We also suggested that, as an added expression of good will, churches might want to put on their bulletin boards phrases such as: "Best wishes to our Jewish neighbors and friends in this holy season," a gesture that costs so little but can mean so much. Today, in New York City at least, such messages are not uncommon as congregations of different faiths exchange holiday greetings in their newsletters and on their outdoor boards.

Even before the High Holyday season began we had planned where to set up an outdoor succah, the temporary booth erected during the festival of Succoth, which falls five days after Yom Kippur. Adorned with fall fruits, plants, leaves, and branches, the booth is a symbol: just as the succah is frail, so is life; and just as the booth grows in beauty when we fill it with nature's bounty, so the days of our years become more beautiful when we bring God into our lives. Moreover, Succoth has also been known as "the Brotherhood festival" ever since the days when King Solomon offered a sacrifice of 70 bullocks for the 70 nations of the world.

With the approval of The Brotherhood Council, we erected our booth near a side entrance to the theater auditorium below the sanctuary. It caught the attention of the theatergoers, including one we did not expect—the fire inspector. He concurred that, yes, the succah was beautiful but noted that it was too close to the door of the theater and thus in violation of the Fire Code. Dr. Stitt and I then related the story of a pious Jew who put up a succah on the roof of his building in a fashionable neighborhood. The landlord took him to court. The judge, who was also Jewish, rendered the following decision: "The holiday of Succoth is celebrated for a week, but nevertheless you must abide by the law of the land and take down the booth. However, I will give you ten days to do so." The fire inspector permitted our succah to remain in place for the balance of the week provided we had fire extinguishers on hand and a guard. After that incident, we always built the succah in our building's courtyard so it would be visible to passersby.

TEACHING THE NEXT GENERATION

Fundamental to Jewish life is the principle that every boy and girl is entitled to receive a religious education and it is every community's duty to provide it. The word "rabbi" means "teacher;" teaching is our purpose and our mission. In the first century, Rabbi Joshua Ben Gamala insisted that it was the obligation of the community to provide schools and teachers for all children, a philosophy that would ultimately lead to universal education.

Within the first weeks of the establishment of our synagogue, we allocated funds ($1,000) for a religious school. Classes began after the High Holydays with one volunteer teacher and 6 children and met on Saturday mornings so as not to interfere with the Village Church's Sunday school. Within two weeks our enrollment had tripled—18 children, four of them in a Bar/Bat Mitzvah class.

The curriculum included a worship service, Bible stories, history, customs and ceremonies, and Jewish music.

There was no stipulated fee; parents were invited to make a contribution for the support of the school, but no child was ever turned away.

The third year we had three salaried teachers and three classes, and our curriculum had expanded to include more intensive Hebrew language instruction. Rabbi Leo Storozum was appointed principal-educator in the fall of 1956, and classes were held on Sundays in a private school nearby because we had outgrown our own facilities.

A year later our enrollment had grown to 30 children and we engaged teachers from Stern College of Yeshiva University. By our fifth anniversary we had a registration of 52 children.

SHARING AND WORKING TOGETHER

As our congregation grew both in membership and in financial strength, we voluntarily increased our contribution toward the management of the property. Over time we raised it from an initial 25 percent to a third, then to half and later, as we were able to handle more, to two-thirds of the maintenance budget. When some members of the Village Church demurred, saying that a partnership should be 50/50, we explained that as they had been gracious to us when we were a fledgling congregation, we wanted to reciprocate their generosity. Isn't that what brotherhood is all about?

Dr. Stitt and I proposed, and The Brotherhood Council agreed, that we should affix a sign on the gate outside the main sanctuary to share our story with the community. It read:

ONE HOUSE SERVING TWO FAITHS

THIS HOUSE OF WORSHIP IS SHARED WITH TWO CONGREGATIONS WHO HAVE ENTERED INTO A COVENANT OF BROTHERHOOD. IT HAS BEEN ARCHITECTURALLY DESIGNED TO SERVE AS A SYNAGOGUE ON THE SABBATH AND JEWISH HOLY DAYS, AND AS A CHURCH ON SUNDAY AND DAYS OF CHRISTIAN OBSERVANCE.

TOGETHER THE VILLAGE PRESBYTERIAN CHURCH AND THE BROTHERHOOD SYNAGOGUE ENGAGE IN COMMUNITY ACTIVITIES TO FOSTER BETTER UNDERSTANDING AND COOPERATION. THESE ACTIVITIES ARE CARRIED ON THROUGH THE BROTHERHOOD COUNCIL WITHOUT COMPROMISE TO THE RELIGIOUS CONSCIENCE AND THE ESTABLISHED TRADITIONS OF THE TWO CONGREGATIONS.

THIS PROGRAM OF SHARING AND WORKING TOGETHER WAS BEGUN IN 1954 AND REPRESENTS OUR EFFORT TO BRING ABOUT A WORLD OF PEACE AND BROTHERHOOD.

At Thanksgiving our two congregations sponsored a community-wide ecumenical religious service. One year clergy and congregants from as many as 20 different houses of worship in Greenwich Village and lower Manhattan joined with us. One worshipper's comment summarized the significance of this program: "I come to these Thanksgiving services because it's the only sane hour in an altogether insane world."

The month of December provided another opportunity to exchange greetings. Both Chanukah and Christmas are celebrated at the time of the winter solstice and both have themes of light, joy, and renewal. An announcement on our Synagogue bulletin board extended "Best wishes to our Christian neighbors and friends for a Merry Christmas," while the Church reciprocated with, "Best wishes to our Jewish friends and neighbors for a Happy Chanukah," simple overtures that touch the heart and create a warm spirit of neighborliness and friendship.

As our two congregations worked together, our innovative programs and joint sanctuary engendered a great deal of interest. Local and national publications carried stories about our partnership, and we received invitations to speak before civic and religious groups in the city and elsewhere in the country, as well as to appear on radio and television. (See Chapter 6.) Wherever we went we were always received warmly, sometimes even with wonder and amazement. While we knew that ours was a unique venture, evidently actually seeing a rabbi and a minister standing and speaking side by side was more impressive than a thousand pictures. On one occasion an elderly Jewish lady said to us, "I've dreamed about this day for a lifetime."

When asked what specific programs and projects we were planning, I replied that life itself would offer us opportunities for joint activities. And that is just what happened.

One day a representative of the New York City Department of Mental Health rang our doorbell and introduced himself. His assignment was to encourage religious institutions to sponsor a series of discussions on a wide range of mental health topics; his department would provide films and speakers. Dr. Stitt and I immediately agreed to participate, for, after all, these issues affect everyone.

In time, The Brotherhood Council established a Family Counseling Service because, in our view, churches and synagogues should be not only citadels of religious values and sanctuaries for prayer, but also resources in the field of human relations. Our panel, chaired by Dr. Sherwin Kaufman, a member of my congregation, included Dr. Stitt and me, other physicians, psychiatrists, psychologists, therapists, and social workers. The initial consultation was available to anyone in the community without charge.

OUR THEATER

For several years prior to our relationship with the Village Presbyterian Church, the building had housed a highly acclaimed playhouse, The Greenwich Mews Theatre (formerly The Lemonade Opera). Stella Holt, its producer, had overcome the limitations of her blindness and, with the able and devoted assistance of her colleague Frances Drucker, had pioneered the concept of Off-Broadway theater as a showcase for new talent. Miss Holt soon acquired a superb reputation, giving many African-American and Hispanic playwrights, actors, and actresses their early professional opportunities. Works of Langston Hughes were a mainstay of the repertory. The Brotherhood Synagogue joined with the Church as a co-sponsor of the theater. One of the stipulations, which Miss Holt readily accepted, was that the plays have social and cultural significance, or, as we used to put it, "that what is performed downstairs should follow what is preached upstairs." Dr. Stitt and I read all scripts and we both had to approve them before they could be staged. Out of respect for the Jewish Sabbath, Miss Holt, whose favorite expression was *Baruch*

Ha-Shem yom yom (Thank God each day), agreed not to schedule performances on Friday nights.

Probably one of our most outstanding productions was "Jerico-Jim Crow" by Langston Hughes, first performed in the sanctuary in 1964 under the direction of Alvin Ailey and William Hairston, with music arranged and directed by Hugh Porter. In song and dance it narrated, as Stella and Frances put it, "the grand symphony of the struggle for human rights" in the South. The show was an immediate success and played to audiences around the country, on college campuses, and at civil rights meetings. It was broadcast in London by the BBC and later in Australia and New Zealand. Critics hailed it as an "important cultural production" and gave credit to The Brotherhood Synagogue and the Village Presbyterian Church.

In 1965 the two major productions were "The Exception and the Rule" by Bertolt Brecht and "The Prodigal Son" by Langston Hughes performed together on one bill. At their 100th performance the audience included Arthur Spingarn, National President of the NAACP, Dr. Ralph Bunche, Undersecretary of the United Nations, and Mrs. Bunche. Before leaving the theater Dr. Bunche penned a note on a copy of our Covenant of Brotherhood: "With warm congratulations on the socially significant and unique theater of The Brotherhood Council." Subsequently "The Prodigal Son" went on a world tour and was performed in Italy at the Spoleto Festival at the invitation of its director, Gian-Carlo Menotti. At all times, the playbills carried the names of our two congregations and thus our message.

In 1969, recognizing that the growing Spanish-speaking population in New York longed for professional performances of the great Spanish classics, Dr. Stitt and I welcomed a new repertory group, later known as the Greenwich Mews Spanish Theatre. The actors also took their productions into the community, playing, literally, on the streets in Hispanic neighborhoods without charge. Under the leadership of Gilberto Zaldivar and Rene Buch, the troupe eventually moved to its own building and continues to play an important role in New York's cultural life.

The Brotherhood Council also organized concerts on the theme "Brotherhood Through Music," featuring choral groups such as the United Nations Singers, a 70-voice children's choir from Our Lady of Pompeii, a nearby Catholic Church, the All-City High School Chorus, as well as Cantor Mirkovic and the choirs of our two congregations. One program featured the noted jazz musician and composer Eddie Bonnemere, along with the Reverend John Gensel of St. Peter's Lutheran Church, who discussed and performed examples of contemporary music in worship services.

For Dr. Stitt and for me, theater and music were an extension of our efforts to inspire, respect, and understand different cultures, another way to spread the ideals of brotherhood.

TEACHING AND PREACHING TOGETHER

Other joint activities developed naturally. We began collecting food for the hungry and organizing bazaars to raise funds for the work of The Brotherhood Council. When the Church held a bazaar for its own needs, Synagogue members gladly lent their support by contributing merchandise and buying at the sale.

Dr. Stitt and I often exchanged pulpits. We would choose a common theme and he would preach on Friday night and I on a Sunday morning. One year our topic was, "If I Were a Rabbi" and "If I Were a Minister." Dr. Stitt, preaching as if he were the rabbi, called our relationship a "valiant undertaking" and the sanctuary a place where each congregation can feel "at home." He exhorted the Synagogue worshippers to learn more about the teachings and beautiful traditions of Judaism, to attend services regularly, and to be supportive of the State of Israel. He also reminded us that throughout history not all Christians have been anti-Semitic and that many Christians, "great and small," sacrificed their lives for their Jewish brethren.

"We should," he urged, "become familiar both with the yearnings and convictions of all the great faiths if we would be truly brothers with one another." He also pointed out that "very long would be the list of names" of those great Christians who worked to help the Jewish people fulfill the ancient prophecies of establishing a homeland.

In speaking to the members of Dr. Stitt's Church, I stated that if I were a minister I would want my congregation to be familiar with the teachings of Moses and Jesus. Both had a common heritage and both taught one and the same message; love of God and love for all people. I lamented that the words of Jesus have been distorted by his followers and led to hatred and prejudice against Jesus's own people. And, like Dr. Stitt, I spoke about Israel and how important it was for Christians to help build the country, so that we could all "be inspired by a revival of the land of the Bible." Together our two congregations had been accomplishing great things because we were going out among the people and "telling them of the joys of working together for the Fatherhood of God and the Brotherhood of Man; that the time is at hand for priests, ministers, and rabbis to work as a team for the glory of God."

It was only natural to invite our members to attend services in each other's congregations, especially on major holidays and festivals, to learn about the traditions and rituals of another faith. "We are twice blessed," said a Village Church member, "by these opportunities as well as by our work together." A former member of Dr. Stitt's church reminisced that, after more than 40 years, she still remembers her first Rosh Hashanah service in our Synagogue, the beautiful voice of Cantor Mirkovic, and how she was inspired to begin to learn Hebrew so she could follow the liturgy.

Dr. Stitt and I also offered a series of lectures entitled "The Minister, the Rabbi, and the Bible." We introduced an essay and poster contest for children in neighborhood public, private, and parochial schools on the general theme of "How Can One Be a Better Brother, a Better Person?" It became a very popular annual event for a number of years and, most importantly, led to discussions by young people, their families, and teachers on the meaning of true brotherhood.

At the outset of our relationship, neither the Minister nor I had expected to do anything more than to try to attain the noble goal of the 133rd Psalm, "to dwell together in unity." As others began to recognize our work, however, letters began pouring in. In December 1955 Dr. Everett R. Clinchy, President of the National Conference of Christians and Jews, wrote to us:

...There are many fine things about this Adventure In Goodwill. It is mutually stimulating to the Congregations. It leads to cooperation on common civic tasks. It results in a sublime competition in spiritual excellence and a friendly rivalry in good works.

I hope that the experiment...is continued successfully. It will be a rich encounter between two cultures, good in itself, and also a reminder that throughout the world congregations of Jews and Christians which worship in separate buildings would do well to cultivate a chain reaction of encounters for their mutual stimulation, growth, and for the discovery of new ways to cooperate without compromise.

By the end of our first year as a congregation our membership was increasing; Religious School enrollment was growing; we had an active Women's Auxiliary and a popular Young Adult League. Several hundred worshippers attended our High Holyday services. We had won the respect of the community, and our partnership with The Village Church was beginning to attract national attention.

A Case of Mistaken Identity

One day as I walked to my office, I was astonished to find work-men on tall ladders painting the columns on the portico of the sanc-tuary building. I was a bit annoyed, since this work had not been discussed by The Brotherhood Council. I immediately went to Dr. Stitt's office and inquired when this work had been authorized. He looked at me in bewilderment. We rushed downstairs, spoke to the workmen, and discovered, to their dismay, that they were supposed to be painting St. John's Church, a couple of blocks away on West 11th Street. Evidently they had misunderstood the address, and, because both buildings were very similar architecturally, they didn't realize they were on the wrong street, in the wrong place. As they started to pack up and leave, we yelled, "Listen, fellas, you can't leave just like that, with some columns painted and some not!" The workmen quickly touched up all the columns so they would appear more or less alike and went on their way.

5

Building a Congregation

*"In a world too often divided,
a rabbi and a minister have set
an example of true brotherhood."*

AMERICAN WEEKLY, FEB. 16, 1958

In Chapter 37 of the book of Genesis, the patriarch Jacob sends his son Joseph to inquire about his brothers, who were supposedly tending the sheep in Shechem. Without hesitation, Joseph goes to look for them; he meets a man who realizes that this young lad is searching for something or someone. He asks, "What is it you are looking for?" and Joseph replies, in one of the seminal phrases of the Bible, "I am looking for my brethren."

If I were asked to state the fundamental philosophy of The Brotherhood Synagogue, it would be to acknowledge that, like Joseph, we are all commanded to seek our brethren—no matter what one's faith, color, creed, or background, for the image of God is imprinted on us all. As Jews we have the task of creating a climate of respect and universality, remembering that although each one of us is a unique individual, we are all God's children, we are all brothers and sisters. The essence of Judaism may be found in the writings of our Hasidic masters: we must always be in search of God, even as God is in search of us.

Prayer and meditation and observance of the holidays and festivals are effective ways of bringing us together with God.

THE OPEN-DOOR POLICY

For many congregations the issue of membership dues often becomes contentious in the weeks preceding the High Holydays, because those who are unaffiliated nevertheless desire to pray and have a place to worship during this season. A number of congregations, therefore, view this time as an opportunity for fund-raising. They argue, "If we sell tickets, we will have more funds to accomplish the synagogue's purposes," and they turn to the pithy saying in the Talmud: "If there is no substance, there is no Torah." I always counter this view with the second half of that statement: "Without Torah, there can be no substance." If congregations worried less about funds and more about bringing people into the synagogue, we would be furthering God's will.

To whom do our prayers belong? I remember that, as a youngster in Bridgeport, I would accompany my father to synagogue before the High Holydays and view a floor plan in the office, just as one would at a theater. The more expensive "tickets" were closer to the Holy Ark, and the less expensive ones were for seats in the back rows. I am still dismayed at the charges for High Holyday seats in some congregations. I vowed that in *my* synagogue no one would have to pay to pray, and no one would be turned away. A person's identification as a Jew entitles that person to be welcomed to a synagogue.

For a synagogue to set a charge for the privilege of worship goes contrary to the very spirit of our faith. Indeed, we are but transmitters of the teachings that we have received; we can do no less than make them available to others as they were made available to us. This approach remains a central policy of our Synagogue today.

At The Brotherhood Synagogue, we have always adopted an open-door policy. We do not sell seats or tickets for admission at the High Holydays. On Rosh Hashanah and Yom Kippur we conduct two evening services, one for the membership, the other for the community. Every year one of the most beautiful and awe-inspiring moments is to see the seemingly endless line, three abreast for several blocks, of fellow Jews—a large number of them young people—waiting patiently to enter the Synagogue for the community services, especially the Kol Nidre. We also arrange *Yizkor* memorial prayers to accommodate the community, and have always held special Rosh Hashanah and Yom Kippur services for children and their families.

Years ago Gabriel Cohen, the editor of the *National Jewish Post and Opinion*, lauded The Brotherhood Synagogue's policy of keeping the doors open to the community. I am proud and gratified that our practice is being adopted by many other congregations to accomplish the larger purpose of strengthening Jewish life.

Over the years many worshippers who attended community High Holyday services joined our Synagogue—some became officers and trustees—because they felt that we *cared* about people. In their letters they thanked our congregation for a warm welcome and appreciated the complete second service for nonmembers.

One couple said that when they arrived at the Synagogue and saw a long line of young, well-dressed people, like an Upper East Side crowd waiting to see a first-run movie, they thought, "Here were Jewish people who felt the need to reaffirm their connection with their faith. It was quite a sight." Former worshippers told us how grateful they were when, as young law students without much money, they had a place with us for the High Holydays and how that experience had shaped their life. They eventually moved out of the city, started raising a family, and became officers in a congregation they helped establish.

CELEBRATING HOLIDAYS AND FESTIVALS

From our inception, as we observed the holidays and festivals in the annual cycle, we were always mindful of their larger purpose, which, in the words of Maimonides, is to promote a feeling of brotherly love toward one another.

Let me review the approach we took in the observance of our holidays. Following Rosh Hashanah and Yom Kippur comes a week of festivals: Succoth, Shemini Atzeret, and Simchat Torah. Because our Greenwich Village building was on a busy residential block with many popular restaurants, hundreds of passersby saw and visited our outdoor succah, always magnificently decorated by the Sisterhood—a cool, leafy oasis providing moments of spiritual refreshment. We regularly hosted school, church, and synagogue groups, and it was evident from their comments that they considered these visits very meaningful. During the holiday week, members of our congregation volunteered to sit in the succah to greet visitors and, whenever possible, I was there too, to meet our guests personally and explain the symbols and the significance of the festival.

On the last two days of Succoth—Shemini Atzeret (the Eighth Day of Assembly) and Simchat Torah (Rejoicing with the Torah)—Jews celebrate our commitment to Torah with seven processions of the scrolls around the sanctuary, including children waving flags, to impress upon us that there is no joy like that of a person who loves the Lord and reveres God's laws.

The 25th of the Hebrew month of Kislev, usually in December, marks the beginning of Chanukah, which celebrates the victory of the Jewish people over the Syrians—the very first battle for religious freedom recorded in the annals of history—the rededication of the Temple in Jerusalem in 165 B.C.E., and the renewal of our faith in *Ha-Shem* (God). The message of Chanukah is that man cannot live without God.

Children, particularly, should hear this story related with as much drama and color as any other exciting narrative, when for a few moments history comes alive. Year after year for 40 years I delighted in donning a specially designed Judah the Maccabee costume, disguising myself with a beard, and, dressed like a warrior, enacting the role of Judah for the children of our Religious School and their friends. Taking the part of Judah's brother Simon, another "actor" in costume joined me in the playlet. When my brother, Allen, was our Associate Rabbi, he played Simon. Later my son, Herbert, took that role. The audience especially appreciated the words I addressed to "Simon" (Herbert) as I sent him off to battle: "Simon, my brother, I love you dearly, like a father loves a son." The children used to cheer us on and applaud when we "found" the little cruse of oil and lit the Menorah.

Beginning in our first year, Dr. Stitt and I used to hold an outdoor ceremony for our two congregations, "Dedication of the Lights," on the portico of the sanctuary. Two tall, illuminated glass panels stood side by side, one with the motif of a five-pointed star and the word "Peace," and the other with an eight-branched Chanukah Menorah and the word "Shalom." He and I each spoke about our holiday and then everyone went indoors for an hour of fellowship. Many people still recall those annual festivities with great affection.

On a much larger and more ambitious level, Dr. Stitt and I decided to visit the executive offices of some of the large department stores to ask if they would arrange for Chanukah displays and play Chanukah melodies in addition to Christmas music for their customers. In some stores we did succeed; with others it would take years for this idea to catch on. We also met with the president of Radio City Music Hall to discuss whether the annual holiday stage show could include something about Chanukah. Although that was not possible, he did offer, out of respect for the Jewish community, to have the Music Hall symphony orchestra play the Kol Nidre during the High Holydays, an annual feature for many years.

I like to think that Dr. Stitt and I pioneered in bringing Chanukah into mainstream American culture; we believed that the way to develop mutual respect and understanding is to learn about each other's cultural and religious traditions. Today Chanukah Menorahs are displayed everywhere—in shop windows, offices, banks, lobbies, plazas, on TV, and in the most elegant stores—and recipes for the traditional holiday potato pancakes *(latkes)* appear in newspapers and magazines.

As Jews we have an obligation to publicize the message of Chanukah—the miracle of faith. As Zechariah proclaimed: "Not by might, nor by power, but by my spirit, saith the Lord of Hosts." Had the Maccabees not recaptured Jerusalem and restored the Temple, there would have been no Chanukah and no Christmas.

In the spring The Brotherhood Synagogue always conducted a congregational Passover Seder. In preparing for the holiday, I followed the custom of "selling" our leavened products *(chometz)* to a non-Jewish buyer. Dr. Stitt himself undertook this responsibility; then, at the end of Pesach (Passover) a week later, he "sold" it back to us. In our early years, when our resources were limited, the Seders took place in our social hall. Although the meal was modest, we had a complete and traditional Seder, with all the ritual foods. Clergy of other faiths and community leaders were our guests, and we were gratified by their spiritual response to the retelling of the story of the Exodus of the Jewish people from Egypt. For many of them it was the first time they had attended a Seder. The pastor of a Lutheran church wrote, "Thank you very much for your warm and deeply spiritual presentation of the Seder.... There were moments when we realize that we are all Semites. This is one of them. We are grateful to you for reminding us of our ancestry and the beginning of our one hope." In addition my brother, Allen, Cantor Mirkovic, and I conducted model Seders for many organizations in the community, including church groups.

Fifty days after Passover comes Shavouth (Feast of Weeks), celebrating the giving of the Ten Commandments at Sinai. One year this festival coincided with Pentecost (Whitsunday), a church holiday that falls 50 days after Easter. The *New York Times* carried a lovely story, with photographs, about how each of our two congregations observed its own holiday on the same morning in the same space. The Synagogue worship service began earlier than usual; then the sexton, assisted by members of both congregations, rearranged the altar for the Church's service, which started a little later than usual. That morning Dr. Stitt began his Scripture readings with a verse from Acts II: "And when the Day of Pentecost was fully come, they [the people] were all of one accord in one place."

SCROLLS FROM INDIA

Whenever I was asked to meet someone, I usually said "Yes." One never knows what blessings may ensue from such encounters.

Let me tell you a story. Sometime in 1957 Uncle Jack asked me if I would speak with a business associate of his who was fascinated by the activities of The Brotherhood Synagogue. The gentleman had told my uncle about his friend Eddie, who had a beautifully designed *parochet* (Ark curtain) from India available for display. Perhaps I would like to see it.

I made an appointment to meet my uncle's friend at the Synagogue. He brought the curtain with him, and as soon as I looked at it, I realized that the workmanship was so magnificent it was probably without equal. I called Dr. Stitt to view it as well. Out of our conversation came the idea to display the curtain to our congregations. I would explain the symbols at a Friday night Oneg Shabbat following our worship service and also on Sunday morning at the social hour after the Church service.

The *parochet* was artistic and elegant, hand-embroidered in gold thread on maroon velvet, skillfully crafted by Jewish women in Calcutta. The central symbol depicted a globe of the world upheld by three columns of the ancient Temple, representing justice, truth, and peace. Across the top of the curtain, in Hebrew and English, was the same phrase from Leviticus, "Love Thy Neighbor As Thyself," that was on the valance of the Ark in our sanctuary. Other symbols on the curtain included the Tablets of the Law, rampant lions guarding the columns of the Temple, and a seven-branched Menorah.

A week later when the businessman returned to pick up the *parochet*, he was accompanied by his friend, Edward S. Abrahams, who shared with Dr. Stitt and me some of the trials and heartaches of his early years. Born in Mesopotamia (Iraq) in 1901, he was six months old when Arabs buried his father alive. Later his mother fulfilled her husband's wish to emigrate to India and moved her family to Calcutta in 1904. As he grew up, Eddie learned to read Hebrew, went to synagogue every morning, and observed the Jewish holidays and festivals. Not long after his Bar Mitzvah, he left home and worked his way around the world, always carrying his *tallis*, *tefillin*, and a *siddur* (prayer book) with him. Eventually he settled in the United States, went into business, married, and raised a family. But he retained strong ties to his relatives and friends in the Jewish community of India.

He told us how excited he was about the program of cooperation between the Village Presbyterian Church and The Brotherhood Synagogue and said that he had written about us to friends in India. As we toured the sanctuary, Eddie asked us a simple question: "What can I do to help you? I'd like to do something for this cause." We suggested a cover for the lectern that could be used in services for both congregations.

Several months later Dr. Stitt and I received a package from India with an exquisite maroon velvet embroidered lectern cover that Eddie had commissioned. It was designed in three sections—one to cover the lectern itself and two detachable sections, one for each congregation. The Synagogue panel bore a Star of David encircled by olive branches with the Hebrew word *Shalom* (Peace) and the words of the *Sh'ma* ("Hear, O Israel: The Lord Our God, The Lord Is One.") The Church panel bore a Cross, the word "Peace" and the phrase "Perfect Love Casteth Out Fear." What was most significant to us was that the same hands that had stitched the Star of David had also stitched the Cross.

The story continues. A few weeks later, in February 1958, this lectern cover was highlighted in color photographs in a feature article, entitled "Where Two Faiths Meet," that appeared in *The American Weekly*, a Sunday supplement in the *Herald Tribune* and other national newspapers. Dr. Stitt and I were shown, during our respective services, standing at the lectern, which was draped

with these unusual panels. The story caught the attention of producers at NBC and soon we were invited to appear on the "Today"
Show.

Mr. Abrahams remained in touch. One day he told me that when
he returned to Calcutta in 1959–1960 he realized that the synagogues of India were in a state of decline because so many Jewish
families and individuals had emigrated, many to Israel.
Remembering the beautiful Torahs from his childhood, he
obtained permission from the Jewish community of India to have
some of them sent to the United States. A number of the scrolls
with their Sephardic silver cases would soon be arriving in New
York.

He asked me to serve with him as their trustee and to help him
determine where they should be distributed. Eddie explained
that he wanted to entrust this task to our Synagogue because he
felt that our congregation would know how to handle the assignment properly and spread the message of Torah.

The day before Thanksgiving in 1963 eight enormous crates
were delivered to the Synagogue office. As my brother and I
opened them, we were dazzled by their contents. The Torah cases
were repoussé in design, fashioned by skilled silversmiths and
goldsmiths who hammered the design into the metal by hand.
The cases were then stored until they could be inscribed for a
donor and presented to a synagogue. The artisans had come to
India from Mesopotamia, Burma, Singapore, Hong Kong, and
Shanghai. Chinese Jews, reputed to be outstanding silversmiths,
inscribed along the edges of some of their cases Chinese symbols
that meant "Holy Object," "Sacred Law," followed by the name of
the craftsman. Many of the cases were 100 years old, and a number of the parchments (the Torah scrolls) may have been at least

twice as old, many written in Baghdad, where the scribes were highly esteemed.

The Brotherhood Synagogue took seriously the responsibility of being a co-trustee. We organized Torah caravans, sending the Torahs out on loan to the International Synagogue at Kennedy Airport, to Central Synagogue in Manhattan, and to other congregations in New York State, St. Croix in the Virgin Islands, and as far as California and Japan. Their rabbis organized group visits for people of all faiths to view these precious scrolls and at the same time learn about the traditions and beliefs of the Jewish people. Whenever we lent the Torahs, it was with the complete understanding that they were "on loan," that they belonged solely to the Jewish community of India, and that no other congregation had any proprietary right other than to enjoy them and magnify and teach the words of God's holy writ.

Mitzvah gorereth mitzvah. A good deed has a ripple effect. The effect of saying yes to a request over 40 years ago continues to enrich not only our congregation but congregations throughout our country and overseas. Eddie Abrahams' association with our Synagogue and his personal friendship continued for many years, until his death in 1989. We bestowed upon him honorary membership in our congregation, and he frequently worshipped with us when he visited New York City. One of these special Torahs has a home in our Ark, and the beautiful *parochet* that initiated our relationship is on display in our Gramercy Park building.

When Pope Paul VI visited New York in 1965, the National Conference of Christians and Jews presented him with an album displaying six photographs of unusually beautiful religious objects in houses of worship in our city. Included was one of the Sephardic Torahs from India entrusted to The Brotherhood Synagogue.

A CLASS FOR SPECIAL CHILDREN

In 1967 a letter from the Archdiocese of New York caught my attention because it was addressed "Dear Colleague." It was an invitation to ministers, priests, and rabbis to attend a meeting at the Manhattan offices of the Archdiocese to discuss religious education for developmentally disabled children. I said to my brother: "Al, if you want to do something important, why don't you attend this meeting? I wouldn't want it to be said that no rabbi was present." He did go—and indeed he was the only rabbi there.

Many parents at the meeting were Jewish and had placed their children in the interfaith classes held on Sundays in a Catholic church, Christ the King, in the Bronx because there were no Jewish programs elsewhere. For this the Catholic Church deserves enormous credit, because it was the pioneer in reaching out spiritually to these special children. The families, however, were exhausted from the long trips to and from Brooklyn and Queens and the Jewish parents longed for a Jewish setting in Manhattan. Seeing a rabbi at this gathering gave them some hope.

After my brother shared with me the needs of these families, I proposed that we plan a program for them at The Brotherhood Synagogue. We discussed the idea with Mortimer Kane, the president of our congregation, who fully supported it, as did our Board of Trustees. Thus we instituted the first special education class for Jewish children (SPEC).

A number of non-Jewish families whose children were attending the classes at the Bronx church asked if they could enroll them in our class; of course we said yes, for these parents too were weary. The experience was so heartwarming that a year later Dr. Stitt asked, "Why can't we do this together as part of the ongoing programs of The Brotherhood Council?"

Our class met on alternate Sunday afternoons with trained instructors and with Rabbi Allen Block as the overall director. By the second year fourteen happy students were enrolled, ranging in age from 5 to 15. There were no fees, and counseling and guidance were available for the parents through our Family Counseling Service and the Association for the Help of Retarded Children (AHRC).

We tried to take a universal approach in our curriculum, planning activities based on the children's abilities and culture. Holiday celebrations were always fun; we read Bible stories and encouraged the students to participate actively through art and music. I remember so well the bright smiles on the faces of the first class as they decorated the succah with leaves. The children looked so happy.

We prepared several of the older children for a Bar or Bat Mitzvah. I had the joy of working with them personally and then conducting the Shabbat service when they were called to the Torah to recite the blessings. A few became proficient enough to chant some of the verses of the Haftorah, and they all delivered the traditional speech, each expressing—some very poetically— what this special moment meant to them. As tears flowed from congregants, families, and clergy, imagine the joy of parents who had never dared dream of such a moment. And of course each child had a party for family and friends.

Writing on behalf of the Board of Jewish Education of New York, Dr. Bennett N. Rackman commented, "I feel that what The Brotherhood Synagogue has done, and is continuing to do, on behalf of the Jewish retarded is worthy of recognition. Last year it was the only program of its kind in the greater New York area."

I remain in touch with some of the children and their parents. In time, more than 90 other congregations, Y's, and Jewish community centers established similar programs, modeled on the SPEC concept we had initiated. Few programs have brought us such happiness and fulfillment.

The mother of one of the first young children enrolled in our SPEC group and a leader in the Association for the Help of Retarded Children wrote to me about her daughter's experience. The young men and women she knew "told me how very welcome they were all made to feel" at The Brotherhood Synagogue and how essential it is that "people with disabilities be seen in as many typical activities as possible."

By the mid 1970s we turned our efforts to mentally retarded Jewish adults living in residences in the east midtown area of Manhattan; we organized social and educational activities appropriate for mature men and women with developmental disabilities. (See Chapter 11.)

I am proud of our achievements in this field and I am grateful to my congregation, its staff, leaders, and members, for their constant support and acts of friendship and kindness to the members of these special groups and their families. In this same spirit, in 1995 my successor, Rabbi Daniel Alder, along with Phillip Rothman, our Executive Director and Director of Education, began a class of religious instruction for Jewish children with learning disabilities. They named this new program *Tikvah,* for there is "hope" for every child.

RECOGNIZING ACTS OF COURAGE

Brotherhood also means showing appreciation. Over the years we honored people who saved Jewish lives at great danger to themselves, as well as others who sought to maintain Jewish culture under hostile circumstances. Because they *cared*, we wanted them to know that we recognized their courage and their humanity.

In 1966 The Brotherhood Synagogue paid tribute to Mrs. Simon Bokma of the Netherlands, and to her late husband, for their efforts in the Dutch underground in saving the lives of refugees from Nazi persecution. They took to heart the call of the resistance movement to the people to "prove our honor is not lost and our conscience is not silenced." Mrs. Bokma had come to New York as a guest of Louis and Betty van Naarden, members of our congregation who had been hidden with other families on the Bokma farm. At a Friday evening service we presented her with a silver-covered Bible from Israel bearing the following inscription, *"To Mrs. Simon Bokma of Holland who, with her sainted husband, saved the lives of countless victims of World War II. Presented with everlasting gratitude by The Brotherhood Synagogue on behalf of the Jewish people everywhere."* Among those present at the service were a representative of the Dutch consulate and a group of German Bible students who happened to be visiting our sanctuary that evening.

Two years later we commemorated the 25th anniversary of the dramatic rescue of the Jewish population of Denmark, with members and government officials of the Scandinavian community as our guests. The speaker was Sir Richard Netter, president of Thanks to Scandinavia, an organization dedicated to fostering friendship and cultural exchanges with the people of Scandinavia in appreciation of their heroism in saving Jewish lives. We had prepared an elegantly inscribed Bible from Israel for Rabbi Marcus Melchior of Copenhagen (who was unable to be present) in recognition of his courage in leading his people to safety, and we had sent a similar Bible to His Majesty, King Frederick IX, which was personally delivered to him. The King acknowledged it with a letter: "His Majesty expressed a great pleasure and appreciation in receiving this marvelous gift." Some months later Danish publications carried stories about our presenting the "Citation for Service to the cause of Brotherhood" to the noted Danish artist Harold Isenstein, whom we made an honorary member of the congregation for his powerful sculptures depicting the heroic acts of the Danish people.

At the end of 1967 the great Yiddish actress Madame Ida Kaminska and her troupe—which included her husband, Meir Melman, and her daughter, Ruth—stopped in New York on the way from Warsaw to South America for an extended tour. Considered one of the finest actresses of our time, she had followed in the footsteps of her revered mother, the great Esther Rachel Kaminska. For her magnificent performance in the film "The Shop on Main Street," Ida Kaminska was nominated for an Academy Award.

After hearing her speak at an American Jewish Congress program, I invited her and her family and the troupe to attend a Saturday morning service at The Brotherhood Synagogue, followed by a Kiddush in their honor. They accepted the invitation. The day before that service I received an urgent call from the composer Sholom Secunda begging me not to call Mr. Melman for an *aliyah* (honor of being called to the Torah). Not all members of the troupe were Jewish, he explained; some might be informers, and overt participation in religious rituals might jeopardize the status of the Jewish actors after their return to Poland. That Saturday morning the sanctuary was filled; there was a Bar Mitzvah and many of the worshippers had heard about Ida Kaminska's visit. (A number of years later she recounted this visit in her autobiography and recalled that the young man had told her that he would always remember that she was present at his Bar Mitzvah!)

Addressing our guests in Yiddish, I welcomed the troupe to our Synagogue. As the worship service proceeded with the reading of the Torah, I decided at the last minute to ask one of our Trustees to approach Mr. Melman about an *aliyah*. Surprisingly, he said yes. When I called him to the altar it was obvious that he knew the blessings well; he recited them in a strong, clear voice—but his eyes were moist with tears.

As I was speaking with the troupe after the service, I could sense that one of the Jewish actors yearned to have a *tallis*. Unobtrusively, I picked up one that was nearby, carefully folded and refolded it many times, put the *tallis* in my hand, discreetly made a fist, put my hand in his pocket and released the prayer shawl. So great was the atmosphere of fear in which they lived and worked.

A year later, when the Jewish population of Poland again found conditions ominous and repressive, Madame Kaminska, Meir Melman, and Ruth Kaminska decided to leave their native land. After a few months performing in Israel, they returned to the United States, and again we invited them to be with our congregation. Remembering The Brotherhood Synagogue with great affection, they accepted our invitation to worship with us. In January 1969 we presented a citation and a prayer book to them with the following inscription: *"In recognition of their great contributions to the world of art, the theater, and the Yiddish language."* We also named them honorary members of The Brotherhood Synagogue, and I expressed our happiness at their return to America, telling them that their presence would surely give great encouragement to a revival of the once great Yiddish theater in our country, especially in New York. It was our hope that someday they would perform in our own Greenwich Mews Theatre, but unfortunately our facilities were not suitable for their productions.

The Kaminska–Melman family maintained an affiliation with our congregation for many years, participating actively in services. In the spring of 1980, after our Synagogue had moved to Gramercy Park, Madame Kaminska starred in *The Investigation*, a play by Peter Weiss staged in our sanctuary and based on the Auschwitz trials. After a number of performances, she came to me one day and lamented, "Rabbi Block, I don't feel so well." She was hospitalized and passed away a few weeks later. Her family, representatives of the State of Israel and of the Jewish community in New York, as well as stars of the Yiddish theater paid tribute to this great woman at a memorial service in our sanctuary, where she had made her final professional appearance.

HANDS OF FRIENDSHIP AROUND THE WORLD

Whenever we learned that somewhere in the world our Jewish brethren needed assistance, The Brotherhood Synagogue tried to respond. In 1969 we sent sets of Jewish encyclopedias and books of biblical commentaries to Singapore following a Sabbath evening talk and request by the Honorable David Marshall, then delegate to the United Nations from Singapore and former president of his country's Jewish community. As he acknowledged when he wrote to thank us, it was a "promise made and a promise fulfilled."

We lent one of the Sephardic Torahs from India to the Jewish community of St. Croix in the Virgin Islands and made a gift of prayer books to them as well as to a synagogue in Nassau in the Bahamas. When Rabbi Samuel Lerer of Mexico City made us aware of communities of poor Jews in the area of Vera Cruz, Mexico, who longed to rediscover their Jewish roots but had no Torah, we responded to their plea and lent them an Ashkenazic scroll, for which they were very grateful.

Our congregation had long been one of the few synagogues to take an interest in Ethiopian Jewry. Ever since my student days, I have been interested in the plight of this impoverished and embattled community struggling to maintain its dignity, identity, and traditions in the face of civil war in the country and the decimation of its ranks by disease, starvation, and military action.

Years before their rescue in Operation Moses and Operation Solomon and long before most rabbis ever spoke out on their behalf, The Brotherhood Synagogue championed the cause of Ethiopian Jews, then scornfully referred to as Falashas (strangers) by their compatriots. Compassionate as always, raising funds on their behalf and sending them religious articles, my congregation unhesitatingly reached out to this long neglected community. Once again, our Synagogue showed the way. (See Chapter 12.)

A JEWISH COFFEE HOUSE

Some of the best ideas for programs have originated with the congregation and community at large. Whenever someone wanted to discuss a suggestion with me, I was always ready to listen.

In 1972 Jeffrey Oboler, a young man living in our neighborhood, spoke to me about the need for an informal setting where Jewish men and women his age could meet for study, prayer, and fellowship; he wondered whether our Synagogue could provide space for a free coffee house. We talked about his ideas, I read what he had written, and I concluded that here was a need we could and should meet.

The goal was to combat assimilation among young people by creating a sense of Jewish community and to focus on what united them rather than on what divided them. Here are excerpts from the proposal prepared by Jeff Oboler, who eventually made *aliyah* (emigrated to Israel):

> The evolving of *Havurot*, small groups that meet to explore Jewish experiences, is a new development in America, one that is having a positive effect on American Jewish life today. Throughout Jewish history such groups have always met for study, prayer or celebration.... The Havurah movement is an attempt to revive this community. Bet Kafe is a Havurah where we hold our own prayer services at the synagogue, and meet in each other's homes later. We reach out to many unaffiliated young people to join us in the warm community atmosphere of our coffee house.

Inspired by the famed Greenwich Village coffee houses of the 1960s, Bet Kafe proved to be a warm, enthusiastic group that exuded love, friendship, compassion, and camaraderie. Every two weeks up to 200 young adults, most of them in their twenties, gathered in our Synagogue to talk, read poetry, play music, sing and dance, and "express themselves Jewishly." On one notable occasion Shlomo Carlebach led them in prayer and song.

After reading about Bet Kafe in a Jewish newspaper, a group of Jewish inmates in an upstate prison wrote to ask if members of the group would come to visit them. A dozen young people responded and later made contact with the families of some of the prisoners. For those behind bars, the presence of these young men and women from our Bet Kafe reassured them that they were not lost to the Jewish community.

Bet Kafe soon became a model for groups in other parts of the city and around the country. Jewish life was enriched because, once again, we were open to new ideas. Perhaps the influence of our philosophy was best expressed by the young man who founded Bet Kafe: "My association with The Brotherhood Synagogue has been one of the most meaningful experiences of my life."

OUR BAR MITZVAH YEAR

When our congregation celebrated its thirteenth anniversary, we invited Dr. Stitt to help us mark this milestone and to give the "Bar Mitzvah" address. His words were so beautiful and so inspiring that we had his speech printed and sent to all the members of our two congregations. Here are a few excerpts:

The subject of the evening calls for a good healthy sincere—"Mazel Tov."...

You know I have been very close to this Bar Mitzvah creature—this Brotherhood Synagogue. I was present when it was born and let me tell you it was a beautiful boy. One looking at it from the very moment it took breath knew that throughout its life it would be led by a pillar of cloud by day, to lead it on the way and by a pillar of fire by night, to give it light.

...I too felt the impact of its importance for the world into which it was born, and for the cosmic commission which was laid upon it. It was to carry the faith of a Moses—enduring as seeing Him who is invisible. It was to have the wisdom of a Solomon, the Song of a Psalmist, the righteousness of an Amos, the tenderness of an Hosea, the pleading of an Isaiah, and the uncompromising loyalty of a David—in all its relationships to all men everywhere, regardless of race, color or creed....

From one who truly knows, let me say it has fulfilled, to this hour, its reason for being, because you, your Rabbi and all those who have been with you in your Synagogue during these 13 years have willed to make it so.

Bless you! *Shalom! Shalom u'vracha!*

The Ketubah

In celebration of our first wedding anniversary, Phyllis and I received a gift of front-row tickets to Fiddler on the Roof, starring Zero Mostel. Being in such close proximity to the stage gave me an opportunity to note small details of costumes, props, and the like, and I realized that the Ketubah (marriage document) held by the "rabbi" was not a real Hebrew document, but a corporate business form in English.

I was upset by the lack of attention to this important detail. The next day I found a Ketubah the right size in my office files and mailed it to Mr. Mostel. What prompted me to send him the document, I wrote, was to make the scene with the rabbi a little more authentic, and I concluded by saying, "Sei mir gezund" (Be well). A few days later I received a response:

Dear Rabbi Block,

I wanted to tell you that the Hebrew Ketubah is in the show and has been in use since the night I received it. I had had an argument with the stage manager that persons of my faith would notice the English text. I was right!

Thank you for your cooperation. It is much appreciated.

As the good book says, Sei mir gezund.

Cordially,
Zero Mostel

6

Rabbi and Minister: Telling Our Story

*"We believed we have a challenge unsurpassed
in modern times to further the concept of brotherhood
by continuing the programs we have set in motion together."*

REV. DR. JESSE WILLIAM STITT

One day as Dr. Stitt and I were talking about the escalating volume of correspondence and telephone calls, which were taking an increasing amount of our time and energy, I mused: "What do you think Moses and Jesus did without a telephone?"

He laughed and replied, "They did great things because they went out among people."

TRAVELING AROUND THE COUNTRY

As our joint programs became known, Dr. Stitt and I received invitations to relate our story to groups in the New York area and in many parts of our country as well as in Canada. We were delighted to accept because we felt we had an important message to convey: religious leaders and their congregations should develop warm, friendly relations with each other.

Whenever we made our presentation, Dr. Stitt and I preferred to use the term "brotherhood" rather than "interfaith." We felt that the latter term, as it was interpreted at the time, might lead to a misunderstanding of our relationship. What we were striving for was a reaching out to one another, working together in harmony and friendship, while at the same time assiduously maintaining our own customs and theology, and carrying out joint programs and activities. If asked, we would point out that it was not essential to share a building in order to accomplish our goal.

I usually met Dr. Stitt in front of his apartment house on Gramercy Park, hopping out of my taxi into his car where he was already in the driver's seat waiting for me. We traveled all over the New York area, addressing religious groups as well as numerous parent–teacher associations in the public schools. One group recommended us to another. If our hosts offered an honorarium, we asked that it be directed to the work of The Brotherhood Council.

In 1956 we were the speakers at the Toronto convention of a national pharmaceutical company, which later printed our remarks in one of its publications. In 1962 Dr. Stitt and I flew to the West Coast, where rabbinic colleagues had arranged for us to speak at synagogues in the Los Angeles and San Francisco areas, in many cases inviting church leaders and their congregants to attend as well. Rabbis Arthur Kolatch and Gerald Raiskin, classmates of mine in rabbinical school, were especially helpful in arranging opportunities for us to share the excitement of our joint venture with religious and lay leaders of many faiths.

From California we headed north to Portland, Oregon, appearing before synagogue audiences and on a radio program under the auspices of the National Conference of Christians and Jews and the National Council of Churches.

Another trip took us to Chicago, where we were welcomed by members of several large synagogue congregations, and then to Terre Haute, Indiana, where my rabbinical school roommate Rabbi Bernard Cohen had planned joint gatherings of church and synagogue congregations. Even the local Holiday Inn announced our arrival on an outdoor sign. In 1968 we traveled to the coastal area around Stuart, Florida, where our good friend Emeline Paige, former editor of *The Villager*, our Greenwich Village newspaper, was living at the time. This trip was a family affair. Nancy Stitt accompanied her husband, and Phyllis, our three-year old son, Herbert, and Phyllis's mother joined with us. Through Ms. Paige's academic and community connections Dr. Stitt and I were invited to speak at a Catholic college, a community college, a temple Sisterhood, and a Kiwanis club, and we were interviewed on a television program broadcast from Palm Beach—a full schedule in a few days—and then my family and I stayed on for a vacation.

I must confess, however, that, hectic as they were, these speaking engagements provided a bit of a respite from the pressures of our day-to-day activities at home, as well as a chance to visit new places, enlarge our personal contacts, and learn the reactions of people in different parts of the country to our Covenant of Brotherhood.

No matter where Dr. Stitt and I went, we were always received very enthusiastically, frequently with a long round of applause. At times the reception was somewhat overwhelming. Even now, after more than 40 years, I remember the Monsignor who turned to me and whispered wistfully, "Is there a place in your program for a Catholic priest like me?"

I asked a member of my congregation, a psychiatrist, why we so often received standing ovations after our presentations. The doctor replied that people are very moved by the idea of a minister and a rabbi standing side by side, and that seeing us together mirrored all their hopes and dreams of a world at peace.

We took great pleasure in addressing many groups, both Jewish and non-Jewish, who came to Greenwich Village from all along the East Coast expressly to visit our joint sanctuary. Many religious institutions made attendance at our Friday evening worship a part their field trip to New York City. Young people seemed especially receptive to our message. A high school senior with a Congregational Church group from Vermont wrote; "Of all the places I visited I found The Brotherhood Synagogue in Greenwich Village the most rewarding because of the warmth conveyed by the people. You ought to try and have all the kids attend Friday night services, as it throws a different light on city life as it is and how it should be."

Another student group had the opportunity of observing the sexton prepare the sanctuary to serve the religious needs of both congregations. Later the children sent us a letter saying, "Your talks made us understand that we should love other religions as well as our own." The teacher told us the class had prepared questions in advance to ask Dr. Stitt and me but the youngsters were so captivated by what they had experienced that they left "speechless."

A number of Presbyterian churches sent their religious school classes to visit our building. What seemed to impress the young people in particular was "the mutual respect, integrity, and unique contributions among Judaism and Christianity." As one of their ministers observed, "Your working brotherhood has shown us new, practical ideas in living, and proves a good, harmonious relationship among honest men is possible." We hosted more than 150 Jewish high school boys and girls from the Boston area and on another occasion a group of 50 young visitors from churches in New York State and New Jersey. Teenagers from Minnesota and Iowa attending a convention in New York City came with their pastors because, they told us, they wanted to meet and encounter people "who really cared." From time to time we welcomed volunteers from The International Center in New York City and their guests from Europe, the Middle East, and Asia, who were eager to learn how to establish similar grassroots-level programs in their own countries.

Writing in a 1995 publication, Dr. Eugene Fisher, Associate Director, Secretariat for Ecumenical and Interreligious Affairs for the National Conference of Catholic Bishops, and Rabbi Leon Klenicki, Director of the Interfaith Affairs Department of the Anti-Defamation League and a member of The Brotherhood Synagogue, reviewed the advances in interreligious relations in the last four decades:

> Today Christians and Jews are called to work together, for the sake of and for the upbuilding of God's Kingdom in this world, ironically one of the points of our most bitter controversies in the past. To do this we need to relate, not just at the top, on the level of the Vatican, and the World Council of Churches, but perhaps more importantly on the local level, the level of community, the level of our two peoples struggling together to discover and to follow God's will for both of us.

This is the goal that Dr. Stitt and I pursued. Perhaps we and our two congregations played a pioneering role in bringing about dialogue on the local level between communities of different faiths.

It saddened us that for too long many in the Catholic Church hierarchy discouraged priests from actively participating in ecumenical organizations and programs. The first neighborhood priest to attend a service in our synagogue was our good friend Father Mario Albanese of Our Lady of Pompeii in Greenwich Village, on the night of President John F. Kennedy's assassination. When I saw him enter the sanctuary, I invited him to come to the altar to share his grief with the congregation, and he accepted. It seemed to me that after those sad days—and under the leadership of Pope John XXIII—priests gradually became less hesitant to speak in houses of worship of other faiths. They were no longer reproved, as had been Father George Barry Ford of Corpus Christi Church, near Columbia University, when in the 1940s, he advocated interfaith dialogue and cooperation. Father Ford proudly noted in his autobiography that in 1968 he had addressed Congregation B'nai Jeshurun on the occasion of his friend Rabbi Israel Goldstein's fiftieth anniversary in the rabbinate. The climate and mood were changing and this time "no one said me, nay!"

ON THE AIR

Television producers began to show an interest in what was happening on West 13th Street. In our first year together Dr. Stitt and I appeared on WPIX (Channel 11), on *News-O-Rama*, on the *Tex and Jinx* show highlighting Brotherhood Week, as well as on religious-oriented programs such as *Lamp Unto My Feet* and *The Way to Go*.

As our reputation grew, we were frequently interviewed for articles in the local, national, and international press and were invited to appear on such popular television shows as *I've Got a Secret*. Dr. Stitt and I revealed our "secret" to the audience while the panel of blindfolded "experts" tried to guess who we were and what made us unique. They couldn't come up with the answer! (We shared the same sanctuary.)

Our most memorable appearance was as contestants in April and May 1956 on NBC's *The Big Surprise*, a widely viewed national quiz show offering a generous prize that could go as high as $100,000. When Dr. Stitt and I were invited to meet the producer, our initial reaction was not to accept. On second thought, however, we reflected that it never hurts to meet new people, and so we made the appointment.

I joked with Dr. Stitt, "We probably won't agree to be on the show; but if they pressure us, let's suggest 'religion' as our category and you answer questions about Judaism and I take questions about Christianity." It turned out that this was exactly what the network officials had in mind. Nevertheless, I still had misgivings and felt very uncomfortable at the thought of standing before an estimated audience of 40 million viewers and answering questions about a religion not my own.

But, I said, "Jesse, we would never have come to them, but they came to us, and who knows if this isn't the hand of God working on our behalf?" Dr. Stitt concurred. We reasoned that if God had shown us the first step, then surely God would provide us with the second. We decided to accept NBC's invitation.

The master of ceremonies, Mike Wallace, was always gracious as he introduced us to the national audience. The first and second questions were on simple religious facts, but as the contest reached the next level the questions became more difficult. I surmised that parallel questions would be asked—for example, the 12 Tribes, the 12 Apostles, the 12 months of the Hebrew calendar. Between the second and third week I sequestered myself in a house in Brooklyn at the invitation of some members of my congregation. In a quiet room with no phone I was able to apply all my time to study, taking a break only to join the family for meals.

The appearance of a rabbi and a minister together on a television quiz show was reported all over the country. We received telegrams and phone calls saying, "We're praying for your success." "We wish you good luck!" A Christian viewer sent a telegram to Dr. Stitt with the encouraging words, "I lit a candle for your joint success." My father told me that on our street in

Bridgeport all the neighbors tuned in, and of course our two congregations followed the contest intently.

In our third session Mike Wallace asked me to quote the last words spoken by Jesus on the Cross. I had anticipated the question so the answer came easily. Dr. Stitt was asked to name the 12 Hebrew months. He knew them but he had a bit of a struggle with the Hebrew pronunciation. Seated in the front rows of the studio audience were members of our families and congregations as well as our dear friend the Reverend Dr. Carl Hermann Voss. Even today I can visualize him wringing his hands with anxiety, praying that Dr. Stitt succeed (as was the whole world, or so it seemed). Everyone applauded jubilantly as he successfully completed his answer seconds before his time was up.

Mike Wallace invited us to return the following week; we then had to announce that we could not continue because the coming change to Daylight Saving Time meant that the Jewish Sabbath would not conclude early enough Saturday night for Dr. Stitt and me to appear on the show at the scheduled hour. Maintaining respect for our Sabbaths was one of the main principles of our relationship.

But we did win $10,000! Half went to the Synagogue and half to the Church, and each congregation then donated $1,000 to The Brotherhood Council.

A few months later, as Dr. Stitt and I were walking across a main street in Greenwich Village, a tour bus pulled alongside and we heard people shouting, "There they are! There they are!" As we looked around to see what was happening, voices cried out, "There's the minister and the rabbi!" A group of high school students poured off the bus and surrounded us, asking for our autographs. We loved it. I signed mine "Yours in Brotherhood."

OUR TRIP TO ISRAEL

Both Dr. Stitt and I were emotionally tied to the land of Israel and prayed for the peace of Jerusalem and for the re-establishment of Israel as a great spiritual center for all the world.

I had spent several months in pre-statehood Israel in 1947 and 1948 studying at the Hebrew University and serving with the Haganah. Dr. Stitt had been an early member of the American Christian Palestine Committee and had become active in it through his friend the Reverend Dr. Carl Hermann Voss. After Dr. Stitt returned from his first trip to Israel—he had gone with a group of U.S. mayors—I immediately asked him, "Well, Jesse, in one word, what do you think?" He responded, "Wonderful!" I knew then that he and I would get along exceedingly well, because love for the land of Israel is a touchstone of brotherhood between Jew and Christian. When he returned from his second trip, he brought the Synagogue a mezuzah, and together with the staffs of both congregations we affixed it to the door of my office.

In the summer of 1959 Dr. Stitt and I made the trip together. Family, friends, and congregants accompanied us to the airport to send us on our way with their blessings and good wishes. While waiting to board, we became acquainted with another passenger, Kate Marshall, wife of Brigadier General S. L. A. Marshall, one of the great American military historians, who had come to see his wife off. They graciously offered to introduce us to some Israeli military leaders.

When we arrived in Israel we were surprised to learn that our trip had been reported in advance in leading newspapers. In an article entitled, "A Priest Wears a Yarmulke, a Rabbi Knows the New Testament," a reporter wrote at length about the relationship and activities of our two congregations. We certainly hadn't anticipated that kind of publicity.

We were staying at a beautiful hotel in Herzliya right on the Mediterranean and as soon as we had registered we hurried down to the beach. It was already dark but we listened to the lapping of the water, took off our shoes and socks and waded along the shore of this land, sacred from time immemorial.

Our travel agent, a close friend of a member of my congregation, took good care of us and arranged for a car and driver to accompany us all the time. The day after our arrival we headed north, visiting Natanya and Hadera as well as Nazareth, where an Arab guide escorted us around the sites sacred to Christianity. From the top of Mount Tabor we viewed the beauty of the land— Megiddo and the Upper Galilee—we spent time in Tiberias, nestled on the shore of Lake Kinneret (Sea of Galilee), gazed in wonder at the panoramic view of Haifa and the azure waters of the Mediterranean from Mount Carmel, and visited Kibbutz Dafna, where I had worked in my student days in the summer of 1947. I envied the kibbutzniks for their large outdoor swimming pool, an amenity we certainly did not have in my time there. And everywhere we marveled at the rapid development of the country.

Later we flew to Eilat, where, thanks to General Marshall, we were able to meet General Avraham Yoffe, commander of the Southern Forces, and other military officials, who briefed us on Israel's security needs from their perspective.

Of course Dr. Stitt and I spent considerable time in Jerusalem. In 1959 it was still a divided city; the Western Wall was in Jordanian hands and inaccessible to Jews. We made a pilgrimage to Mount Zion, recalling the biblical prediction, "Out of Zion shall go forth the Law, and the word of God from Jerusalem," and in a candle-lit room paid our respects at what is believed to be the tomb of King David.

At dinner that night Dr. Stitt and I talked about making a condolence call to the Chief Rabbi of the Sephardic community, Yitzhak Nissim, who had lost his sister and was observing the *shiva* (a 7-day period of mourning). Dr. Stitt consulted our driver about what to wear to the Rabbi's home—a regular business suit, shirt, and tie or a dark suit and clerical garb. The driver appreciated the Minister's sensitivity and opted for business attire, but I objected. It seemed to me that his answer was based on the assumption that the Chief Rabbi would not be comfortable with symbols of other faiths. I prevailed upon Dr. Stitt to wear clerical garb. When we arrived at Rabbi Nissim's home, we entered the room quietly and, as is the custom, sat silently for a while and then prepared to leave. Mrs. Nissim saw us and we spoke together briefly. Looking back, we noticed that the Chief Rabbi was now alone in the room, so we returned to be at his side. He engaged us in a long and fascinating conversation, even discussing the question of what to wear to his home. As Chief Rabbi, he commented, he received visitors of different world religions, and many prominently displayed the symbols of their faiths. Obviously this did not offend him in any way. On the contrary, he thought it was natural for them to do so.

I have often reflected on that conversation. So powerful is the bitterness of centuries of religious persecution that many Jews cringe at the sight of someone wearing clerical garb in their home or synagogue. There are rabbis who will not participate in an ecumenical program if there is a cross in the room. While I understand their emotions, I for one do not take offense at symbols sacred to someone else's faith.

For our last Sunday in Jerusalem we had scheduled visits to a number of religious institutions. I rose early and said morning prayers at the Great Synagogue, returned for breakfast with Dr. Stitt, and then accompanied him to the Baptist Church and the Ethiopian Coptic Church, and later to St. Andrew's Presbyterian Church, which overlooked a valley known as Gai Hinom, the "Valley of Hell" (Gehenna), so named because historically this was a major site of human sacrifices.

We also included a visit to Me'a Shearim, the Hasidic neighborhood, where I took a few minutes to purchase religious articles, such as yarmulkes and mezuzahs, to take home as gifts. I invited Dr. Stitt to come into the store with me, but he preferred to remain outside. He was wearing a dark suit with a white clerical collar and a black felt fedora. Every now and then when I glanced out of the store window to be sure that all was well, I noticed that as Hasidim passed by Dr. Stitt would wave his hand and greet them. When I rejoined him and our driver, I saw a young Hasid approach, a handsome man in his late twenties, elegantly attired in a traditional *kapate* (long black silk coat) and wearing a luxurious *shtreimel*. He looked regal. As he neared the Minister, he did something none of the other Hasidim had done: he stopped, stretched out his hand, and asked in Yiddish, "From where comes such a handsome-looking Jew?" The eyes of the young Hasid had gazed beyond the clerical collar, observing only a face that mirrored love for humanity, the smiling and friendly countenance of my friend the Reverend Dr. Jesse W. Stitt.

A MISSION TO WEST GERMANY

In March 1960 Dr. Stitt and I traveled to West Germany at the invitation of the Bonn government following an alarming resurgence of anti-Semitic incidents there. West German officials, who had read about the activities of our two congregations and learned about our Covenant of Brotherhood, hoped we could be "goodwill ambassadors," bringing our message of brotherhood to the people and, perhaps, determine the reason for this disturbing turn of events.

On December 25, 1959, swastikas had been smeared on the exterior walls of a new synagogue in Cologne, built a few years before by the West German government as part of the reparations agreements. The young men responsible for this despicable attack had evidently been under the influence of the neo-Nazi party and the quick transmittal of the news over international wire services on Christmas Day gave rise to widespread outrage and concern. Not long after, the Cologne incident was repeated in other cities in West Germany as well as in Europe, South America, the United States itself, and even in Israel. West German leaders must have envisioned the possibility that a visit by a minister and a rabbi who were friends and traveled and spoke together might encourage their citizens to develop programs of cooperation rather than confrontation. And so Dr. Stitt and I prepared to do something that had been inconceivable to me: travel to a land whose people had engaged in acts of such horrendous brutality against the Jewish people that I never imagined I could ever walk on their soil.

Our departure date was one I can never forget—Thursday evening, March 17, 1960, my 37th birthday. We were booked on the first transatlantic flight of Air Lufthansa, No. 421 from New York to Frankfurt, but boarding and departure were delayed four hours because of a bomb scare. By the time we arrived in Frankfurt, it was Friday afternoon, we were five hours behind schedule and had missed the earlier connecting flight to

Nuremberg, our first stop before the oncoming Sabbath. As we walked to the arrivals building, we were met by reporters and photographers who had been waiting for several hours to interview us about the purpose of our trip, our itinerary, and what we hoped to accomplish.

On the way into the city I explained to the officials accompanying us that I could not take an evening flight to Nuremberg because that would be a violation of the Jewish Sabbath. We decided that Dr. Stitt should continue the trip as planned and that I would meet him in Nuremberg after Shabbat. When our hosts offered to arrange hotel accommodations for me, I mentioned that I had friends in Frankfurt and asked them to call the family and at least let them know I was there. As soon as we arrived at Lufthansa's main office, a representative made the call and returned shortly, saying, "Please, Rabbi Block, be seated. Everything is going to be just fine."

Hardly had twenty minutes elapsed when Heinrich Bloch came bounding in and embraced me. The last time we had seen one another was in Jerusalem in 1948. "You must come to our home," he urged, "and not stay in a hotel. You will make us very happy if you stay with us for Shabbat."

We took a tram to his apartment house, which was some distance away. The ride gave me a chance to see the people and come face to face with a question I knew I would constantly have to raise in my mind: What were these people opposite me, in front of me, next to me, doing twenty years ago during the war? Where had they been? What terrible secrets did they carry in their hearts? Had they participated? Had they known? When we reached our stop, I stared at the cobblestone streets and for a moment I could almost hear the clump of the Nazi troops goose-stepping through the city.

I waited outside Heinrich's apartment for him to share the news with his wife, Maryla, so that she could have a few minutes to prepare for a surprise guest. When I came in, she took a look at me and cried, "Irving, Irving, what a joy to see you! What a joy!" So I spent Shabbat with the Bloch family.

How life sometimes comes full circle. Thirteen years before, I had come to Jerusalem as a student and unexpectedly spent my first night in the land in their home; and now, my first night in West Germany, I again found myself their guest. We spent the time reminiscing and catching up with our news. Heinrich, it seemed, had returned to West Germany from Israel five years before, using their reparation funds to enter the import-export business selling Israeli made clothing. But Maryla's heart longed for Israel. I was sorry that Heinrich and Maryla's son, Benjamin, now a teenager, was away from home working on a new *aliyah* project. I remembered him as a small child that summer of 1947 crying with fright as British guns were being fired under the windows of the building in which the Blochs lived.

The next morning Heinrich and I went to synagogue. I was introduced to the congregation, and when it came time for the mourner's *Kaddish*, I rose to say it on behalf of the Six Million. From then on whenever I attended a synagogue service in West Germany or visited a Holocaust memorial, I recited the *Kaddish* if there was a *minyan* present, or one of the Psalms in their memory. I shuddered when Maryla told me about a neighbor, an outwardly pleasant man, who maintained that the figure was only four million, not six.

At the time of our visit, most of the Jews in West Germany were either survivors who had been released from DP (displaced persons) camps after the war or German Jews who had left before World War II and returned to reclaim what remained of their homes and businesses. Others were administrators of social service agencies and a few religious leaders who had come to the country to offer their assistance.

To understand the crisis that had brought us to West Germany, Dr. Stitt and I met with government officials, ecclesiastical leaders, heads of Jewish communities, and representatives of associations for Christian and Jewish cooperation. Wherever and whenever possible, we also spoke with taxi drivers, waiters, and ordinary people, young and old, in their homes and offices. Our itinerary took us first to Nuremberg, the city ill-famed for the severe anti-Jewish laws that became Nazi policy and the site of the war crimes trials of the defeated Nazi leaders. In 1933 Nuremberg had 9,000 Jewish residents. There were three deportations in 1941, and by the end of the war the Jewish population numbered only 200, most of whom had not been residents in the prewar years.

We spoke with the director of Nuremberg's Jewish community, who expressed a positive outlook, telling us that he felt much freer now than he had before 1933 because now the government reacted severely to all anti-Semitic incidents. He also commented that as a representative of the Jewish community, he was received everywhere with genuine friendliness.

From there we drove to Munich, where in the early days of the rise of Nazism Hitler's followers plotted the "final solution." During our visit I worshipped in the synagogue and spoke with Jewish leaders, who thought that most West Germans, including young people, agonized over the anti-Semitic acts that had been committed around the country and attributed them to neo-Nazi groups attempting to determine what the reaction would be to such vicious attacks. Here, too, the Jewish leadership seemed confident that the Bonn government was determined to bring the culprits to justice as well as those who, in speech, action, or in writing, incited others.

A twenty-minute train ride from Munich, followed by a ten-minute taxi ride from the railroad station, brings one to Dachau, the notorious concentration camp. Dr. Stitt and I approached the dreaded site with some apprehension. Green farmland bordered the bleak enclosure of wooden huts and high towers, beyond which stood the crematoria. We noticed the landscaped grounds and a stone bearing the inscription, "Out of night and horror this monument was erected to the honor of God and those who had to die because they were Jews." As we stood before the open furnaces, staring in horror at the long metal stretchers which had borne hundreds of thousands of Jewish and Christian bodies into the depths of the incinerators, I lifted up my voice and chanted the traditional Mourners' Prayer: *"El Maleh Rahamim"* ("God, full of compassion, have mercy upon these souls...").

Seared into my mind is the view from the cemetery on a hill near Dachau. In the center of the valley below stands a church, its white steeple piercing the sky. I kept asking myself whether it is conceivable that the pastor and the parishioners were unaware that the smoke belching forth from the camp chimneys was the smoke of human flesh. Were they so terribly oblivious or were they unconcerned because it was not their personal problem, not their own people being tortured and suffering? The questions still haunt me.

Our next stop was West Berlin, where we met with such outstanding figures as Bishop Dibelius, Evangelical Bishop of Berlin, and Willy Brandt, the Mayor of West Berlin. One of the Jewish religious leaders, Cantor Martin Weil, accompanied us through the Brandenberg Gate to East Berlin, where we stopped to visit the imposing Russian war memorial. What struck me in particular were the faces of pedestrians in East Berlin—sullen, unsmiling, grim, in contrast to the animated expressions of the West Berliners.

Later we went on to Cologne to visit the synagogue that had been defaced. Built after the war by the West German government at a cost of over a million dollars, it was probably one of the most beautiful synagogues in all of Europe, we were told.

From there we drove to Bonn, the legislative capital of West Germany, and went to the Foreign Legation Office, stopping first at a nearby small, exquisite synagogue, also built as part of West Germany's reparations to replace the one that had been destroyed by the Nazis. The Jewish community of Bonn dates back to the twelfth century, but its existence was constantly in peril and the people endured persecution and murderous attacks until 1794, when the city was occupied by the French revolutionary army. Then the Jews were declared citizens with equal rights and the gate of the ghetto was publicly torn down.

Our last stop was Frankfurt, once a great center of Jewish life and learning. Some in the Jewish community told us they were convinced that there was latent anti-Semitism among the masses and still many Nazis among the population. However, they also acknowledged that the government was doing everything possible to denounce and renounce anti-Semitism.

If teenagers were responsible for desecrating synagogues and public buildings in West Germany—there were more than 600 such incidents—an even greater number of fine young men and women were dedicating themselves to the challenge of reconciliation. One example: a month after the Cologne incident, 40,000 boys and girls marched in a spontaneous demonstration through

the streets of West Berlin and stood before the Jewish community center in silent reverence. Never in the previous 500 years had
anything similar occurred. When Dr. Stitt and I met with Willy
Brandt, he told us that German youth were asking questions such
as; What is the meaning of life for the individual and for the country? Isn't it something more than material wealth and buildings
and prosperity? Isn't it also morals and intellectual ideas?

It was West German young people, all Protestants, who founded the Atonement Movement. Twenty of them went to France, to
the town of Villeurbanne on the outskirts of Lyons, and there,
with food and lodging provided by local Catholic institutions and
supplies and materials furnished by a West German army field
unit, they spent two years building a synagogue with their own
hands. I learned about the project, completed in May 1963, from
a friend of our congregation, Margo Wolff, a German-born United
Nations correspondent who traveled around Europe speaking on
behalf of the Atonement organization. Wherever she went she
spoke of the relationship between a synagogue and a church in
New York City, and many people queried, "Why can't we build
such a brotherhood program here in Germany?" The synagogue
in Villeurbanne was later named La Synagogue de la Fraternité
(literally, The Brotherhood Synagogue).[1]

Some religious leaders with whom Dr. Stitt and I spoke suggested that the future of Germany would lie in an answer to the
question, "What is the moral role of the church?" Half of the
German population was Catholic and half Evangelical Protestant,
but most of their church leaders were publicly silent on
Kristallnacht ("Night of Broken Glass"), on November 9 and 10,

---

1. In May 1971 my family and I visited this synagogue and spent a day with
leaders and members of the congregation.

1938, when synagogues in Germany were set ablaze, Jewish shops demolished, and Jewish citizens beaten, imprisoned, and put to death. It would take half a century for German religious leaders to admit their culpability. (See Chapter 13.)

In Munich one distinguished member of the Jewish community had maintained that "there would never be close cooperation between churches and synagogues" until [the church] refrains from teaching the crucifixion story in schools. The way it is presented "sows seeds of hatred in German boys and girls." Other Jewish people we met stressed the character of German friends who did help save many lives during the war. As one observer put it, "Germany not only has its murderers but also its righteous."

After Dr. Stitt and I returned home, we submitted a report on our trip to our State Department and to the West German government and also discussed our experiences with our congregations. It was difficult to state conclusively whether the anti-Semitic acts in West Germany had been isolated incidents or were deliberately organized. Some attributed them to neo-Nazi propaganda making inroads among German youth, while others viewed them as a vehicle for old Nazis to attack the Adenauer government. One Jewish leader characterized the attitude of West Germans this way: "On the level of social exchange there is some cooperation, but in the area of religious brotherhood there is just tolerance."

PUBLIC RECOGNITION OF OUR WORK

During the 1960s our two congregations continued their joint activities and were the recipients of honors from many civic and religious organizations. Two events were particularly memorable.

The weekend of May 3–4, 1968 Bucknell University in Lewisburg, Pennsylvania, held a convocation on the theme "Individual Responsibility in a Free Society," at which one of the honorees and the main speaker was Vice President Hubert H. Humphrey. An awards ceremony would recognize a number of individuals for their "exemplary concern for the quality of community life." The University President, Charles H. Watts II, notified Dr. Stitt and me that our two congregations had each been selected to receive a special award because they "typify what can be done to effectively advance the cause of brotherhood by a substantial group of individuals collectively exercising responsible leadership." His letter certainly took us by surprise. It was just a month before the fifteenth anniversary of my ordination.

Dr. Stitt and I, our wives, and leaders of our congregations received VIP treatment all weekend. Our hosts had thoughtfully arranged for Phyllis and me to have Shabbat meals with a young faculty couple who kept a kosher home, and I was invited to conduct a Sabbath service on campus since there was no rabbi in residence.

The ceremony was a highly emotional experience, but it offered us an opportunity to bring our message to a broad and influential audience as well as to honor our two congregations, whose members supported our pioneering programs so actively and wholeheartedly. We each received, on behalf of our congregations, a special medallion as well as an Award of Merit, which read:

Man's responsibility to man through free, unfettered worship is the ideal cornerstone on which is erected the shared sanctuary of the Village Presbyterian Church and The Brotherhood Synagogue in Greenwich Village, New York.

Heralds of the ecumenical spirit, a Christian and a Hebrew congregation have joined not only to worship in the same physical setting, but to demonstrate that religious truths are more universal than their traditional definitions.

To the Reverend Jesse W. Stitt belongs the inspiration to convert the sanctuary he served as pastor for the use of church and synagogue. To Rabbi Irving J. Block belongs the vision of those infinite dimensions of the spirit created by this act of faith. To the congregations both men serve belong the grace and strength of belief whose wellsprings lie in the individual conscience.

Bucknell University is proud to present this Award of Merit for Service in the Cause of Brotherhood to the Congregations of The Brotherhood Synagogue and the Village Presbyterian Church, through their spiritual leaders, Rabbi Block and the Reverend Stitt, whose acts of faith have brought us to a new understanding of those deeper communal bonds that unite all men.

In the spring of 1971 we received another joint award, one that was particularly meaningful because it was presented by a neighbor, The Salvation Army, whose national headquarters was then located on West 14th Street, just around the block from our joint sanctuary. Moreover, The Salvation Army Evangeline Residence for young women was a few doors away from our building, and many of the residents attended our services. Sometimes together, and other times individually, Dr. Stitt and I were frequently invited to speak at the weekly vesper service at the residence.

In the course of my rabbinate, I calculate that I have addressed residents at least a hundred times at various Salvation Army facilities in the city. I have always admired this organization because it epitomizes brotherhood in action, and I cherish my friendship with many of its officers and their families. One of the officers once commented that I probably know more about The Salvation Army than any other rabbi in the city.

One of the highest honors The Salvation Army presents to community leaders is the much coveted Golden Doughnut Award, which Dr. Stitt and I each received:

> The Salvation Army presents its Golden Doughnut Award for 1971 to Rabbi Irving J. Block and the Reverend Jesse W. Stitt, co-partners in the ministry of preaching brotherly love by practicing brotherhood in action to a loving God and serving people as joint occupants for 17 years of a unique New York institution.

This would be the last award that Dr. Stitt and I received together. That summer he retired.

The Village Presbyterian Church now faced a formidable task: to choose a successor who not only would lead the congregation but would continue the joint programs with our Synagogue in the spirit of our Covenant of Brotherhood.

The Consul, The Rabbi, and the Little Train

In May 1971 I took a short sabbatical—our destination was Israel—with Phyllis, our son, and my mother-in-law. Our itinerary included a few days in Paris and then a trip by train south to Marseilles to board the Israeli ship Dan to the port of Haifa.

Since the train made a stop at Lyons, we thought it would be important to visit the synagogue in Villeurbanne, built by West German young people of the Atonement Movement. Our friend Margo Wolff, a journalist with contacts in the German government, arranged for me to meet the German consul there. When the train arrived at the station, there was a delegation waiting to greet us, including the rabbi of the congregation and other Jewish community leaders—all French-speaking immigrants from North Africa— along with Rudolf Teske, the West German consul. Phyllis was our French interpreter as we conversed in English, French, and Hebrew.

We were very impressed with the lovely synagogue sanctuary, modern in design but not stark, which could accommodate about 300 worshippers. The Holy Ark housed beautiful Torah scrolls with bells and crowns from North Africa. I was also deeply moved by the name of the congregation, "La Synagogue de la Fraternité."

Mr. Teske had already set up an appointment with me in his office the next day, but as a parent himself, when he saw that we had a young child with us, he made a wonderful suggestion: Why don't we all go to the zoo in Lyons so our family could remain together.

The family enjoyed the exhibits and the lovely park, while the consul and I talked and strolled at our own pace. Then we saw the miniature train that took sightseers around the zoo. It was just ending its last run for the day, but the consul persuaded the engineer to make one more trip to accommodate special visitors from America.

We all boarded the train on that delightful warm and sunny May afternoon, the consul and I seated several rows behind, talking seriously about how to foster an even greater spirit of reconciliation and atonement. Truly an unforgettable day.

7

Dr. Stitt Retires
New Minister Spurns Covenant

"I grieve with you! Something beautiful has been lost."

RABBI MORRIS S. LAZARON

On April 21, 1970, Dr. Stitt announced to his Boards of Elders and Trustees (the Session):

After painful mind, heart and soul-searching, I have decided that my ministerial relationship with the Village Church has to terminate as of July 1, 1971....Much has to be done between now and then. What the future will be? What the decisions will be?... There is one matter which I want to bring to your attention, as far as I am personally concerned. You, as a Session, and I, as your minister, and the members of the congregation of the Village Presbyterian Church have been in constant relationship with, and bound by, a Covenant of Brotherhood with The Brotherhood Synagogue since May 1954.

This Covenant must be held completely inviolate. The word of the Covenant cannot and must not be held lightly by this Session or by our Congregation.

If by any stretch of the imagination, this Session, or this Congregation should not fight to the bitter end, and to the highest authority, for the rights and privileges of The Brotherhood Synagogue for the use and ownership of this property... then my ministry, this Session and our Congregational commitment to the Brotherhood program with The Brotherhood Synagogue will have been in vain.

The news of Dr. Stitt's impending retirement in the summer of 1971 filled the heart of the Synagogue's members with sadness, anguish, and dismay. We had to decide how best to express our love, admiration, and respect for him. At a Friday night service on February 19, 1971, our Synagogue proudly conferred honorary membership in our congregational family upon Rev. Dr. and Mrs. Stitt, in recognition of their labors of love for all the children of God and for their dedication to the community of mankind. We also gave them a gift from Israel, a replica of a Torah, our Synagogue's highest award, adorned with silver bells, breastplate, pointer, and an Ark to house it.

At home that night, Dr. Stitt penned a letter to me:

...you all were so generous in your praise for all the years we have had together.... For Nancy and me to have received the Certificate of Honorary Membership as members of The Brotherhood Synagogue would have been long, long, long remembered, but to have placed in my arms the Sefer Torah which you put there was beyond belief and beyond anything that could enter into one's imagination or expectations. I truly do not know how I can be so fortunate with the blessings of so many.

Four months later Dr. Stitt preached his final sermon to his congregation, which he titled "Exit Only":

There was a minister who stood in this Pulpit in November 1900 who believed with his congregation that our Church had a distinctive ministry to perform just where it was.

There is a minister now who stands in this Pulpit who believes, with you, that our Church has a distinctive ministry to perform just where it is...it is a ministry of brotherhood with The Brotherhood Synagogue unparalleled in this country in any denomination—which must be accepted and commended by the Presbytery of the City of

New York to whom we turn for guidance—and from whom we expect an uninhibited blessing.... it is the sponsorship (along with our colleagues and partners of The Brotherhood Synagogue) of the Greenwich Mews Theatre. These actors and actresses have sought to interpret the great social and religious truths which the Rabbi and I have tried to interpret to you from this pulpit. This must be continued.

...The years we have had together—let them speak for themselves.... The years you all have before you—may they be many and may they be greater than you can ever imagine... God bless you all. Amen.

Unfortunately, he and Nancy were not able to enjoy their retirement. The malignancy he had been battling silently weakened him and he grew frailer and frailer. On the evening of November 23, 1971, at the age of 67, Dr. Stitt passed away. We mourned along with members of his Church, reciting our traditional mourner's prayer, the *Kaddish*, for him throughout the year, and we tried to comfort Nancy as much as we could.

What was unique about Dr. Stitt's ministry was that so much of it was shared with a rabbi and his synagogue. He was a Christian Zionist, a sincere friend of the Jewish people, and was uplifted by his every visit to the State of Israel. His ministry reflected his love for all humanity and his vision of religious brotherhood. As the Minister of his church, he would speak of our respective and differing traditions saying, "My job is to make better Christians out of my people; and the Rabbi's job is make better Jews out of his congregation." Jesse Stitt was a friend, a dedicated servant of God, and a devoted shepherd. He was respected by his fellow clergy, who elected him to positions of leadership, and was respected in the communities that he served. On the pulpit he was an imposing figure, tall and elegant, a superb and popular preacher. He was a caring husband, a man with a good sense of humor who enjoyed life and made friends easily. To me he was a brother, a beloved colleague, and a mentor, always at my side at my family's life-cycle events, in times of joy and sorrow. Jesse Stitt was a dreamer who believed in the exhortation of the prophet Malachai: "Have we not one Father? Hath not one God created us? Why do we deal treacherously every man against his brother?" As he preached, so he lived.

The Connecticut *Jewish Ledger* eulogized him in an editorial:

> For every person whom he may have influenced in the direction of good will toward his fellow man, he will be remembered for having lived in accordance with the highest ideals one strives for. We in Connecticut, who have seen these principles in action in so many of our suburban communities... will certainly record Dr. Stitt's name among the righteous friends of the Jewish people.

ILL WINDS BLOWING

Knowing that he was gravely ill, Dr. Stitt arranged for a new minister to be "called," as the church procedure for selecting a new minister is described. He and I had spoken from time to time about the attributes required for his successor, and he reassured me that whoever was selected would have a similar commitment to our brotherhood program, its philosophy, and its ideals and would maintain the friendship which had bound our two congregations together for seventeen years. I eagerly looked forward to working amicably and effectively with the minister who would accept this rather unique pulpit.

Pastor William Glenesk was called to be Dr. Stitt's successor, with the approval of both the Session of the Village Presbyterian

Church and the Presbytery of New York. The two men had known each other through The Players, a club on Gramercy Park, and shared an interest in theater. The Pastor, a few years younger than I, had been serving Spencer Memorial Church in Brooklyn Heights on a part-time basis and, coincidentally, had even once invited me to address his congregation on a Sunday morning. At one time a synagogue had temporarily used the facilities of his church.

Pastor Glenesk had a reputation as a man of artistic talent, somewhat flamboyant and avant-garde in his approach; he had caught the attention of *Life* magazine, which featured him in an article on new trends in church leadership. What I did not know was that some of his programs had alienated Christians as well as Jews in his Brooklyn community, but it did not take long after his arrival on West 13th Street for me to realize that William Glenesk was the wrong minister to continue the unique relationship between the Church and our Synagogue. I had only to sit down with the new Pastor once to realize that everything was about to change.

As we sat together on the couch in his office—and without any preliminary pleasantries—his words jolted me: "My people tell me that they feel like little Israel surrounded by her Arab neighbors." I shuddered, and I stammered, "Pardon me, but I don't think I quite heard what you said." He repeated, "My people tell me that they feel like little Israel surrounded by her Arab neighbors." I couldn't fathom what he was driving at, but I quickly and strongly objected to such a distorted analogy. He went on to tell me that he was receiving complaints from the church people and that they were unhappy with our relationship. That was the very first time I had ever heard anything like that or had any inkling of such an attitude on the part of members of the Village Church. I just could not believe it. I knew at once that great "Trouble" was sitting next to me on the couch.

When I came home, my wife saw at once that I was pale and trembling and terribly agitated. I shared with her my conversation with the Pastor and predicted that our relationship would be tumultuous and adversarial. Only Heaven knew where it would lead. How I missed Dr. Stitt.

Shortly after Pastor Glenesk officially began his ministry at the Village Presbyterian Church in September 1971, Herbert Plaut, President of our Synagogue, and I had lunch with him. Repeatedly, the Pastor emphasized a twofold objective: to build up the Church congregation and to develop their own individuality. We asked him to kindly explain the phrase, "their own individuality," but the more he talked the more bewildered we became. I remember retorting, "Who ever stopped this Church from being a Christian congregation, and what does individuality have to do with brotherhood and friendship?"

A few weeks later, when the Synagogue was celebrating Succoth, the Pastor complained about "vibrations" during his Sunday morning service caused by the presence of Synagogue women seated in the succah. We had given them that assignment precisely to prevent any noise or loud conversation on the street from disturbing the worship service. The Pastor, however, viewed their presence as an intrusion. On the other hand, the Church office was now open on Saturday mornings and the typewriters clacked away during our Shabbat service, but *we* had not complained about that act of disrespect.

One day the Pastor visited me in my study. We spoke about programming, and when I called attention to what we had done in the past, he retorted, "It's in the past, all right; you said it, you made your point. Brotherhood is passé. It's bad enough that your Friday nights kill our theater."

In spite of the fact that for years the Greenwich Mews Theatre had been a joint cultural project of the Church and the Synagogue, as the playbills clearly acknowledged, the Pastor insisted that the theater was a project of the Church alone. He denied that any co-sponsorship of the theater had existed even though Dr. Stitt had acknowledged it in his final sermon to his congregation and had clearly urged that this arrangement be continued. There had been a specific understanding that neither nudity nor obscenity would be permitted on the stage, but the Pastor viewed this agreement as artistic censorship and refused to comply. He assumed the title of "Artistic Director" of the theater, characterizing it as a ministry to the arts. When I tried to explain that we had been partners, "Show me proof," he demanded, "not hearsay!"

On another occasion the Pastor objected, in his words, to the "obtrusion and omnipresence of the Holy Ark," contending that it interfered with the use of the altar for theatrical presentations that he wished to incorporate into his religious services and limited the use of the sanctuary for rehearsal space. He complained that our Religious School classes utilized too much space and, contrary to the regulations of The Brotherhood Council, he began to schedule theatrical rehearsals during school hours, making it very difficult for teachers and students alike. People were continuously running around the building and using inappropriate language. Even Cantor Mirkovic and our choir were unable to practice on Friday nights prior to the services because of theatrical rehearsals at that hour, something that would have never been permitted in Dr. Stitt's time.

When we called these matters to the attention of the lay leaders of the Village Church, they demurred, advising us to be "patient," to give the Pastor a chance. He's not Dr. Stitt, they said, and he does things his own way. It was not the response we had expected.

At a meeting of The Brotherhood Council, the Pastor indicated that he was about to introduce a number of changes, which he anticipated would irritate the Synagogue. He stated that he did not consider himself bound by the Covenant of Brotherhood since he was not the Pastor when it was adopted; he implied that the Synagogue had usurped the larger office space; he protested that the Synagogue was not supporting the theater and the Saturday Church bake sales. And he contended that we ought to contribute a far greater portion than two thirds of the maintenance costs of the building. "You are here on a steal!" he shouted. We were stunned by his anger and his vehemence.

In another incident, as he walked by the Synagogue office one day, the Pastor yelled an imprecation or threat at me. When I suggested he ease up, he screamed while descending the stairs, "My people are going to come here and break down the doors!" I no longer recall what precipitated such an outburst. Perhaps he was piqued at the refusal of The Brotherhood Council to allow the sexton to take on the added burden of cleaning the Spencer Memorial Church in Brooklyn, where the Pastor was still serving on a part-time basis.

BROTHERHOOD UNDER SIEGE

By October 1972, a year after the Pastor's arrival, our President, Herbert Plaut, felt compelled to report to our Board of Trustees: "Those to whom the Pastor's actions towards the Synagogue and the Rabbi for the past year seem sporadic bits of bad manners, lack of respect, and a single-mindedness of promoting theatrical enterprise without concern for others, are to be informed that these, I strongly believe, were fitted together by him into an over-all plan to damage, if not entirely undermine, the concept of the Covenant of Brotherhood."

It became increasingly evident that the Village Presbyterian Church now lacked effective lay leadership. Many staunch propo-nents of our brotherhood concept had either passed on to heav-enly realms or moved out of the city. Membership had dwindled and funds were limited. The Church was reaching a turning point where it had to take measures to insure its future; at the same time we were concerned about our status in the building.

In 1962 The Brotherhood Council had proposed an arrange-ment for a long-term right of occupancy by The Brotherhood Synagogue, inasmuch as the property would, according to Church regulations, revert to the Presbytery of New York should the Village Presbyterian Church cease to exist. This proposal was sub-mitted to the Presbytery, but somehow, over the years, in spite of all the discussions by the Village Church, the Synagogue, and the Presbytery, the issue was never resolved. In 1970 Dr. Stitt again sought to introduce the question of our tenure to the Presbytery in the hope that it would be forced to discuss it "with a sense of serious determination." He assured The Brotherhood Council that "we will fight together, we will work together and we may cry together—but we will stay together."

These questions were brought up again in May 1972. A sub-committee made up of two Village Church leaders and two Synagogue presidents proposed a 50-year lease when and if the Village Church could no longer continue as an entity at its pre-sent location. Pastor Glenesk was asked by his Session to advocate this plan to the Presbytery. When Herbert Plaut was told three months later that the Executive Presbyter had disapproved of the idea, he was so chagrined that he telephoned the official to express his dismay and sorrow at the decision. To his amazement, the official said that he had personally favored the suggestion for tenure, either through lease or sale, but since his term as Executive Presbyter was concluding, he lacked authority to move the request through the proper channels. This was totally different from the statement we received from the Pastor that the plan for a long-term lease had been disapproved on its merits.

At the end of 1972 the Clerk of Session of the Village Church, Mrs. Eunice Currie, wrote to the new Executive Presbyter asking that the matter of tenure, "which is of deep concern to us," be given prompt consideration. During this same period a number of long time Church members, deeply disturbed by what they felt was mismanagement of Church affairs and concerned over the Pastor's antagonism toward the Synagogue, were meeting with the Presbytery to petition for his recall.

The friction and disagreements never abated. Six months later, in July 1973, the Pastor charged that for the past two years his

> uphill work of building the Village Church congregation... has met with an unbelievable intransigence on the part of the Rabbi which leads to the question of the honesty and integrity of the Covenant relationship. It would appear that the Synagogue desires a token relationship to a token Christian congregation who occupy a very minor part of its own facilities, as if we had given away our birthright without any substantial investment toward equity, not unlike Isaac, Jacob and Esau.... We will not be the token house Christian or second class citizen in priority and needs to implement our program.... If the relationship is broken it will be the doing or undoing of those who lead the Synagogue, but it cannot continue at our expense.

A month later, on August 16, 1973, William Cohen, Mr. Plaut's successor as our President, wrote to Mrs. Currie:

> We are terribly outraged at your present Pastor's continuing slurs against the integrity of our Synagogue, and we deeply resent his impugning our motives and his repeated carping about the presence of our religious objects. We can no longer tolerate these disdainful attitudes....
>
> From time to time we have met with you and expressed to you our concern at what we have seen as a deterioration of our program of religious brotherhood. We have also been aware that you, too, have been increasingly disturbed by such acts and attitudes on the part of the Pastor which willfully disregard our regulations and traditions.

Mr. Cohen went on to charge that the Pastor had violated

> our longstanding regulations by... the unauthorized use and rental of rooms in the Community House...
>
> He further implies that the Synagogue is merely a tenant in the buildings, and that he has a right to do with the property whatever he wishes, whenever he wishes and however he wishes...
>
> Let us state categorically and unequivocally that we are not, have never been and would never consider ourselves as tenants of 139–143 West 13th Street....[1]

YOM KIPPUR WAR ON 13TH STREET

That fall began the battle of the written word. In the Village Church bulletin of September 9, 1973, the Pastor, writing about The National Museum in Barcelona, Spain, stated that it "holds

---

1. While the building was legally the property of the Presbytery of New York, our Covenant of Brotherhood established a partnership, not a landlord–tenant relationship.

Europe's best collection of Romanesque early Christian art... expressing the early experience of the followers of Christ in an alien environment, persecuted by the Jewish theocracy and the Roman oligarchy, comparable to our situation as a minority and remnant in New York City...."

But it was the Yom Kippur War, which Egypt launched on Saturday, October 6, 1973, that even more clearly revealed the depth of the Pastor's hostility not only toward our congregation but to Israel and the Jewish people. Taking into account that Israel had been attacked by massive military units that crossed the Suez Canal on the most sacred day of the Jewish year, as soon as our worship services were over I placed a notice on the Synagogue's outdoor bulletin board: MAY THERE BE VICTORY AND PEACE FOR ISRAEL.

On the following Sunday the Pastor responded in his Church bulletin: "To our friends, Arab, non-Zionist Jews and all who are offended by the arrogant, self-righteous sign posted outside our sanctuary by the Synagogue re 'Victory for Israel' we offer our regrets and prayers for peace."

That Sunday was an intermediate day of Succoth and I was at the Synagogue when someone handed me a copy of his bulletin. As I read that outrageous text, I was so infuriated and shaken I could hardly speak. The Church service was over, the coffee hour had just ended, and I saw the Clerk of Session leaving the community house. I immediately confronted her with this bulletin. "This goes beyond the Pastor's ill-tempered manner," I asserted. "This is a declaration of war against the Jewish people!"

A couple of weeks after the Yom Kippur War, a community-wide rally in support of Israel was planned for October 23. A number of local Christian clergy had indicated that they too wished to participate. The rally was to take place outdoors on West 13th

Street, in front of our building, so that in case of inclement weather the event could easily be moved indoors, since ours was the largest synagogue sanctuary in the neighborhood. Early that afternoon the United Jewish Appeal staff brought down banners, flyers, pledge cards, and the like, and left several boxes of material in the first-floor meeting room of our community house. Later in the day, when the UJA staff returned, the boxes were nowhere to be found, but anti-Israel posters were now hanging in the hallway. The sexton searched all over and finally, in the meeting room, his eyes caught something protruding from behind the drape that covered a small Ark. There were the missing boxes.

Needless to say, Pastor Glenesk strongly opposed this rally. "Why is this rally being held since it deals with another political state?" he asked. When someone he met on the street—obviously unaware of the Pastor's attitude—asked if he were going to attend, he angrily countered, "I am not in Israel, I am in Syria!"

I was at home preparing for the rally when I heard my wife talking excitedly on the phone. Phyllis called out to me that the sexton was terribly upset because the Pastor had instructed him to lock the gate in front of the building before the event got under way. I immediately picked up the phone and assured him that the use of the sanctuary, if necessary, had been discussed with Mrs. Elizabeth Moore, a member of the Village Presbyterian Church, who was the current President of The Brotherhood Council, and that the plans had her full approval. Furthermore, we had all the necessary permits for holding an outdoor program.

Mrs. Moore and the Pastor had often clashed on a whole range of issues, so I immediately called her to discuss this latest crisis. We agreed that under no circumstances should the sexton lock the gate. I hurried over to the building; the gate was open, and

the rally took place as planned. Ministers, rabbis, and public officials spoke, and there was no further confrontation. But with this
episode the Synagogue's relationship with the Village
Presbyterian Church had reached an intolerable state.

TAKING THE DECISIVE STEP

Our Board of Trustees—which had followed with anguish the
deteriorating relationship with the Pastor—and I decided the
time had come to call an emergency meeting of our congregation
to share with our members all the disturbing remarks, canards,
and incidents of the last two years. We acted with a dire sense of
urgency, and the Board passed the following motion: "Resolved,
that it is the sense of this Board, *unless there is a change in the leadership of the Church*, that we make arrangements for a new location for our Synagogue, subject to approval by our membership."
We wrote to our members, urging them to attend a special meeting on Wednesday evening, November 7, 1973, to confront this
looming crisis.

The members of the congregation who had come together, plus
some friends, heard my heart cry out that in the last two years we
had been made to feel unwanted here. For seventeen years the
Village Church and its Minister did not find the Ark objectionable,
and now we hear from the Pastor that he sees the crucifix being
carried in and out "like a theatrical prop" while the Ark stays on
firm as Gibraltar, very visible, imposing and immutable, a symbol
of arrogant piety." Then our officers enumerated a whole litany of
grievances. The congregation was appalled at these revelations,
but everyone listened very intently, anxiously waiting to speak
and ask questions.

Somehow, unbeknown to us, the press had learned about this meeting and sent reporters to cover it. In her article "The October War on West 13th Street" in *New York* Magazine, Dorothy Rabinowitz wrote, "Of the 250 or so members at the meeting there was not one who failed to join the applause when member after member got up demanding to know why this insult had been allowed to drag on. They wanted out, now. They regarded the silence of the Presbytery as an answer to them." I had replied that our congregation had invested so much time and effort to realize the dream of brotherhood that we didn't want to come to a hasty decision but rather wished to try to give everyone a chance to work out the problems.

It was a long meeting. Many expressed their distress at this unforeseen turn of events and everyone saw no option other than to separate, because the situation had become unbearable and a threat to our existence as a synagogue. Our elected officers, President William Cohen, and Chairman of the Board Howard Westrich, presented the resolution to leave West 13th Street and asked for a vote. The Talmud says, "Even silence is an affirmation." When the motion was presented, there was a long silence before the vote. However, we did accept a suggestion to make one final attempt to meet with the Presbytery before going on our way.

I was proud of the congregation that night, and I assured our members that brotherhood had not died, that our dream was still alive, and I pledged that we would continue to spread our message of brotherhood wherever we might go and would continue to reach out to the community. On the way home from the meeting one member reflected to a reporter, "Those two [referring to Dr. Stitt and me] had a dream. That's what those two had. But this is the way it really is."

Our decision, while not unexpected, was heart-wrenching for many in the Village Church. Pastor Glenesk certainly did not enjoy the wholehearted support of his congregation. Dorothy Sulsona, President of the Women's Society, stated; "What I want is for Glenesk to leave and for the Rabbi and the Synagogue to stay. We have had a beautiful thing here for nineteen years. We've prepared a petition of recall to the Presbytery."

What I ultimately understood was that the Presbytery of New York, representing more than 100 Presbyterian churches, had permitted a minister with decidedly anti-Jewish and anti-Israel attitudes to be the new spiritual leader of the Village Church. Surely the Presbytery must have been aware of the Pastor's opinions and inclinations, yet it failed to forestall the dissolution of what one reporter called "the only ecumenical experiment of its kind."

After the difficult decision we reached that evening, we were left with the inevitable question: Was our pioneering experiment in religious brotherhood a little ahead of its time? I went home heartbroken and distraught, but sustained by the love and support of my congregation and my family and convinced that what we had done was right. For us, *ein breira*, there was "no alternative" to the decision we had made.

THE FINAL BREAK

I knew in advance that a story would probably appear in the *New York Times* the following Saturday, November 10, 1973, and I arranged to have someone bring me the early edition of the paper on Friday night so that Phyllis and I could read it. At the head of the article were two photographs, one of the Pastor and one of me. We both looked grim. The headline read, "War Dispute Helps End Brotherhood Effort." The reporter reviewed the partnership between the Village Church and The Brotherhood Synagogue that had begun in 1954 with Rev. Jesse William Stitt. The Pastor attributed the breakdown to the "intransigence" of the Rabbi, and the Rabbi was quoted as saying: "Dr. Stitt's successor was abrasive and insulting and never became attuned to the melody of his predecessor."

Phyllis and I realized that we faced an immediate problem at home: what to say to our young son? Though he was only eight and a half, he flipped through the *Times* every day, and we didn't want him to see and read the article until we had discussed it with him. We were particularly concerned that he not become embittered toward the Village Church and toward Christian people. Early Saturday morning, before I left for synagogue, we called Herbert into our room. As he sat on the side of the bed in his pajamas, we told him about the article, emphasized that there were many good people in the Village Church, that Dr. Stitt had been a marvelous person, but that the new Pastor did not have the same ideas, concepts, and sensitivity. Then we read the article with him, explained that the Church congregation was overwhelmed with problems and that it would be better for us to leave. He seemed to accept our explanation, nodding quietly; but later he asked about certain Church members he had come to know. We assured him that most of them were supportive of our congregation's position but, surprisingly, others were not. The child's face became flushed and he ran to his room to hide his own anguish.

The administrative office of the Presbytery of New York City was located at 7 West 11th Street, on the corner of Fifth Avenue, on the grounds of the First Presbyterian Church. I couldn't recall ever seeing anyone enter or leave the Presbytery office, but now, suddenly, offices usually dark at night were illuminated, people were coming and going. Officials of the Presbytery had been in contact with us either to request information or to meet with the Elders of the Village Church and then with the Board of Trustees of our Synagogue. We agreed that on January 14, 1974, members of the Executive Committee of the Synagogue would hold one more meeting with a special seven-member commission of the Presbytery. Louis Rivkin, a past President of our congregation, would speak for the Synagogue. Neither the Pastor nor I was to be present. I had asked Mr. Rivkin to stop by our apartment before going home, to share the discussion with us, and we waited anxiously for the doorbell to ring. The time seemed endless. Finally he came. Hardly had he taken off his coat when he burst out, "Rabbi, get ready, we're moving!"

As he reviewed the conversations with Phyllis and me and the direction of the discussion, I gathered that this special commission had been directed to compile facts about the dispute and report back to the Presbytery. However, given the frequent changes in the Presbytery staff, the commission members felt that they were not in a position to support our program in the future. Exasperated, Mr. Rivkin decided to ask a direct question: "Forget the immediate problems," he told them. "Forget the need to apologize to the Synagogue. I realize that you can't speak on behalf of the Presbytery but, as individuals, do you think it is good for churches and synagogues to join together and work for a common cause as we have done?" After a long pause, only one member of that Presbytery commission openly expressed the thought that it was a good idea. It was time for us to be on our way.

That night I thought back to the numerous occasions when Dr. Stitt had been asked about the reaction of his "higher ups" regarding our program of sharing. He would usually respond,

"How can anyone be against brotherhood? It's like being against motherhood." In response to the same question, I would answer that I was sure that our goal, "Love thy neighbor as thyself," would surely have the full approval of the Lord. It doesn't get any "higher-up" than that!

EXODUS FROM 13TH STREET

I was determined that the final act of leaving the building, our Synagogue home for almost twenty years, be conducted with great dignity.

We set March 19, 1974, a Tuesday, as the day for moving. (Many Jewish people choose a Tuesday, the third day of the week in our tradition, as a moving day because in Genesis the phrase, "God saw that it was good" appears twice in the creation story of day 3.) We had two months of frenzied activity ahead of us. A real estate committee was formed to locate a suitable building, preferably in Greenwich Village. I called a number of my rabbinic colleagues and asked them to care for our Torahs in the interim, and I invited them to join with us at the ceremony of carrying the Torahs out of the building.

On the Friday night before our departure my sermon topic was "The Need for Moral Courage." I had chosen it to commemorate the centennial that weekend of the birth of Rabbi Stephen Samuel Wise, whose prophetic voice always guided me. I proclaimed that the honor of the Jewish people must not be stained and that we could no longer worship in a sanctuary that had been profaned by acts that had taken place there during the preceding months. There was a large attendance, including many members of the Village Church, who had come out of respect and friendship for us and who, in a way, cast their lot with us—they too had chosen to leave.

There was a Bar Mitzvah on Saturday morning, an especially poignant time for us all, for this was to be our final service in this sanctuary. The young man, Jonathan Todd Weiner, offered a special prayer for peace, for Israel, for the children of the world, and for his congregation, "That their next home will be a permanent and secure house of worship which will truly know the meaning of brotherhood that they have practiced and taught for so long."

Ironically, the last telephone call received at the Synagogue office, just minutes before the scheduled ceremony of departure on Tuesday, was from a Western Union operator reading aloud a message from Dr. Harry Phillips, the new Executive Presbyter, who extended good wishes to our congregation.

The ceremony was scheduled for 5:00 P.M. My remarks had to convey our pain at the separation, and at the same time reaffirm our commitment to the concept of religious brotherhood. It seemed that every radio and television network had dispatched a battery of reporters and camera crews to West 13th Street to record the event, and the police closed the street between Sixth and Seventh Avenues. As Synagogue members and Church congregants, family, neighbors, and friends gathered outside the building, some residents on the block strung a banner across several brownstones down the street expressing sorrow at our leaving and wishing us well. At my side stood an armed guard because, as I later learned, there had been death threats against me.

Parts of my speech were televised on the evening news broadcasts on most TV channels. I reviewed our twenty-year history as a Synagogue and explained why we were leaving:

In 1954, together with the late and beloved Rev. Dr. Jesse William Stitt of the Village Presbyterian Church, we entered into a Covenant of Brotherhood between our two congregations unique in the annals of church and synagogue relations. We took this pioneering step because we realized the painful fact that over the years—and even today—peoples of different religions have fought each other and caused great anguish and suffering. Our aim was to show that the universal dimensions of religious faiths can, and must, bind us all into a common humanity.

This ideal is as old as Abraham, who moved to a new land where he could preach compassion. It is an ideal as old as the biblical injunction in Leviticus to "love thy neighbor as thyself," as old as the Psalmist's song and dream "behold how good and pleasant it is for brethren to dwell together in unity." It is an ideal more valid today than ever before, and I pledge to you that my congregation and I shall never abandon it.

Have we succeeded over these twenty years? I say *yes*—because we *tried*. Had we not tried at all, then we would have indeed failed as a House of God.

But now this noble experiment has come to a pause, but not because the principle is inoperative or unattainable. Sadly, two and a half years ago, after the retirement and then the death of the Rev. Dr. Stitt, a new minister came to the Village Church and, like Pharaoh of old, knew not nor understood the children of Israel. For these two and a half years we have protested and resisted his hostile attitudes toward our synagogue and the sacred symbols of our faith. *Never, never,* for seventeen and a half years, had such attitudes ever been manifest on these premises.

Our going forth today, without having waited to attain a permanent home for our synagogue, is meant to demonstrate that neither I nor my entire congregation could any longer tolerate or accept the continuing slurs and offensive remarks against the faith of Judaism and the homeland of the Jewish people, the Land of Israel. *Enough is enough!*...

The atmosphere was tense with anticipation and anxiety. I realized that I would never again return to this street or this building where I had spent two decades, where I was married, where our son had had his *pidyon ha-ben* (service for a first-born son), where other family life-cycle events had been celebrated, and where I had made so many friends and been blessed with the opportunity to pioneer new approaches in religious life. For all of us, this was a very emotional and solemn moment, the heartbreaking end of a dream of a shared house of worship.

With the blowing of a number of shofars, and my cradling a Torah in my arms, Cantor Leib Mirkovic and I led the procession of the Torahs down the steps of the sanctuary, out of the gate, and onto the street. Cars were waiting to receive the sacred scrolls and take them to their host congregations, Orthodox, Conservative, and Reform, for how long no one knew. As the Torahs went forth under a *chuppa* (canopy), tears flowed freely down the faces of the onlookers, as though we were reliving the history of the Jewish people, and in their grim and mournful expressions was the reflection of the anguish and pain Jewish communities have had to endure for centuries.

The cameras focused on the Synagogue's outdoor bulletin board, now completely blank except for the one-word message my wife had suggested: SHALOM.

Reporters began interviewing people in the street to try to ferret out how they viewed the Pastor's attitude toward the Jewish people. One prominent TV anchorman happened to ask a long-time, active member of the Village Church whether in her opinion the Pastor was anti-Semitic. It took this brave churchwoman but a split second to respond affirmatively.

Scenes of our departure were carried again the following morning on nationwide television, and the phrase in my remarks that was highlighted was *"Enough is enough!"* The event would continue to be a source of conversation for a long time;[2] it inspired the noted columnist Nat Hentoff, who had been one of our members, to reminisce in *The Village Voice*:

> It was the manner of The Brotherhood Synagogue's leave-taking that made the event one of the most glorious continuations I have ever witnessed of the "Do Not Tread on Me" ethos that is supposedly endemic to the American as well as the Jewish psyche. There was no scuttling away, carrying the Torahs out by night. Just before sunset, on the steps of the Sanctuary, the rabbis, the elders, swarms of children, a couple of Christian ministers who had come by... these and scores more listened to speeches of proud farewell as the Torahs were lifted high. And on the top step, a dream of my boyhood, not just one shofar, but six, a mighty blare of defiant rams' horns.

Several months later I was invited to offer the invocation at the annual dinner of the Avenue of the Americas Association. After the program I joined my wife, who, coincidentally, was seated at the same table as the wife of a Presbyterian minister. He had evidently not caught my name earlier, so he asked, "Rabbi, what is your congregation?" I replied, "The Brotherhood Synagogue, which used to be in Greenwich Village." He looked at me and

---

2. Recently, when I consulted a medical specialist for the first time, he asked me, "You're Rabbi Block, aren't you? I remember when you left Greenwich Village. I was a young doctor and happened to be walking on 13th Street that afternoon and stopped to see what was going on." He said he had never forgotten the occasion or the passion of my remarks.

shouted, "I apologize to you! I apologize to you!!!!" I looked around and said to myself that it was a good thing that only a few guests were still present in the large ballroom. The four of us then went downstairs for tea and he expressed his pain at what had occurred, in words that still ring in my ears: "The church is sick! The church is sick!" The controversy on 13th Street represented, in his view, another failure on the part of his church community. I empathized with his sense of outrage and anger, for I have always believed that world peace can be achieved only when our religious institutions are strong. What the Presbytery should have done was demonstrate support and encouragement for our program of brotherhood.

In the words of a neighborhood Episcopalian minister, who was a good friend of mine:

> The candle you and Dr. Stitt lit has now been snuffed. And the people of The Brotherhood Synagogue now know that there are Christians in Greenwich Village and New York City who prefer the darkness of prejudice to the light of acceptance. May The Brotherhood Synagogue relight that candle in another place during the coming years.

The most resolute challenge to the Presbytery came from the Anti-Defamation League of B'nai B'rith, under the leadership of Seymour D. Reich, then Chairman of its New York Regional Board (and later international President of B'nai B'rith) and Robert C. Kohler, Director of the ADL's New York regional office. After many meetings and correspondence with Presbytery officials, they asserted that its moral failure to take disciplinary action against the Pastor "was distressing to those of us committed to building understanding between Christians and Jews."

Weeks after our departure I received a letter from Rev. Phillips, the new Executive Presbyter, indicating that the Presbytery of New York City had voted without dissent to "express to The Brotherhood Synagogue its regret that the relationship of twenty years existing between the Village Church and itself had been severed." He continued by noting that this brief formal action did not "begin to reflect the strong feeling of genuine dismay" voiced by Presbyterians at the termination of the relationship between our Synagogue and the Village Church, and he concluded by saying that the Presbytery joined him "in the hope that a bright future unfolds for The Brotherhood Synagogue and its commitment to interfaith understanding.... May God's blessing abide with you and your people." Had such a man been at the helm of the Presbytery earlier, the confrontation might have been resolved differently.[3]

Some cautioned me, "Rabbi Block, this may be the end of your synagogue." To them my reply was, "I don't know what the good Lord has in store for us, but I do know that we cannot remain in a place which is no longer sacred for us." I am a strong believer in the adage *Gam zu le'tova* (This, too, is for the good). I maintained a sense of hope and faith that surely some good would come of our pain.

3. The Pastor resigned the following year. In the fall of 1975 the Presbytery of New York voted to dissolve the Village Presbyterian Church. The building was ultimately sold, but because of its location in a landmark district, the exterior could not be altered and remains as it has always been. The interior, however, was converted into apartments.

Three Masonic Brothers in Jerusalem

In the summer of 1959, the Reverend Dr. Jesse William Stitt and I ascended Mount Zion, one of the seven hills comprising the City of Jerusalem, with shrines holy to both Jews and Christians. One is a medieval-looking building where, according to Jewish tradition, King David is at rest, his casket covered by a dark cloth, upon which is inscribed in Hebrew, "The spirit of King David lives and endures."

Two distinguished representatives of the Committee of Mount Zion stood behind the alcove with the casket and offered prayers and greetings to visitors. One of the two gentlemen asked, "Do you wish me to recite special prayers for the souls of your loved ones?" "Please do," I replied, "for my father, who passed away just six months ago, and for my mother, who died shortly after the State of Israel was born." As he concluded, he placed his hand upon my shoulder and expressed prayerful wishes for health and peace.

My eye fell upon his Masonic ring, a blue stone in a gold setting. Grasping his hand in the fraternal manner of Master Masons, I excitedly whispered, "We are brothers!" Dr. Stitt also stretched out his hand in the Masonic clasp. The representative drew us near and embraced us. As we briefly told him about our joint efforts for brotherhood, he responded; "I wish there were time for us to speak at length. God be with you, and may you succeed in all that you do."

We could not help but reflect on the surprising coincidence of three Masonic brothers standing together in a room hallowed by memory, on a hill made sacred by history, in a land reborn by the spirit of King David, whose son, King Solomon, was the master builder of the great and glorious Temple.

8

In Search of a New Home

*"Weeping may tarry for the night,
but joy cometh in the morning."*

PSALM 30

When I saw our Torahs being carefully and gently placed in the cars of members of other synagogues and driven away to temporary homes, I truly understood the pathos of the midrashic statement, "When Israel went into exile, God followed Israel into exile." The congregation wept, and my heart cried in anguish and grief. But a verse from Psalm 30 was a source of strength, enabling me to look beyond the immediate problem. It was not only one of my favorite verses, but also Dr. Stitt's: "Weeping may tarry for the night, but joy cometh in the morning."

As camera crews took their final pictures and reporters queried bystanders for last-moment reactions, the police reopened the street to traffic and, little by little, people went on their way, still dabbing tears from their eyes. My family and I went home to comfort each other and to try to rest after this harrowing day.

THE KINDNESS OF FRIENDS AND COMMUNITY

The task of finding a new synagogue home in Greenwich Village was daunting. Either the location or the size was not appropriate for our needs, or the buildings did not possess that intangible spiritual character that could enhance the mood of worship. In the interim, we rented temporary offices in a commercial building on 14th Street and Fifth Avenue, where we could manage our administrative affairs, conduct Religious School classes, and hold Board meetings.

Two Orthodox congregations in the neighborhood invited us to worship in their sanctuaries. On Friday nights we gathered at Congregation Darech Amuno in the West Village, which held Sabbath services at an earlier hour than our usual 8:00 P.M. Also known as The Charles Street Synagogue, it is the oldest Jewish congregation in the area, a small structure whose sanctuary still conveys an Old World feeling. Rabbi Walter Neumann and President Harry Zager were very accommodating and graciously offered us the use of their *k'lay kodesh* (holy objects).

The first Friday night after our exodus, as my family and I walked the few blocks west to Charles Street, we were joined on the way by many congregants and neighbors. Inside, the main sanctuary and balcony were full, a wonderful demonstration of affection and solidarity that buoyed our spirits.

Saturday mornings we joined with Congregation Emunath Israel on West 23rd Street, where, despite some differences in the prayer service, our two congregations joined together in worship. Here, too, our hosts were warm and friendly, and Rabbi Meyer Leifer invited me to sit at his side on the altar and to offer Torah commentary.

For the several Bar and Bat Mitzvahs that had been scheduled long in advance, we were invited by Rabbi Dennis Math of The Village Temple on East 12th Street to use its facilities. This was the congregation I had served briefly before founding The

Brotherhood Synagogue. Rabbi Math had recently accepted this pulpit, and old tensions had receded into past history.

Other religious leaders in Greenwich Village extended a hand. Among the first were the Rev. Charles Graf of St. John's In The Village (Episcopal) on West 11th Street, and Sister Helen, the administrator of St. Vincent's Medical Center on West 12th Street, who called to say they had space available for us in their buildings. I was especially moved by my conversation with Father Graf, because his church had recently been partially destroyed in a fire; yet he wanted to find some way to help.

We were literally "wandering Jews," trying to keep our congregation intact and to conduct our day-to-day activities as best we could. As I walked home after services one Friday night with our President and the Chairman of our Board, we talked about our lack of success in locating the right building. Would there be any objection to extending our search to neighborhoods east of Fifth Avenue, they wondered? I replied with a favorite quotation from Yehuda Halevi, "I am in the West, but my heart is in the East." "So," I said, "we should have no hesitancy in expanding our search to the East Side."

Not long after, there was a story in the newspaper, with a photograph, about the landmark Friends Meeting House on Gramercy Park, which was vacant and for sale. Since so many people were looking out for our interests, it was no surprise when friends called this story to my attention: "Rabbi Block, maybe this place is for you." That evening a past President, Herbert Plaut, phoned about the same building and encouraged me to look at it. Coincidentally, Dr. and Mrs. Stitt had lived just two doors away, so I must have passed the Meeting House many times but had paid scant attention to it, since I usually went to their home in the evening and the Meeting House was set back from the street and dimly lit. Who could have predicted then that this historic building would someday become a synagogue, our Synagogue?

By the time summer came, Phyllis and I were emotionally and physically exhausted and looked forward to a quiet vacation and a respite from turmoil and tension. We decided to try a new beach resort in the South, with reasonable rates and a day camp; it proved to be just the right place.

However, I did take along a tape recorder to answer a hundred or more letters and calls from all over the country, and even other countries, from people who had written to console us and encourage us not to abandon our dreams. So many letters began with a lament: "I felt heartsick in reading about the crisis that you are facing"; "I know how upset and disappointed you must be"; "My dear colleague, keep your chin up, the good Lord is on your side!"

A rabbi had phoned to tell me that our difficulties had prompted a discussion in his Hebrew School and that the children would be writing to me. I was very moved by their understanding letters. Some were bold enough to offer advice: "Try and talk it over with him [the Pastor]. If you already did and it didn't work out, try to stay away from him. You made it to be a great rabbi and you will make it to be a greater rabbi." Another student was complimentary: "There should be more people with guts to help people as you have." One youngster assured me, "As long as you stand up for what you believe in, you'll make everything OK!" I treasure these letters and commend the teachers.

A minister friend poured out his heart to me over the phone with tears in his voice. "Irving, listen to me. There are times when the idea of religious brotherhood is at its zenith, and there are times when latent anti-Semitism screams from the wellsprings of

Christian life like an epidemic." Then he wistfully added; "As a Christian minister, I feel lost. This noble experiment, my dear brother, must not fail!" The same anguish gripped a Catholic professor of history: "Once again I feel homeless!"

A college president lauded our work as "something that inspired us all" and hoped that the Presbytery "will come to its senses and find the kind of leadership that is needed."

FAILURE TO REPUDIATE PREJUDICE

On June 11, 1974, after six months of hearings, the Presbytery of New York ruled that no charges would be formally filed against Pastor Glenesk, on grounds that the allegations against him were not supported by sufficient testimony or evidence.

The Anti-Defamation League labeled the outcome of that investigation a "whitewash" of charges of "repeated, willful undisguised bigotry." The chairman of ADL's New York Regional Board, Seymour D. Reich, questioned "how the [special Presbytery] committee could be so insensitive to Jewish concerns as to dismiss clear, substantiated and unequivocal evidence." He cited as one example a written statement by Elizabeth C. Moore, President of The Brotherhood Council, declaring that the Pastor "certainly has been guilty of anti-Jewish words and actions." The Presbytery's action, Mr. Reich observed, was in marked contrast to a "Declaration of Faith" proposed at the denomination's national General Assembly, which had repudiated the rejection of Jews as "shameful prejudice" and called for "dialogue and cooperation with mutual respect and love."

Given the Presbytery's previous attitude in this controversy, I was not overly surprised at the decision, but I was disheartened. The church had lost a unique opportunity to speak out against the highly offensive remarks that had demonstrated disrespect for the Jewish people. A church must evince a moral stand; it must be God's messenger, doing God's work.

OUR NEW HOME

Before we left on vacation, Phyllis and I, along with some of our officers, had an opportunity to walk through the Friends Meeting House. It appeared so gloomy and vast, with cracked walls, peeling paint, floors with holes and ankle-deep fallen plaster, and a decaying stairwell. Leaks had obviously taken their toll over the years. But the meeting room was large—with space for 700–800, it was just the size we needed for a sanctuary—and the location could not be better: a 15- or 20-minute walk from Greenwich Village, a few blocks from Stuyvesant Town and Peter Cooper Village where many of our members lived, and in one of the most notable and elegant neighborhoods in the city. Perhaps the Lord had heard our petitions.

While we were away, our officers made a thorough study of the building. Could this 1859 edifice, steeped in history and considered an architectural jewel, be properly renovated and restored to make it once more a beautiful and vibrant House of God? Since Quakers display no religious symbols, the Meeting House could readily be adapted for use as a synagogue. To paraphrase the English author Israel Zangwill, "A building without a congregation was awaiting a congregation without a building."

The Quaker group that had constructed this building dated back to an early nineteenth-century (1828) split in its ranks. The Orthodox favored delegating theological questions to the Elders, while the liberalists, known as the Hicksites, were motivated by the spirit of an "inward light." The more traditional (Orthodox) faction left and built a new home on Henry Street, on the Lower East Side. In 1840 they sold it to a synagogue and moved to Orchard Street. Eventually they sold that building for $30,000, enough to purchase four lots on newly developed Gramercy Park for $24,000 and build this Meeting House. The Friends had to obtain special permission to construct the Meeting House, since only residential buildings were permitted on the Park. (The Hicksites remained on the Lower East Side (Hester Street) until they built a Meeting House on Stuyvesant Square and East 15th Street in the early 1860s.)

Built of Dorchester olive stone on an almost square plot 106 feet deep by 109 feet wide and set back 16 feet from the building line, the Gramercy Park Meeting House was designed by the eminent architectural firm of King and Kellum in the neo-Italianate style so popular in New York in the pre-Civil War period. Entry was, and still is, through an iron gate that opens into a flagstone-paved courtyard. Above the wide, wooden doorway is a curving pediment, while a symmetrical, triangular pediment crowns the building itself. Construction began in 1857, and the first worship service was held on December 18, 1859. The Quakers pointed out that the building reflected the good judgment of the building committee and skill of the craftsmen, who were all members of the Meeting.

On either side of the first-floor rotunda a pair of curving staircases with mahogany banisters leads up to the 40-foot-tall meeting room, just one foot short of square and described by *New York Times* architecture critic Ada Louise Huxtable as a place of "classical, formal elegance and spare simplicity." Twelve tall, clear windows, most of which still have the original glass panes, are almost the full height of the two-story high sanctuary.

Many rows of pews are older than the building itself, since they were brought from their former 1840 home on Orchard Street. Benches were placed under the sounding board in the front of the meeting room and elevated to allow the Elders to face the congregation and rise, in Quaker tradition, to share their thoughts as the spirit moved them. The third-floor balcony rests on twelve iron columns painted to match the walls, and the building itself is supported by strong, massive brick arches in the expansive basement. The building committee records note:

> In getting up [its] plans, great care has been taken to endeavor to produce such a building that every person who shall see the house after it is erected will say this is exactly suited for a Friends Meeting, entirely plain, neat and chaste, of good proportions, but avoiding all useless ornament, so much so as to not wound the feeling of the most sensitive among us.

Though some Quakers considered the building too severe, it was actually less "plain" than other meeting houses. As the Secretary of the Meeting observed in an interview at the time landmarking was being officially considered, "They couldn't help making it less severe, because they put too much love into it."

The Gramercy Park Meeting House would become an important New York institution, with a long record of social as well as religious involvement. It was dedicated in December 1859, the year John Brown attacked the government arsenal at Harper's Ferry, Virginia, hoping to provoke a slave insurrection. A year later Abraham Lincoln was elected President of the United States.[1] Members of the Meeting took an active role during the Civil War,

---

1. Two great figures in Jewish life were born at this time: Sholom Aleichem, the Yiddish writer and humorist, in Russia in 1859, and Theodor Herzl, founder of modern Zionism, in Budapest in 1860.

sheltering, clothing, feeding, and training fugitive slaves in a room on the third floor. (Some people claim the building may have been a stop on the Underground Railroad and the tunnels in the basement escape routes.) It was in this building that the eastern division of the Travelers Aid Society was founded in 1905 and New York City's first vocational high school had its genesis in 1861.

Decades later, sewing machines were set up in the large first-floor workroom, where volunteers repaired and packed clothing[2] to be shipped by the American Friends Service Committee to the war-ravaged European countries after World War II. In this spirit the Synagogue uses this room not only for classrooms but, during the winter, as a homeless shelter.

A HISTORIC NEIGHBORHOOD

Gramercy Park, situated between what is today East 20th Street on the south, East 21st Street on the north, near Park Avenue South on the west, and near Third Avenue on the east, was once part of a vast tract of woods and farms purchased from the Dutch West India Company in 1651 by Peter Stuyvesant, the Dutch Governor of New York. The original name of the area was Crommessie, derived from the Dutch words *krom* (not straight) and *messje* (small knife), descriptive perhaps of the path of a small brook that meandered through the property. A century later in 1761, James Duane, Mayor of New York from 1784 to 1789, pur-

---

2. In 1947 the Nobel Peace Prize was awarded to the Friends Service Council in Great Britain and to the American Friends Service Committee. The formal attire worn at the Oslo ceremony by Henry Cadbury, Chairman of the American Friends Service Committee, came from the clothing warehouse and was repaired and tailored to fit him for the occasion.

chased four acres of the tract from Gerardus Stuyvesant, Peter Stuyvesant's grandson. Duane later acquired an additional ten acres and anglicized the name to Gramercy Farm.

Prior to World War II the neighborhood had very few Jewish residents. Yet Samuel Ruggles, the brilliant lawyer and real estate investor who established Gramercy Park in 1831, had a Sephardic Jewish friend, Seixas Nathan, who became one of the first residents on the new park.

Foreseeing the northward expansion of the city, Ruggles, in a masterful and visionary deal, bought Gramercy Farm from Duane's heirs and others. Although many mocked his purchase of this hilly swampland, others shared his vision, and in time well-to-do, prominent families in government, banking, and the arts bought lots and built stately red brick and brownstone houses, some decorated with lovely wrought-iron grillwork. Today Ruggles would be called a developer, city planner, and environmentalist, but he was also a pragmatist. Recognizing that an "ornamental private park" would increase the value of the residents' property, he designated 42 lots to provide "free circulation of air" for the lot owners, no matter how densely populated the surrounding neighborhood might become. Even then air pollution, dirty streets, and overcrowded living conditions had become major concerns. The handsome, eight-foot-tall iron fence that encloses Gramercy Park, New York City's only remaining private park, was erected in 1844.

According to Mr. Ruggles' deed, Gramercy Park is managed by a group of five Trustees, and there is a substantial mandatory annual assessment for each property owner for the maintenance of the Park, based on the number of lots purchased. The Quakers had bought four of the 61 lots. Lot owners are entitled to two Park keys per lot, which we gladly make available to our members for the day. Who knows how many members have joined our Synagogue because access to the Park is a delightful plus—a serene, safe place to play, read, stroll, or jog amid shade trees and flowers.

Residents of the area included such luminaries as the Stuyvesant Fishes, who entertained lavishly in a corner mansion just up the street from the Meeting House; James Harper, Mayor of New York from 1844 to 1845; the writer Edith Wharton; Peter Cooper, the founder of Cooper Union; and the eminent architect Stanford White. It was also home to actors John Barrymore and Edwin Booth; Cyrus Field, who laid down the transatlantic cable; and Samuel Jones Tilden, the 1876 Democratic nominee for President of the United States, who won the popular vote in the election but lost by one vote in the Electoral College. Ruggles' friend Washington Irving and, later, Theodore Roosevelt lived nearby, and the future President played in the Park as a child. His niece, Eleanor, who became the wife of President Franklin D. Roosevelt, was baptized by the Rector of Calvary Church, which anchors the northwest corner of the Park.

The Meeting House was used for 99 years, until 1958, when the congregation merged with the other Friends Meeting on Stuyvesant Square and 15th Street, thus healing the century-long rift between the two Quaker groups.

The Friends did not immediately sell the 20th Street building after the merger, but they could no longer afford its upkeep and moved most of their activities to 15th Street. In 1965 the New York Monthly Meeting of Friends decided to sell the Gramercy Park property to a private contractor, whose plans were to erect a 30-story apartment house on the site. Thus shortly after its 100th anniversary, inconceivable as it seemed, the building was on the verge of being demolished. What an outcry that provoked!

Fearing a high-rise that would alter the nineteenth-century character of the neighborhood and block the sunlight to the Park, local residents mobilized and banded with other activists to form the Committee to Preserve the Gramercy Neighborhood. Historic preservation had already become a hotly debated issue in New York City political life following the demolition of Pennsylvania Station. Intense lobbying and pressure from the community led to the designation in 1965 of the 20th Street Friends Meeting House as a city landmark[3] by the newly established New York City Landmarks Preservation Commission, which cited "its clean-cut lines, sound construction and admirably restrained design" that provide "a significant building which respects the outlook of the important group which built it." The Quakers continued to own the building.

Many churches and synagogues have opposed landmark designation because of the restrictions it imposes—and I understand their reservations—but for The Brotherhood Synagogue it was a blessing. Without it, the building would never have been available to us. In May 1966 the streets around the Park were designated the Gramercy Park Historic District. Fifteen years later it was listed on the National Registry of Historic Places, and our Synagogue was given the honor of receiving the certificate of registration on behalf of the community.

In 1967 the Quakers sold the building for $400,000 to a group of wealthy neighborhood residents—among them the influential publicist Benjamin Sonnenberg, owner of the former Stuyvesant Fish mansion—who called themselves "Friends of the Friends." They had an ambitious plan to convert it into a center for the performing arts, but the demise of one of the principal investors

3. It was the second building in the city to be landmarked. The Pieter Claesen Wyckoff House (1652) in Brooklyn was the first.

forced them to abandon the project. The group, also known as The Meeting House Foundation, then considered selling it either to the Ninth Church of Christ, Scientist, which had been worshipping there temporarily, or to the United Federation of Teachers (UFT), whose main office was two blocks away. Many in the neighborhood preferred the Christian Scientists because the building would remain a house of worship, but the Foundation regarded the UFT as a more financially stable buyer. The UFT bought the Meeting House in 1973, intending to renovate it as a community and educational center and headquarters for some union operations. A year later, however, realizing the building would not be suitable for the union, the UFT put it on the market once again. That is when the Meeting House came to our attention.

We were very anxious to purchase it, but the required $15,000 down payment was far more than we could afford. With the very limited funds we now possessed, we could manage only $5,000. Although other buyers were being considered, the UFT accepted our offer.

Why was The Brotherhood Synagogue selected? After all, the sale price was fixed, so there was no question of competing bids. The explanation would come several years later, at the time we paid off our mortgage obligation to the UFT: The Brotherhood Synagogue's reputation for integrity and our appreciation of historic buildings persuaded the UFT that we would respect the character of the Meeting House, restore it, and use it for the benefit of the community.

Not long after we acquired the Meeting House, a new member of our congregation confided to me that he had been the broker for the proposed sale to a contractor back in 1965. At times he would cup his face in his hands and shake his head in dismay. "Rabbi, what I almost did! If that sale had gone through, there would be no synagogue here." This family, whose home and business were on East 17th Street, was possibly among the first Jewish families in the Gramercy Park neighborhood, and the presence of a synagogue was therefore all the more meaningful to them. I remember the first time I met the gentleman's mother, then close to 90. She was ecstatic: "I never thought I would live to see the day that there would be a synagogue on Gramercy Park."

RESTORING A LANDMARK

Our building committee had consulted James Stuart Polshek, then Dean of the School of Architecture at Columbia University and an expert on historic preservation, regarding the restoration. A frequent visitor to Gramercy Park, he so admired the building that he offered his personal services pro bono, as did the general contractor, Lawrence Held and Son, which oversaw the construction and the work of the subcontractors.

Thanks to the unsparing efforts and abilities of our Synagogue leaders and the generosity of our members, as well as of community residents and people everywhere, Jewish and non-Jewish, The Brotherhood Synagogue raised the necessary funds and had the determination and persistence to bring this project to fruition. We developed a "Bricks for Brotherhood" campaign to encourage people to contribute at various levels, and we in turn gave the donors a wallet-sized card acknowledging them as leaders in the cause of brotherhood.

We were especially touched by the gifts from longtime friends from the Village Presbyterian Church. After the Presbytery officially closed the church on September 30, 1975, a year and a half after our move, these friends sent us the remaining pieces of altar furniture we had left behind, which our two congregations had purchased jointly. As one of the stalwart members of the Village Church stated, she was insistent on "closing the church with grace." The chairs and lecterns were eminently suitable for our new sanctuary and remain a precious link to our past history.

One major gift, designated for cleaning the exterior of the building, came from a non-Jewish neighbor, who explained, "I like to see the buildings around the Park look nice." Other donors hoped that we would continue our open-door policy, so characteristic of the spirit of a Friends Meeting House. The concept of historic preservation is very much in keeping with Jewish tradition, which seeks to preserve the past while making it relevant to modern needs. The critic Ada Louise Huxtable lauded the architect's "skillful recycling of an older structure for contemporary life."

The building had been unoccupied for so long that we were especially concerned about the roof. Was it sturdy? Did it leak? The UFT dispatched an engineer to inspect the roof, who reported that indeed it was in poor condition and should be replaced. The UFT agreed to do so and, in effect, used our $5,000 down payment to cover the cost.

Meantime, I had spoken with the rabbis in the neighborhood to assure them that we were not coming as rivals but as partners for the benefit of the entire Jewish community.

Neighboring churches reached out in friendship. The parishioners of Epiphany Roman Catholic Church and their pastor, Msgr. Francis M. Costello, wrote in his church newsletter, "Welcome and Shalom to the congregation of The Brotherhood Synagogue whose motto is 'Brotherhood—Still the hope of the world.' " The Reverend Dr. Thomas F. Pike, Rector of Calvary/St. George's Parish

(Episcopal), who had invited me to preach at a Sunday morning service at his church even before we moved in, put on his outdoor bulletin board the message, "Warm Greetings to The Brotherhood Synagogue." Boy Scouts from Calvary Church helped scrape and paint portions of our iron fence in fulfillment of Eagle Scout merit badge requirements, and Epiphany Church's Troop 422 completed the assignment for community service credit. Ecumenism in action! I knew right away that we were acquiring not just a historic building, but new friends, who were doing everything possible to make us feel at home in the community.

MOVING IN

On August 8, 1974, at 6:00 P.M., we held a symbolic ceremony of signing the contract of acquisition in front of the building. Joan Davidson, a prominent advocate of landmark preservation, chaired the ceremony. Over 200 members and community leaders witnessed Jules Kolodny, Secretary of the United Federation of Teachers, sign the papers that would transfer ownership of the Friends Meeting House to The Brotherhood Synagogue. Then Howard D. Westrich, Chairman of the Synagogue Board of Trustees, who had skillfully and professionally handled the negotiations with the UFT, affixed his signature, making the purchase official. The President of the congregation, William Cohen, announced the start of a $500,000 fund-raising campaign to restore and refurbish the building. When I addressed the gathering I stated:

> We affirm in the presence of this community that the noble tradition of independence of spirit that characterized those who worshipped here for over a century will be continued by this Synagogue.

Since its founding two decades ago, this Synagogue has pioneered, and symbolized to all, the concept of religious brotherhood in action.

Recognizing the attachment the Quakers still had to their former Meeting House, I had written to the Administrator of New York Quarterly Meeting of the Religious Society of Friends, C. Frank Ortloff, "We hope to be true to the magnificent heritage of the building and in every way be a good neighbor and friend to all in the community... to do otherwise would not be in keeping with the noble ideals of our religious traditions."

Since the building required so much work to make it safe, comfortable, and suitable for our needs—new lighting, plumbing, wiring, kitchen, and fire doors had to be installed—we had to decide where to conduct Rosh Hashanah and Yom Kippur services just a few weeks later, in mid-September. Dr. Leon Brody, immediate past President of our congregation and a professor at New York University, arranged for us to use the large auditorium in the Loeb Center on the university's Greenwich Village campus. Again, *Ha-Shem* (God) was with us.

During Succoth we erected a succah in the courtyard of our new synagogue home, not only in fulfillment of a religious requirement, but as a symbol of our presence and our optimism about the future. A few weeks later, on November 12, 1974, we officially took title to the Friends Meeting House.

At the end of the year the building was still not ready for occupancy. We held our Chanukah party at the neighboring Parkside Evangeline Residence of the Salvation Army, at the invitation of Major and Mrs. John Lambert, the administrators, whom I had first met years before when our congregation was on West 13th Street and they were in charge of a similar residence on the same block. The residents and staff joined us as we lit the Menorah, spun *dreidels* (tops), sang the traditional melodies, and enjoyed *latkes* (potato pancakes).

Just one year almost to the day after our painful departure from Greenwich Village, the front page of our Synagogue bulletin heralded, in large, bold type: "With thanks to the Almighty, The Brotherhood Synagogue joyfully announces Sabbath Services at 28 Gramercy Park South, Friday, March 21, 1975, at 8:00 P.M." It was Shabbat Hagadol (the Great Sabbath, just before Passover) and my sermon topic was "A Great Sabbath Indeed." That evening we honored our contractors, their workers, and their families to express our gratitude for their enormous effort to have the building ready in time for Passover. It was a joyful Sabbath of fellowship as we celebrated the end of our wandering. A year before who could have predicted such a happy ending so soon?

Later on we gave a tea for Congregation Darech Amuno and Congregation Emunath Israel and presented them with pulpit *siddurim* (prayer books) engraved in their honor, and we invited The Village Temple to a joint worship service. On our first Simchat Torah service (Rejoicing in the Law) in the building we honored and expressed our appreciation to Dean Polshek, our architect, and Joseph Stuhl of Lawrence Held and Son, our contractor.

Just as there had been a Bar Mitzvah ceremony on the last Shabbat morning in our 13th Street sanctuary, so too there was one on our first Saturday morning on Gramercy Park. That honor fell to Michael Weprin, whose father, a realtor, sent his own maintenance crew to help prepare for the weekend festivities.

Two weeks later, on April 6, we formally welcomed back all the Torahs that had been cared for by other congregations for the past year. Arthur Jacobs, a new member of our Synagogue, highly respected in the community and business manager of Gramercy Park at the time, had obtained permission from the Park Trustees to allow us to gather inside the gate to assemble our Torahs and form our procession into the sanctuary. (Never could Samuel Ruggles and Seixas Nathan have envisioned such an event.) The day was blustery, but the skies were clear and sunny and the mood warm and festive.

In front of the Synagogue, as a prelude to the main indoor ceremonies, a choir of our members expressed in song the exultation in our hearts, and we affixed a mezuzah to the front door and recited the traditional prayer of gratitude, *Shehecheyanu* (Thanks to God who has kept us alive, sustained us, and brought us to this glorious moment). Dr. Leo Storozum, our congregation's first Assistant Rabbi, blew the shofar to signal the start of the procession of the Torahs, carried under a *chuppa* by an honor guard of members of the Jewish War Veterans. My wife and 10-year-old Herbert were at my side as he proudly carried one of the small Torahs.

Over 700 members, friends, and dignitaries were waiting in the sanctuary to greet the Torahs. As Cantor Emeritus Leib Mirkovic, Cantor Ira Fein, and I led the procession from the Park, my mentor and friend Rabbi Edward E. Klein, our principal speaker, joined me at the head of the procession. The shofar was sounded from the altar to herald the arrival of the Torahs. Everyone rose and tears flowed freely as the Torahs proceeded down the center aisle in the arms of Synagogue officers; but these were tears of happiness and rejoicing. What a glorious sight to see Torahs held by our officers and Trustees across the entire span of the altar. It was a triumphant moment and I thanked God for enabling me to reach this great day.

In my address, I made a pledge to the congregation and community:

The Brotherhood Synagogue has come to Gramercy Park to establish here a new home for our congregation, which a little more than a year ago, just before the Passover season, began its exodus. We had willingly elected to sacrifice our former home and risk an unknown future in order to uphold the honor of the Jewish people...

Now, a year later, we have reached our Promised Land.... Our being here on Gramercy Park is the result of an act of faith.... As we look back over the past year, we realize more than ever that we have made the right decision and that the Lord has been smiling upon us.

Now morality takes courage. Houses of worship must always speak with courage and morality.... We shall never forget the past, which is a forewarning of the future. We promise this community that, as we have not been silent in the past, we shall not be silent in the years to come, because we recognize that what happens to the Jewish people ultimately happens to the rest of humanity....

Our Synagogue has always been committed to the community of which we have been a part, and we shall continue that commitment. Our Synagogue has always been concerned about the events unfolding in America, for we are part of America, and that concern shall continue. Our Synagogue has always directed its heart toward our brethren in the Land of Israel...and we shall continue to work for the State of Israel. Our Synagogue has always had an open door and an open heart, and we shall continue to keep our door and our heart open....

Rabbi Klein spoke eloquently on the role of a synagogue; James Stewart Polshek discussed the restoration of the building, and John Maynard, Clerk of the 15th Street Monthly Meeting of the Religious Society of Friends, conveyed the good wishes of the Quakers. Among the guests was a very special group, former members of the Village Presbyterian Church who had been pillars of support to us. An entire week of festivities followed, with tours of the building and talks by distinguished rabbis and lay leaders.

The saga of The Brotherhood Synagogue had remained a compelling story. News of our move in the national and local press prompted people everywhere to express their delight that our wandering was over and that our congregation finally had not only a new home, but one that was truly unique and beautiful. Rabbi Robert I. Kahn, President of the Central Conference of American Rabbis, wrote: "My congratulations to you and the congregation on the persistence which has kept you alive, and sense of principle which has led you to relocate." A message from Rabbi Harold H. Gordon, Executive Vice President of The New York Board of Rabbis, stated: "Your pioneering efforts in brotherhood will always stand out in the history of American Jewry." Selma Rattner, an architectural historian and preservationist, declared: "The city owes you and your congregation a huge debt of gratitude for your courage in saving and maintaining at considerable cost this major landmark."

PLANNING FOR THE FUTURE

We were encouraged at the number of new members, many of whom offered to assist in developing cultural programs that would, at the same time, help raise the funds we required to meet our financial obligations, especially our two mortgages. The first mortgage was due in just four years.

The expenses and diminished income of the past year after leaving Greenwich Village had so depleted our coffers that sometimes it was difficult to meet the payroll, and three months before the mortgage was due we were still short $40,000. But the rabbis, officers, Trustees, and staff sacrificed and persevered, and members as well as foundations interested in the work of our congregation and in historic preservation rallied to help us in this crisis.

On February 25, 1979, as we prepared to mark the 25th anniversary of the founding of our Synagogue, we made the final payment of $175,000 on our first mortgage to the Society of Friends at a joyful ceremony in the sanctuary. We now had seven years before the second mortgage would come due.

The Quakers had built on only two of their four lots. When we acquired the property, we found two deep, bleak, rock-strewn plots, one on either side of the building, and realized that some day they would have to be landscaped. Not long after, one of our Trustees, Marvin Levy, later Chairman of the Board and then President, discussed options for establishing memorials. He wondered if Jewish tradition would permit an outdoor memorial. I encouraged him to think in that direction, and he began to conceive of a Garden of Remembrance, a memorial both to the departed loved ones of our members and to the victims of the Holocaust.

Marvin Levy did not live to see the completion of this project. On Friday afternoon, December 16, 1977, just nine months after he was elected President of the Synagogue, he was fatally shot by an unknown assailant as he was leaving his office to return home and prepare for Shabbat. The congregation, and indeed the whole city, was horrified at this enormous tragedy and we mourned him deeply. I had known four generations of the Levy family and had officiated at many of their life-cycle events. At his funeral I remembered Marvin Levy in my eulogy as a man "endowed with an agility of mind and a sensitivity of heart, a man of compassion whose life personified *menschlichkeit* (being an upright, honorable person). He richly deserved all the encomia bestowed upon him.

The events of the 1970s had tested our faith and our emotional fortitude as we coped with Dr. Stitt's retirement and death, our departure from Greenwich Village, the search for a new building; the unexpected loss of a Synagogue leader. And in the midst of it all in my own family we mourned the untimely passing of a young cousin and a brother-in-law.

But then "joy [came] in the morning"—the providential acquisition of a new Synagogue home more magnificent than we could have anticipated, and then in May 1978 the celebration of Herbert's Bar Mitzvah. When the young man is the rabbi's son, the event becomes a sentimental community occasion, and we were delighted and proud to share it with our congregational family. Cantor Mirkovic and Herbert had developed a special fondness for each other. When the Cantor moved to Florida the year before the Bar Mitzvah, he promised Herbert that, God willing, he would return to sing at the service. And he did. Six weeks later Cantor Mirkovic surprised me by returning for a program celebrating my 25th anniversary in the rabbinate.

To mark that anniversary, I was proud to be awarded the degree of Doctor of Divinity, *honoris causa*, by my seminary, Hebrew Union College–Jewish Institute of Religion, and gratified that the citation recognized my service in Israel during the struggle for independence and my commitment and leadership in the cause of interfaith brotherhood.

As the decade drew to an end, our membership and Religious School were growing, we had developed new programs and others were being planned; the building was taking shape; and we had established a good reputation and warm relationships in our new community.

Although I looked to the 1980s with optimism and faith, hoping for a period of calm so we could continue to move forward, I became increasingly aware that another turbulent period lay ahead.

A Mother's Wish

One day shortly after our move to Gramercy Park, one of our new members came for a tour of the Synagogue. She was an exuberant woman who took a great delight in the beauties of our faith and the loveliness of God's house. Like all who entered our building, she admired the elegant pair of curving staircases in the rotunda leading to the sanctuary on the second floor. "Oy, Rabbi," she sighed. "How I'd love to see my daughter walk down those steps as a bride."

Little did she realize that Heaven was already listening to her heart and that a young man her daughter was dating would soon propose marriage. Their wedding, in our sanctuary, was the first since we had acquired the Meeting House.

Following the custom of breaking a glass at the end of the ceremony, and the exclamations of mazel tov (congratulations, good luck), I led the recessional. Just when the bride and groom were about to descend the stairs, the mother's wish flashed through my mind. I momentarily halted the recessional, took the bride's mother by the hand and walked down with her to the rotunda. I nodded to the bride and groom to continue down the steps and then turned to the mother and said, "Look up. Your wish has come true."

9

Conflict and Crisis

*"The gem cannot be polished without friction,
nor man perfected without trials."*

CONFUCIUS

A Talmudic proverb states: *Meshane makom meshane mazal—*A
change of place often brings with it a change of fortune.

The months of anguish preceding our leaving West 13th Street
so traumatized us that my family and I have never gone back
there.

Our three-year struggle had taken a devastating emotional—
and in some cases, physical—toll on everyone in the congregation. I was able to draw strength from my faith in the Lord and
from the love and support of my wife and family and the affection
and loyalty of our members and friends everywhere.

As time went on after our departure from the Village Church,
my sorrow was assuaged by pride in knowing that we had fought
for the cause of brotherhood and the honor of the Jewish people,
and that we now had a new home more beautiful than I could
ever have imagined. My sleepless nights were over. The Lord had
answered our prayers "to bring to naught designs of those who
seek to do me ill."

It was time to move forward. But I soon recognized that some
of our officers and Trustees were so disillusioned about the future

of Christian–Jewish relations that they could not rise above the hurt and anger all felt. Although the threats to our existence as a congregation had been resolved, it became apparent that we would soon be embroiled in another conflict—this time from within.

TROUBLING SIGNS

When my family and I left on vacation in July 1974, we looked forward to a respite from stress and tension. Still we kept in touch with our officers to follow the progress of the projected acquisition and restoration of our new Gramercy Park building. We were excited to learn that the Synagogue would be able to take title in August and that a prominent architect had been engaged to plan the necessary renovations. Nevertheless, I began having a nagging feeling that major decisions were being made without consultation with me.

After I returned home in August, I heard that important matters had indeed been decided. Time and again I would hear about plans only when they became general knowledge, and I had a strong impression that my role as Rabbi was being relegated primarily to the conduct of worship services.

I was not invited to meetings between the architect and officers. During one conversation with the Chairman of our Board I found myself pounding on the table and insisting on sharing my own ideas with the architect. The Chairman finally consented to arrange a meeting.

I had anticipated a one-on-one conversation with the architect for, after all, we *were* designing a house of worship, and I was the founding Rabbi. Instead the architect presented his projected plans—including modifications to the sanctuary—to a group of

Board members. I was present but it seemed to me that I should have had the opportunity for a personal discussion of his proposals and my suggestions beforehand.

At that meeting, I did, however, raise the important issue of installing an elevator. The two-story high sanctuary was on the second floor, with a third-floor balcony. The staircases were long and steep—one had 17 steps, the other 22—and many of our members were reaching an age where an elevator would be essential. I was told that it would be impossible at this time because of the cost involved, but I continued to press the point. To install it now, I urged, before we moved into the building, would not only make our Synagogue more accessible to our members and people in the community, young and old, but avoid a major disruption in the future. I argued that an elevator was a fundamental necessity, not a frill, and that we should proceed with the same fortitude and faith we had shown in the past. I was sure that many people would contribute to such a worthy cause, because I firmly believe that if one does the right thing people will respond, as the Talmud exhorts, "Do God's will so God may do your will." But there was no listening to me. It would take ten years and cost many times as much to accomplish what could and should have been done then.

There would soon be other points of conflict. For a July 1975 article in the *Jewish Week–American Examiner* titled, "Village Synagogue Gets Gift from Christians Who Regret Pastor's Attitude," the reporter asked me whether I would "consider inviting a church congregation to share the facilities of The Brotherhood Synagogue." I knew it was a difficult question and that my reply could be misinterpreted, but I did not want to be vindictive in my response:

Yes, we believe that brotherhood is still the hope of the world…if we found a congregation that would respect thoroughly the interests of Judaism, the Jewish people and the land of Israel. All my life I have wanted to bridge the chasm between religious communities and make it clear that we are all one family of mankind.

What an outburst of criticism followed, leading to rumors and fears on the part of some officers and Board members that I was unilaterally considering inviting a non-Jewish congregation to share our building, and soon. These rumors persisted for several years despite my assurances that I had no group in mind and that, if ever such an arrangement were even contemplated, it could come into effect only with the fullest concurrence of the officers, Board of Trustees, and ultimately the congregation.

That summer at a Board meeting one of the officers admonished me for reading aloud a number of letters I had received from Christian clergy, among them a very cordial letter from the Executive Presbyter, which I considered an expression of his own personal good will. I also pointed out that we had received more letters from churches than from synagogues, which reflected a painful truth that the Jewish community should focus more on *intra*faith relations.

PRINCIPLES AT STAKE

What really disturbed me the most were statements and actions of some officers and Board members that negated the philosophy of our Synagogue. For example, on 13th Street we had had an innovative program of religious education for retarded children, which had attracted several non-Jewish families, who appreciated

our universal approach in teaching Bible stories and holiday traditions. Discussion at a Board meeting about continuing this program precipitated an angry debate over enrolling non-Jewish children. Henceforth, the Board decided, despite my objections, the
program would be limited to children of the Jewish faith.

To my religious way of thinking the Board had taken a course of
action that was unworthy of the name of our Synagogue. If any
child smiles, that child beckons us, and I pleaded that we make
every attempt to retain the present composition of the class. It is
one thing to initiate a program and set certain criteria for participation; but it would be heartless to turn away from an existing
program even a few of these special children, who had already
made friends in the group and eagerly looked forward to their
weekly class. At an August 1975 meeting I stated my opinion very
forcefully:

> ...As your Rabbi, I must tell you how distressed and saddened I am
> by the inclusion in the minutes of the last Board of Trustees meeting
> of a statement [regarding our retarded children's program] which I
> consider to be contrary to the philosophy of this synagogue.... to
> negate that generosity of spirit and heart that has nobly character-
> ized our work in the past. The approach expressed by the committee
> on retarded children, if it does indeed reflect the policy of the Board,
> is certainly not my approach. I therefore wish to go on record... that,
> first as a Jew, and then as the spiritual leader of this congregation, I
> strongly disapprove of such an attitude and approach.

I offered a compromise: All the children would continue to
come to us on Sunday mornings and I would arrange for the few
non-Jewish children to be instructed part of the time by a minister from a neighborhood church. But the Board rejected even that
proposal.

As we prepared for our move to Gramercy Park, fund-raising and congregational finances became major topics on the Board's agenda. The officers put forth what they considered a relatively easy way to raise funds: setting aside one evening a week for duplicate bridge. While I agreed that bridge was not gambling, I was not pleased. Was this to be the first major program we would offer the congregation and community? I asked to be excused from any involvement in this project. Although there was some profit in the first months, by the end of the year the Synagogue was losing money, and bridge evenings were discontinued.

Board meetings became increasingly characterized by the incivility and discourtesy of members toward each other and to me, with such statements as, "The Board is the congregation. The Rabbi is just an employee here." Concerning my activities in the community: "If the Rabbi spends 99 percent of his time on Synagogue and Jewish affairs and 1 percent of his time elsewhere, that 1 percent is already too much." This should have been a happy time for me, but all the disagreements and arguments with the Board—so totally unanticipated—were wearing me down, and there were even times when I was reluctant to go to my office, so disheartened had I become.

By the fall I could no longer restrain myself. I addressed the Board of Trustees:

Before any committees are appointed to review existing programs or planned ones, the Rabbi is to be consulted...so that I may have the opportunity to offer my suggestions as well.

Board meetings must be conducted with dignity, without the histrionics, recrimination, and name calling that have unfortunately characterized recent sessions. I will no longer tolerate it, and I am sure the congregation would not want to either, for it vitiates all the good we are seeking to do and for which so many are giving all their strength.

Everyone was startled by the vehemence of my words. Of course, they were not directed to all Board members, but only to a group whose attitude was causing confrontation and dissension.

TO AFFILIATE OR NOT

Early in 1978 one of our officers posed a question: "For the past 25 years we have been an independent congregation, but why should we remain an eclectic institution? Isn't it time to affiliate with a synagogue union?" I had heard that question many times before; but particularly while we were sharing a joint sanctuary, I thought it best not to be identified with any one branch of Judaism. Brotherhood is an obligation of *all* the household of Israel, not just the purview of any one group.

I responded that we *have* had an affiliation—with the Almighty, and you can't improve very much on that. Yet it is always proper to reconsider current practices in the light of new circumstances. Before I knew it—I had no inkling in advance—there was a motion before the Board of Trustees to make a formal application to the United Synagogue of America (Conservative movement). As soon as the motion was introduced, it was evident that it would pass without a full discussion. Since such a motion would have to be approved by the entire congregation, I asked; "Why would you want to make your proposal from the position of weakness rather than from strength? How are you going to respond to members who might favor the Orthodox, Reform, or Reconstructionist unions? Why not ask each of the four groups to meet with us? If they don't wish to, the advantage would be ours." The Board decided to accept my suggestion.

We invited each of the four Synagogue unions to come to our Synagogue for a light supper and to make a presentation of their programs. Each one accepted. In our conversation with the Orthodox spokesman, I explained forthrightly that a number of our worshippers, because of their age or the distance from the Synagogue, came by car or taxi on Shabbat. He responded that while his union did not encourage it, that would be no reason to deny affiliation. I continued, "We haven't provided for a *mechitzah*" (a physical barrier to separate men and women at services). Again he replied; "There are a number of Orthodox congregations throughout the country where they have not yet done so. That too would not be reason for exclusion." Then I took a deep breath and informed him that the congregation was going in the direction of egalitarianism and inviting women for an *aliyah* (to come forward to the Torah). He looked at me and sighed, "Rabbi Block, that is a fundamental difference." Nonetheless, we were all greatly impressed with the extensive educational and community programs of the Orthodox Union.

The Reform movement sent two representatives, who explained the scope of its education and social action departments and new dimensions in liturgy and approach to *Halakhah* (Jewish law) designed to bring the unaffiliated into Jewish life. As we reflected later on this meeting, however, we realized that our congregation preferred a more traditional stance in worship services and religious practices.

Our guest from the Reconstructionist movement informed us that an increasing number of congregations were swelling its ranks, in search of a theology with emphasis upon humanism.

The Conservative movement appealed to us because of its adherence to tradition and its ability to reinterpret ancient laws and make them applicable to modern life. One of our officers commented, "Rabbi Block, you have been taking us in that direction all along."

A motion to affiliate with the United Synagogue of America was presented to the congregation at the next Annual Meeting, but its advocates had no easy time trying to convince the membership to relinquish our independent status. I sensed the mood of the congregation and, recognizing that the motion might not pass, I rose to express my opinion: that affiliation was probably a worthwhile step, that the decision would not be an irrevocable commitment, and that the next couple of years could be a trial period. The motion passed.

TAKING A STAND

In February 1979 we received a scroll of affiliation with the United Synagogue of America just at a time when a constitutional crisis in our congregation was about to explode. The Board of Trustees had decided that, given our new house and other changes, it was time to review our constitution and by-laws. The major revisions concerned the roles of the rabbi, the Board, and the President and revolved principally around the issue of authority—namely, who is authorized to give direction to synagogue affairs: Is it the Board of Trustees, the rabbi, the congregation, or all of them? Is the role of the rabbi to be limited to leading prayers, officiating at life-cycle events, and delivering sermons? Is the rabbi free and unrestricted to assume the role of teacher and preacher, expounding Judaism's moral and ethical concepts to the congregation and the community at large?

Discussions about the proposed revisions exacerbated the conflicts and tensions of the previous five years, and the continual arguments consumed so much time and energy that it had become almost impossible for me to function and therefore for the Synagogue to function.

The vote on the new constitution was scheduled for April 25, 1979, at the Annual Meeting. Some of the suggested changes deeply disturbed me because they blurred the lines of authority and contravened the accepted practice of synagogues as well as the Religious Corporations Law of New York State, and they regarded the synagogue more as a commercial corporation than as a House of God.

[The proposed revisions are in italics, with the most controversial changes underlined. The text of the then existing constitution and by-laws are in parentheses.]

"The Rabbi shall enjoy the freedom of the pulpit, and subject to the responsibilities of the Board of Trustees and to the advice and guidance of any committee or committees thereof, he shall have the responsibility of implementing the objective and purposes of the Synagogue." ("The Rabbi shall preside over and direct the spiritual affairs of the congregation.")

One other section referred to the powers of the Board of Trustees:

"The Synagogue shall be managed by the Board of Trustees. Without limiting the generality of the foregoing, the Board of Trustees shall have custody and control over the name, temporalities and property of the Synagogue including their use for purposes other than those set forth in these By-laws, for example, fund-raising, public meetings; awards, prizes or other honors; and affixing of plaques or other signs within or without the property of the Synagogue. The trustees shall act only as a Board of Trustees, and the individual trustees shall have no power as such."

("The Trustees shall have jurisdiction over and custody, control and administration of all the temporal affairs and property of the congregation.")

Another section defined the scope of the authority of the President of the congregation:

"The President shall be the <u>chief executive officer</u> of the Synagogue and shall have general supervision over the affairs of the Synagogue, subject, however, to the control of the Board of Trustees." ("The President shall be the lay leader... and shall exercise all powers and authorities of the executive officer in accord with parliamentary rules of procedure.")

These proposals underscored the divisiveness that not only had caused dissension within the Board, but had set members of the congregation against each other. So passionate were the emotions that phonathons were organized by the proponents and opponents to lobby the members for weeks before the meeting. People were baffled and confused by this controversy. It was so completely out of character for our congregation.

I had to take a stand. There was a principle at stake. I could not allow a Board of Trustees to limit and determine the role of the rabbi—not just my role, but I was thinking of so many of my colleagues who sacrifice themselves and then are often needlessly castigated and harassed.

The night of the Annual Meeting the sanctuary was filled, the atmosphere tense. Never in our almost 25 years as a congregation had we faced such a contentious meeting. I felt compelled to bare my personal feelings to the congregation as a whole, the pain and sorrow that had often overwhelmed me since our move to Gramercy Park but that I had never openly expressed.

As I rose to speak, I prayed I would be strong but not scathing, and would focus on issues not personalities.

On May 14, we will mark the 25th Anniversary of the first Shabbat service held by our congregation… we have earned the… reputation of being a Synagogue with a sense of warmth and respect for all… the potential is here to make ours one of the great synagogues of the country. We came to Gramercy Park with an already established reputation, and yet, we can even go higher.

In the past four years we have accomplished many great things… but the opportunities of our new location have been far from realized [and] discourtesies and provincialism have diminished the spirit of warmth and friendship which have always been our hallmark. During the past years, I have regrettably often been disturbed by the acrimony in our Board of Trustees' meetings, the discourtesy toward each other and toward the Rabbi. I have sought to do whatever I could to alter the climate, to change its direction and to avoid confrontation, because I have never liked to see Jew fighting Jew…. More and more I hear people saying that they have become disenchanted with the Synagogue. The tense atmosphere at Board meetings and in some committees has caused a number of Trustees and committee members either to resign or to lose their *chaysheck*—their desire to attend meetings.

Repeatedly, the impression is distinctly left with me that the Rabbi must confine himself to matters of the sanctuary, while the Board will take care of running the Synagogue, because "this is a business" that needs money to run….

Let me tell about our local clergymen's group, which meets once a month and over coffee discusses matters of common interest in the community… In 1977, the group…asked me if I would consent to conduct a Passover Seder, and whether it could be held in our building…. I indicated that I would be very glad to conduct a Jewish Seder, and indeed there were precedents for that in the Third or Community Seder, but that I would not involve myself in anything which was other than [strictly] Jewish. They assured me that that was sincerely their intent. But the Board of Trustees said that such a Seder could not be held here, and there were strong and angry reactions to the idea that we might sit at the [Seder] table with our non-Jewish brethren.

That Seder had to be held at the Parish House of the Calvary Church [on the north side of Gramercy Park] during *Chol-ha-Moed Pesach* [the intermediate days of Passover]; [it was] a strictly kosher Passover Seder... and with a *mashgiach* (a religious supervisor), for I would have it no other way. And in 1978 again it [the Seder] had to be held in another church. And I cannot tell you what I had to endure, and the rantings and the ravings, and the imprecations hurled at your rabbis for being present at such Seders. I remember how painfully I had to explain to our committee of religious leaders that the Seder could not be held in our Synagogue, and one minister said to me, "Do you mean that there are no gentiles allowed in your Synagogue?" I looked at him and with all of the sensitivity and all of the philosophy and theology I could muster, I gave answer, trying to explain that perhaps this was a reaction to our problems on 13th Street.

This year the committee proposed...an evening program of food and fellowship. "Rabbi, do you think it could be held at The Brotherhood Synagogue?" And I said to them the President of our congregation has the master calendar and would know the availability of our rooms.... *And for one whole hour* the matter was discussed at a meeting of our Board....

I posed the question: Can it be that we may not have tuna fish and tea with members of the community? *Are my hands to be so tied that I cannot even invite a group for an evening program?...* I find myself stifled and repelled by an attitude of provincialism. In recent days, remarks such as these have been passed on to me; 'The Rabbi likes *goyim* (non-Jews) more than he likes Jews.'

I yield to no one in this room a sense of my love for Judaism. I yield to no one in this sanctuary my love for Jewish life and Jewish causes. And no one can question my sensitivity to Judaism and our people... this pin on my lapel is an indication that I was willing to give my life for our people when I joined the Haganah, and I would be willing to do so again![1]

Now brotherhood between Jew and Jew is primary.... Our Synagogue stands out in trying to breach the barriers between synagogue and synagogue. You show me another synagogue that has made the attempt to bridge the gap, to bind the hearts, to cement the ties of Jewish life, and I will show you The Brotherhood Synagogue!

Before we actually moved here I went to all of the rabbis in the community in order to tell them of our plans and to assure them that we were not *Masig-ha-g'vul*—[that] we would not encroach upon their membership or their spiritual programs in the slightest, but that we could develop many wonderful areas of cooperation. I remember how I was mocked at a meeting of the Board.... "What do you have to ask another rabbi for? We are an independent, free congregation and can do whatever we will." And my answer was, "I do not want to diminish what another synagogue is doing and gain at their expense...."

Now comes an attempt to stifle the rabbi even further in his work, his actions and his presence, subjecting the rabbi to the dictates not of his own conscience, or to the law of the Torah, but to others!

Well, I have learned from the teachings of my mentor, Rabbi Stephen Samuel Wise, that... "The rabbi, in the household of Israel, does not regard his utterances as infallible. No rabbi will refuse to correct an opinion, though he takes the utmost pains to achieve correctness, in form and substance, before speaking, when cogent reasons are advanced to convince him of his error. Nor will a rabbi fail to welcome criticism and differences of opinion, to the end that the truth may be served." But I can only emphasize the words of Rabbi Wise, "to declare that in the event of a conflict of irreconcilable views

1. A menorah-shaped pin was awarded by the Israeli government to those who had served during the War of Independence.

between the rabbi and the Board of Trustees, that it is the rabbi who must yield in the domain of religious activities, is to assert the right not to criticize the rabbi, but to silence him," and a rabbi is not an ox, who should be muzzled or penned in....

The rabbi and the Board of Trustees must find a way to work together as equal partners. *We must find a way to work together in a constructive manner, the Board of Trustees, the Congregation, and the Rabbi.* There are so many wonderful things that we can do in the next years, so let us put aside divisiveness... and strive for a *sense of unity*, encompassing the Board, the Rabbi, and the Congregation....

When I concluded, it was obvious that most of our members had not been aware of the gravity of the issues. Advocates of my position jumped to their feet to demonstrate their support, while those who sought to limit and control the Rabbi's outside activities were taken aback by the vigor of my exposé and shouted to counter my views, even to the point of stalking out and using ugly language. They had come to the meeting "to clip the Rabbi's wings," as someone described their intention, but they did not prevail.

UNRESOLVED CONSTITUTIONAL DIFFERENCES

When order was restored, the Chairman of the Constitution and By-laws Committee presented the revised constitution. One member called particular attention to Section 5 of the Religious Corporations Law of the State of New York, which requires a notification of revisions in advance at two meetings. The section provides:

By-laws may be adopted or amended by a two-thirds vote of the qualified voters present and voting at the meeting for the incorporation or at any subsequent meeting, after written notice, embodying such by-laws or amendment, has been given at a previous meeting at which such proposed by-laws or amendment is to be acted upon.

A distinguished federal judge and longtime member of our congregation, who was present, concurred that we would be unable to vote upon the constitution at this Annual Meeting because the text had not been submitted to the members in advance and the congregation "cannot rise above the law enacted by the legislature." A motion to table discussion of the proposed revisions passed overwhelmingly.

It was imperative to resolve our differences with all deliberate speed. At the next Board meeting the Trustees adopted a resolution to appoint a committee to seek the advice and guidance of the United Synagogue of America.

Among the topics we hoped to discuss was the right of the rabbi to direct and preside over the spiritual affairs of the congregation, to participate in community activities, to be consulted and directly involved in planning the activities of the congregation, and to supervise the educational programs for children and adults. In other words, how to resolve conflicts between the philosophy of the rabbi and decisions of the Board.

During the summer, officers of the congregation summoned a special membership meeting to discuss these issues. The day fell at a time when my family and I had planned to be on vacation; but, much to the surprise, and perhaps chagrin, of some of the officers, we interrupted our Canadian trip and returned home to ensure that all points of view would be presented. A Board member summarized the whole conflict very succinctly: "*We* tell the rabbi where he may go and which organizations he may be active in. The rabbi has to abide by our decision."

THE CONGREGATION DECIDES

That fall a number of longtime members who feared that the continuing divisiveness would ultimately imperil our synagogue proposed that the only solution would be to present the membership with an opposition slate of officers and Trustees at the next Annual Meeting, in accordance with procedures set down in our constitution. This was the first time in our history that a Nominating Committee slate had been challenged. A committee led by a highly respected physician spearheaded this effort. The nominees were carefully selected to include first-time candidates for office as well as incumbents who accepted the basic principles on which the congregation was established. There was no intent to suppress honest debate, because the strength of a synagogue rests upon the expression of diverse views.

The election of officers and Board members was scheduled for March 1980, and both sides campaigned intensely by phone and mail. Regrettably, a number of members resigned; they couldn't find the peace they sought in a house of worship filled with strife. And I couldn't blame them.

Over the years when colleagues had poured out their hearts to me about similar feuds with their Boards, I had always been proud and happy that my congregation was different in that regard. Now I too was no longer spared, but I found solace in the words of Talmud: "Every controversy which is waged for the sake of Heaven will lead to abiding results; but the controversy which is not waged for the sake of Heaven will not lead to abiding results." This was probably the most painful period of my rabbinate, even more so in many ways than the crisis on 13th Street that led to our leaving Greenwich Village. Then we were united;

now we were a house divided. Nevertheless I had confidence in the good judgment and good will of our membership.

There was a large turnout at the meeting. We had prepared printed ballots, which were carefully tallied by a special committee. When the results were announced late in the evening, the alternate slate had won overwhelmingly. I felt as if a stone had been lifted from my heart.

Unfortunately, some who were not elected interpreted the results to mean that they would no longer be welcome in the congregation. I have always regretted any words of mine or those of others that might have prompted their departure.

Even though we had met frequently with leaders of the United Synagogue of America, our discussions had produced no clear resolution to our frictions. By the end of 1981 our Board suggested a review of our affiliation, and not long after that our members voted to revert to the status of an independent congregation.

I have often reflected on what brought about the confrontation. Why did men and women who had long been active members and leaders in our congregation reject the principles on which our Synagogue was founded and which seemingly they had accepted in the past?

No doubt, and to a great extent, the ordeal we had endured on West 13th Street with the new minister and the upheaval of our decision to leave, the search for a suitable new location, our extremely limited funds—all led to feelings of frustration and often to angry discussions about our future. All of us reacted to the events according to our own emotional, psychological, and spiritual propensity. Obviously, I was painfully disillusioned and distraught. My dreams and hopes had been dashed. But I was determined to keep my congregation together and to rebuild, and I refused to allow acrimony to dominate my thinking.

There was another factor, I believe: Our founders were men and women who shared my vision of achieving brotherhood among world religions. In our early days, many of our officers and Trustees brought to our congregation years of experience and leadership in synagogue life, whereas the attitudes of our Boards in the 1970s reflected their inexperience in that domain. By then the Board was more preoccupied with the pragmatic matters of synagogue finances and administration. At the time there was also a general trend in the Jewish community to participate less in intergroup activities and focus on educational and cultural programs, to become "more Jewish."

Perhaps I was naive and unrealistic, but I had always hoped that The Brotherhood Synagogue would be different from other congregations. I took to heart the injunction of the Torah "to love thy neighbor as thyself," and the admonitions of our sages to promote good will between Jews and non-Jews. For me, this too would be a way to live more Jewishly.

It would still take a while to restore *sholom bayit* (peace in the house), but with renewed enthusiasm, we were able to move ahead, pay off our mortgage, expand our programs, and reach out to the community in new ways. We completed the Garden of Remembrance, planted a Biblical Garden, and installed an elevator. The 1980s would be a decade of achievement.[2]

---

2. I have not mentioned any of the officers and Board members by name in this chapter because I believe it would serve no purpose. All of them had worked very hard in establishing our new Synagogue home and had contributed in many ways to the growth of our congregation. This dispute was not between persons and personalities, but about principles and philosophies.

On the other hand, in the chapter on the breakup between the Village Presbyterian Church and our Synagogue, I did mention some people by name because that controversy had been widely reported in the press.

Only in America

One summer evening my wife and I were taking a stroll along Third Avenue when we happened to meet our dear friend Msgr. Harry Byrne, Pastor of nearby Epiphany Roman Catholic Church. As we were chatting and laughing and enjoying our conversation, a young man passed by. After a few steps, he turned back and remarked to the Monsignor, "Excuse me, Father, but do you know that you are talking to a Jewish rabbi?" Msgr. Byrne replied, "Yes, I know that; and he's also my good friend." The young man turned away, shook his head, and audibly commented, "Only in America."

"Only in America" would a church parishioner ask a rabbi (myself) to write to the Archdiocese requesting that her pastor not be reassigned because he is so beloved by his members. Whether my letter helped or not, I may never know, but Msgr. Byrne remained at the parish for a few more years until he retired.

10

A Decade of Achievement

"Communal activity is as meritorious as studying Torah."

TALMUD

Be involved! Hillel's mandate not to separate ourselves from the community is a fundamental principle of Judaism. What then is the role of a synagogue? In addition to being a house of worship and a house of study, a synagogue is also a house of assembly (a "meeting house").

The Brotherhood Synagogue has always been a congregation sensitive to the needs of the community. In Chapters 10 and 11, I want to focus on several of our special outreach efforts during the 1980s. In that ten-year period we accelerated our activities with projects that included sheltering the homeless, instituting additional classes for the developmentally disabled, assisting new immigrants through acculturation programs, making our building more accessible to the physically handicapped, designing two beautiful gardens, and presenting cultural programs and holiday observances for congregation and community—all planned to develop an understanding of the richness of our Jewish heritage.

To accomplish all this required strong leaders. Our sages understood that "as the generations, so the leaders, and as the leaders, so the generations." In the 1980s the Synagogue drew upon the strength and abilities of members of our congregation, and those who provided exemplary leadership and counsel as officers and Board members. We are enormously indebted to them.

I want to express my abiding gratitude to our dedicated and distinguished Presidents: to Gerald J. Friedman, M.D., for decisive leadership at a critical time in our history, and to those who followed him: Dr. Bernard Esrig, Professor Julius J. Marke, and Irving Statsinger; to M. Milton Glass, a Vice President, and to Arthur J. Greenbaum, Chairman of our Board. They and their families worked with me very closely as together we strove to build an even greater Synagogue.

OUR RELIGIOUS SCHOOL

The purpose of education, stressed Rabbi Samson Raphael Hirsch, is revealed in the word *chinuch*, which literally means dedication, preparing our children for a life of dedicated service to God and humanity. Thus we are commanded by the Book of Proverbs to "train a child in the way to go," by precept and example, taking into account each child's own capacity and ability.

Much of the success of our Religious School has been due to the love of children and a strong commitment to Jewish life by our Principals, first Dr. Leo Storozum, and then Phillip Rothman, and our talented and dedicated teachers, as well as Inge Dobelis, who served for many years as President of the Parents' Association. They made religious education exciting for each and every child.

The 1980s was a period of expansion for the school, in enrollment, curriculum, and programming. I attribute this growth to a great extent to the ability and warm, genial personality of Mr. Rothman, who in the fall of 1981 became Principal as well as Executive Director of our Synagogue. Previously he had been a teacher at a downtown Manhattan day school, the East Side

Hebrew Institute (ESHI), and later its Principal. A gifted educator, Mr. Rothman developed new programs such as the "Tichon" group for post Bar and Bat Mitzvah students, which focused on continuing Judaic studies and community service; he expanded the music and art curriculum, and he encouraged the active involvement of a Parents' Association. Under his direction the children conducted food, clothing, and toy drives, entertained the homeless with songs at a drop-in center, and raised funds for a memorial in our Garden of Remembrance for children who perished in the Holocaust. Classes marched in Salute to Israel parades and came to Synagogue with their families for special Friday evening Shabbat dinners. During the year the children helped decorate the succah; reveled at the Chanukah skit when Mr. Rothman and I played Simon and Judah Maccabee in costume; enjoyed fun-filled Purim carnivals, where every child is a winner; conducted model Seders; and enthusiastically raised thousands of dollars for the school with their annual Passover candy sales. They learned Hebrew to the songs of Hanna Levy and made their own "Judaica" under the tutelage of their art teacher, Avi Zukerman. Donna Josephs, Mr. Rothman's talented associate, added classes for parents, video presentations, and creative writing, and she further expanded the curriculum.

The centrality of the State of Israel has always been a focus of our children's studies. Most of our teachers have studied or traveled in Israel, and they share their experiences with the children. Through art, drama, and song, as well as in classroom studies and discussions, the children learn to love the land and understand its significance to the Jewish people over the centuries. One year, on Yom Yerushalayim (Jerusalem Day), the children were asked to explain what Jerusalem meant to them. One perceptive youngster saw it as a place "where you can wear your yarmulke and nobody makes fun of you." Another observed, "It is really what Israel is all about." Still another child remarked that although Jerusalem is very far away, "I feel very close to it." One of the important programs Mr. Rothman initiated was the establishment of a Young Judea chapter at the Synagogue. In this program, sponsored by Hadassah, preteens and teens socialize and at the same time learn to be proud of their Jewish heritage and identity while developing self-confidence and leadership skills. In 1985, in recognition of our achievements, the Board of Jewish Education honored our Religious School and Parents' Association with a Merit Award.

There is a palpable feeling of affection and respect between Mr. Rothman and the children. Parents often contrast the pleasurable experience of their children with their own unhappy memories of Hebrew School and have told us stories that reflect their children's love for the school. For example, a student is sitting at home with his yarmulke on and watching television. Realizing he is still wearing his skullcap, the child turns to his mother and says, "You know, I'm really proud to be Jewish."

The scene of parents gathering to pick up their children in the evening and the animated conversations about school projects and assignments is, to me, one of the most uplifting times of the school day.

A parent races into the Synagogue and anxiously asks Mr. Rothman, "Is my child here?" "Yes," he answers, "she's studying in the community room." The mother rushes in, takes her child out of class, and tells Mr. Rothman that her daughter had been home all day with a 102-degree fever but left on her own because "she could not bear the thought of missing Hebrew School."

Developing compassion and sensitivity to other people's needs and situations is an important element in the philosophy of the school. In a Synagogue bulletin article Mr. Rothman wrote about a school talent show. What moved him most was not each individual performance, but rather "the respect each child had for his or her fellow participants. They watched each act intensely and applauded with sincerity." There was no feeling that you had to be better than anyone else.

A core principle of the Religious School is that each child is a member of our congregational family and that the Synagogue belongs to the children as much as to their parents. A student invited some neighbors to join her and her family for a Shabbat dinner at the Synagogue and to attend the evening service. As she escorted her guests on a tour of the building, she proudly declared, "This is *my* Synagogue, not just my mommy's and daddy's."

At a Shabbat service shortly before my retirement, the children were invited to speak about what our Synagogue meant to them personally. Some reminded me that I had named them in the sanctuary and that my door was always open to them, that I made them feel they were important members of the congregation, and that they had learned from me the joys of their Jewish heritage and the paths to brotherhood and peace. Accepting their gift of a beautiful *tallis* adorned with a silver *atara* (collar), I responded, "I could receive no finer tribute than the loving words of the children."

Even in retirement I try to stay in touch with the children, attend Bar and Bat Mitzvahs, and, as often as I can, look in on our Saturday morning junior congregation. And when I do, Mr. Rothman invites me to take part and do what I love—dramatize for a new generation the stories and Midrashim (legends) of the Jewish people.

By the fall of 1998 the school had about 225 children, and it continues to grow. A program initiated by Mr. Rothman and one of our members, Dr. Stephen Benardo, a school superintendent and special education supervisor, provides a religious education for learning-disabled children. The program, called "Tikvah" (Hope), opened in 1995 with a single class of four boys, ages 10 to 13, with learning disabilities. A year and a half later the program had 13 children and three special education teachers. One boy has already celebrated his Bar Mitzvah and others are preparing for theirs. For one child, according to his mother, Sunday (the day when the class meets) is the best day of the week.

On the day the attorney for the Synagogue met with the officers of the United Federation of Teachers and exchanged legal documents acknowledging that our mortgage obligation on the building was now paid in full, I addressed the Religious School at an assembly in the sanctuary. "It is now official," I declared to the children. "This Synagogue belongs to us, to you." Even though the adults had raised the funds to pay the mortgage, I explained the building truly belongs to the children, for they will be the next generation of synagogue leaders.

ACCESSIBILITY

The nineteenth-century scholar Chaim of Volozhin, the leading disciple of the Vilna Gaon and head of the renowned Volozhin Yeshiva, once bought a pair of leather boots that reached up to his hips. Why had the rabbi bought such unusual footwear? After the first heavy snowfall, neighbors saw the rabbi in his high boots trudging through the snow in the early morning hours. "Why are you out so early?" they asked. He responded, "I am making a path so it will be easier for others to come to the synagogue."

The primary task of a synagogue is to bring people closer to God; providing access to houses of worship for people with disabilities is surely the moral and right thing to do. The Baal Shem Tov, founder of the Hasidic movement, mandated, "No one must ever feel left out." If the secular community is obligated by law to make public buildings accessible, should we in the religious community do less?

Accessibility has many interpretations. When The Brotherhood Synagogue was established, we were guided by the principle that everybody would be welcome and our doors would be open to all who wanted to worship with us.

Thirty years ago we welcomed a group of young mentally retarded Jewish children whose families anguished that no synagogue was responding to their needs; we organized a pioneering religious education class for them. Years later we instituted a similar program for Jewish adults with developmental disabilities who were living in group residences in our community.

We were also the first synagogue in Manhattan to open a shelter for the homeless. In addition we have made our facilities available to a number of support groups, for it is not only people with physical problems but also those suffering mental and emotional conflicts who often seek a synagogue setting in which to meet.

In 1974 we acquired our handsome, historic landmark building on Gramercy Park, which Ada Louise Huxtable, the noted architecture critic, extolled, "In art and amenity it is beyond price." However, the Quakers who built it situated the sanctuary on the second floor, up a flight of 17 steps, with another, and steeper, flight of 22 steps leading to the third-floor balcony. There are also four steps leading down from the main floor rotunda into the community room. For a number of our members these became major obstacles, and they found it increasingly difficult to attend services and other programs.

In 1987 we undertook a major fund-raising campaign, headed by a wise and sensible former Board Chairman, Arthur J. Greenbaum, both to meet our second mortgage and to install an elevator. The plans originally called for an exterior elevator housed in a brick and glass structure attached to the west side of our building and providing access to all floors while maintaining the integrity of the sanctuary and preserving our limited class-room and office space.

As in many historic neighborhoods, the residents of Gramercy Park do not hesitate to take strong positions, pro and con, on any changes that might affect the architectural character of the com-munity. The proposed elevator design became a highly contro-versial issue and, to our dismay, met with vociferous opposition from historic preservationists as well as some of our neighbors.

The dispute might appear to be another example of a religious institution pitted against the preservation community. However, this was not the case here. We never insisted on our "right" to do with the building what we would. Instead, we felt it more appro-priate to hold an "open house" and actively solicit the opinions of our neighbors. As a practical consideration, I knew we would have to obtain approval for the design from Community Board 6, which would hold a public hearing, and then from the New York City Landmarks Preservation Commission.

The open-house discussions were frank and forthright as we sought to explain the main advantage of an exterior elevator: it would enable us to retain classrooms for our growing school. While some offered to help defray the projected costs, others were hostile and uncompromising. One visitor looked at the steep, curving stairway leading to the sanctuary and scornfully commented, "Is this what the fuss is all about?"

There was a large attendance at the Community Board meeting the night our Vice President, M. Milton Glass, FAIA, and I formally presented our plans. Mr. Glass, a prominent architect and a Fellow of the American Institute of Architects, was in charge of our elevator project and had developed the design. In the tense discussion that followed, someone coldly asked, "If your school has outgrown your building, why don't you move?" Most people, however, were understanding of our needs, but nevertheless strongly opposed an exterior structure that they felt would clash with the architecture not only of our building but of the whole Gramercy Park Historic District. One of the outspoken community advocates rose and offered a passionate defense of our plans on the grounds that people and their needs, rather than buildings, should be the prime concern. To no avail.

Supporters and antagonists of the proposed elevator design soon mobilized for letter-writing campaigns to the New York City Landmarks Preservation Commission. At the hearing Mr. Glass posed the fundamental question: "Are the religious, educational, and social activities of the members of the congregation who saved the landmark and maintained its bricks and mortar to be compromised for the sake of a sterile concept of historic purity?"

I too addressed the Commission. "At the time that The Brotherhood Synagogue acquired the building, I implored our Board of Trustees to consider the inclusion of an elevator in the plan.... I only regret that my opinion did not prevail." I added wistfully as an aside, "I wish people would listen more to the rabbi." Nevertheless, the Commission, while truly encouraging our efforts to make the building more accessible, pointed out to us the overwhelming negative reaction expressed by the community and rejected the Synagogue's plan.

Mr. Glass revised his design and an interior elevator was dedicated in October 1988. It could accommodate twelve passengers, or one person in a wheelchair with two other passengers; an outdoor ramp on the west side of the building led directly to the elevator. Although we lost office and classroom space, for the most part the compromise satisfied all the concerned parties. A long-time member, Professor Leonard Kriegel, who relies on a wheelchair, had found access to the sanctuary virtually impossible. "The ramp and the elevator have made it feasible for me to maintain my membership in the Synagogue," he said.

At the dedication ceremony speakers congratulated our congregation on achieving its goal and for our determination to preserve and restore this historic building. The President of the Municipal Art Society, Kent Barwick, observed that it was "resonant with vitality." Manhattan Borough President David N. Dinkins praised our many pioneering programs for the disabled and commented that we demonstrated how a historic landmark can be adapted for contemporary needs. The Reverend Thomas F. Pike, Rector of neighboring Calvary–St. George's Parish, remarked that "access" is a hallmark of The Brotherhood Synagogue, whose doors are ever open to the entire community.

Two members of our congregation whose disabilities had often prevented them from worshipping in the sanctuary brought tears of joy to the gathering. Florence Ward, whose family had often literally carried her up the stairs in her wheelchair, expressed her delight at being able to ride up, and Helen Leibler called the elevator her "stairway to heaven." "Rabbi," someone asked, "what is the *bracha* (blessing) for riding in our elevator for the first time?"

To make people aware that our premises were accessible to the disabled, we included the universal wheelchair symbol on our stationery, bulletins, ads, and on the front door. We also offered large-print prayer books, provided Braille texts, and upgraded our audio system.

In 1991 we received Manhattan Borough President Ruth Messinger's Access New York Award, the first offered to any synagogue, and The New York Landmarks Conservancy lauded our good taste in planning the restoration of the building.

In 1994, in celebration of the 40th anniversary of the founding of the congregation, we installed a magnificent new Holy Ark in the sanctuary, designed by Ismar David, one of America's finest creators of Hebrew type and Judaica. Since he would have to make some changes on the altar to accommodate the wider Ark, we asked him to help us solve the problem of enabling those in wheelchairs to mount the two steps to the altar or go up to the *bima* where the Torah is read. He developed an ingenious design that included an unobtrusive ramp leading to both the altar and the *bima*. Thanks to the generosity of Mr. David, a longtime friend of the congregation, who offered his personal services pro bono, and also to the efforts of the Ark Committee—Susan Capaldo, Donald King, and Phillip Rothman—we are blessed with a majestic Holy Ark and artistically and inconspicuously solved the problem of accessibility while at the same time greatly enhancing the beauty of the sanctuary.

How overjoyed a bride was to be able to have her disabled sister at her side on the altar during her wedding ceremony. At High Holyday services as I began my retirement, it was the fulfillment of a dream to see congregants wheel up the ramp in the sanctuary to receive honors they were never before able to accept. In the words of Isaiah, we had truly become "a house of prayer for all people."

GARDEN OF REMEMBRANCE—*GAN HA-ZIKARON*

In 1975 when the Synagogue officers began reflecting on ways to memorialize our loved ones in the Synagogue, our architect, Dean James Stewart Polshek, stated his position very firmly: no bronze plaques on interior walls! They would be out of place, given the history and character of the building. Marvin Levy, soon to be President of the congregation, had often broached the idea of an outdoor memorial. I too was intrigued by the concept. It was a creative approach and I encouraged him to pursue it with Dean Polshek, who accepted the challenge. The architect envisaged a garden that would be a living memorial to the generations that preceded us as well as a testament to the Six Million Jewish victims who had perished in the Holocaust.

Tragically, Marvin Levy would never walk in this garden. A gunman's bullet ended his life on a Sabbath eve in December 1977. (See Chapter 8.)

After the *shloshim* (30-day period of mourning), we commissioned Dean Polshek to develop a design to fulfill Mr. Levy's proposal of an outdoor memorial, to be known as the Garden of Remembrance. He recommended locating it on the east side of our building and advised us that the plans would have to be approved by the Landmarks Commission. Construction began in 1980 and the cornerstone was dedicated a year later, an eternal legacy to Mr. Levy's vision and wisdom.

Entrance to the Garden is through a portal of stone pillars in line with the front exterior wall of the Synagogue and adorned with a trellis of vines. This portal opens to a series of graveled terraces bordered in stone, gently stepping down toward the rear of the property and culminating at a stone-paved area with benches for repose and meditation. Honey locust trees mark the western border of the Garden and frame the wall that encloses it at the southern end.

A $7\frac{1}{2}$ foot-high limestone wall slopes down with the stone terraces and screens the Garden from the neighboring property. It was designed as a Wall of Memory, to be engraved with the names of loved ones and friends, with a special section for names of Holocaust victims. When we dedicated the Garden in the spring of 1982, the architect emphasized the living, growing nature of the Garden. "I hope it will never be completed," he said. "That is its very spirit."

Because the Garden of Remembrance would thus be a memorial to the Six Million, we invited the West German government to contribute to it. This participation would thus be a way to acknowledge the unique contribution made to the rehabilitation of the Federal Republic of Germany by its trusted public relations counsel in the United States, the late L. Roy Blumenthal, brother of one of our Trustees, Jerome Blumenthal. Roy Blumenthal's initiative and efforts after World War II led to a meeting in New York between Chancellor Konrad Adenauer and Prime Minister David Ben-Gurion that fostered a rapprochement between Israel and West Germany and resulted in the payment of more than $800 million in reparations to Israel.

And so it was that on June 3, 1979, the Ambassador of the Federal Republic of Germany, Berndt von Staden, and members of his official staff traveled to Gramercy Park from Washington to present to The Brotherhood Synagogue a check for $10,000 in memory of Roy Blumenthal. At the ceremony a telegram was read from former West Berlin Mayor Willy Brandt, later Chancellor of the Federal Republic of Germany: "Today I think of my friend Roy Blumenthal who contributed in such an exemplary way to the reconciliation of the United States and Germany with deep emotion."

The special section listing the names of victims of the Holocaust is particularly poignant, for in many cases this is their only physical memorial. A young Christian minister visiting the Garden remarked that when she saw the names of twelve people in just a single family, she first began to comprehend the extent of the tragedy that had befallen the Jewish people, including a million and a half children.

A group of German nuns in Arizona wrote: "The very name Garden of Remembrance touches us deeply and reminds us of the unspeakable sorrow which you, our Jewish brothers and sisters, received through our German nation. In our weekly prayer of blessing for Israel we will remember your Garden with the prayer that the Lord Himself may heal the wounds and bless you."

Many community residents sent gifts toward the construction of the Garden. One neighbor commented, "It so appeals to me— truly meaningful, a lasting tribute and memorial to that awesome blot on history. You bring, too, added beauty to our Gramercy Park neighborhood."

Seven years later, in May 1986, we installed a colorful mosaic in the semicircular niche in the southern end of the Garden, a gift of one of the earliest members of the congregation, Mrs. Flora Landsman, to memorialize her son, Stanley, a highly respected figure in the art world. Under the supervision of M. Milton Glass, who had designed the building's elevator and ramp, we held a competition for a suitable work of art, and selected a design by Dr. Irene Rousseau, entitled "From Destruction to Peace." Skilled artisans transformed Dr. Rousseau's concept into a permanent memorial of small tesserae mosaics, chosen for their brilliance of color and durability.

Although the artist is not of the Jewish faith, she was inspired by stories she had heard from Holocaust survivors and resolved to create a work of art to reflect the courage of righteous gentiles who reached out to save Jewish people. Several abstract symbols convey her message. Red flames symbolize destruction yet also represent a reaffirmation of faith through Hebrew letters in the flames reading *"Yit-ga-dal v'yit-ka-dash sh'-may ra-ba,"* the opening words of the *Kaddish*, the traditional mourner's prayer ("Extolled and hallowed be the name of God..."). Blue doves on a white background, flying through the wisps of smoke arising from the flames, represent Israel, their small geometric shapes presenting a feeling of movement as they float upward toward *"Shalom"* and "Peace," to welcome an era of hope for mankind.

At the dedication I reiterated, "The Brotherhood Synagogue seeks to demonstrate the kinship of modern Jewry with its predecessors and to enunciate clearly the indestructibility of Judaism. This artistic mosaic expresses both our tragedy and our hope."

Many members of the congregation are Holocaust survivors, some bearing the scars of torture in the concentration camps. Several were "hidden children," sheltered in convents, in monasteries, on farms, and in cellars and attics. Others belong to Second Generation groups, keeping the memory of their relatives alive and lending support to each other. A Chairman of our Board and past President, Professor Julius J. Marke, related that when he served in the Army in World War II his unit had been among the liberators of Buchenwald.

A dignified bronze marker near the portal explains the meaning of the Garden, the gift of Erwin T. Basch, a past officer of the congregation, who had managed to escape Europe on *Kristallnacht*, the night of November 9 and 10, 1938.

Over the years the Garden has become a great source of comfort, as people stand in contemplation in front of the names of their loved ones and run their hands across the letters. About a thousand names of relatives and friends of the congregation have already been etched into the Wall, a number of them not Jewish, including our beloved friend Rev. Dr. Jesse William Stitt.

Embedded in the cornerstone of the Garden of Remembrance is a large rectangular stone from the city of Jerusalem with three Hebrew words engraved into it: *Even May-Har Tzion* (a stone from Mount Zion), a gift in 1960 from my friend Dr. S. Z. Kahana, the former Director General of the Ministry of Religious Affairs in Israel. I had personally carried it back to New York. It is a symbol of the covenant between our patriarch Jacob and his father-in-law, Laban, as they gathered stones for a "heap of witness," saying, "May the Lord watch between me and thee when we are absent one from another." The stones in the Garden are our witness that the generations past will not be forgotten.

The Garden symbolizes the eternity of the Jewish people and stands as a silent sentinel, reminding us that God demands that we strive for peace, justice, good will, and friendship among people everywhere.

A BIBLICAL GARDEN IS BORN

A garden, lush with beautiful flowers, plants, and trees, suggests the ultimate state of happiness. "One is nearer God's heart in a garden than anywhere else on earth," said the poet Dorothy

Gurney. Legend holds that when God took Adam on a tour of the Garden of Eden, He said: "See my works, how fine and excellent they are! Now all that I am going to create for you I have already created. Think about this and do not corrupt and desolate My world; for if you do, there will be no one to set it right after you."

Just how was the idea of our Biblical Garden conceived? As a member of our congregation, Sandra Levine, who lived directly across the street from the Synagogue, looked down from her apartment, she was dismayed at the physical condition of the lot along the west side of our building. One day she came to me with a proposal to beautify the plot by removing the debris and stones and planting a flower garden.

Unhesitatingly I concurred, but I asked with a twinkle, "Why not make it a Jewish garden and display flora of the Bible?" Surely some of the flowers and plants that grow in Israel could withstand New York weather, I thought. Mrs. Levine spoke enthusiastically of a Biblical Garden she had visited uptown at the Cathedral of St. John the Divine. Could she invite her friend Deborah Peterson, an expert horticulturist, to assist her? "Absolutely."

The Synagogue had limited funds available for a Biblical Garden, but once news about the project reached members and friends who loved gardening, their personal gifts helped defray the expenses. Although the site is narrow, 108 feet deep by 13½ feet wide, the results proved what can be accomplished with talent and persistence. Landscaping divided the garden into basically four sections: a flower bed just inside the front gate, next an orchard, then a fragrant flower garden, and toward the back a woodland section. As a result of painstaking planning and research, as many as 60 species were planted and identified with small signs.

On a sunny September afternoon in 1983, during Succoth, we dedicated the Biblical Garden in an outdoor ceremony attended by congregants, friends, neighbors, and representatives of the Jewish National Fund, who hoped this project would be a forerunner of biblical gardens all over the country. The children of our Religious School were bedecked in Biblical Garden T-shirts they had designed and, together with youngsters from local churches, planted three saplings—a cypress, a fir, and a box tree—covering the roots with a mixture of local soil and earth from the Land of Israel.

"Here we have a little bit of the Garden of Eden," I told the gathering, "a place to feel the power of creation in nature working harmoniously, and that is certainly a lesson for us." A simple story expresses it best. One day a parishioner invited his minister to visit him at his farm to enjoy his beautiful garden. The pastor was very impressed. "See what beauty God hath wrought." "Yes," replied the farmer, "but you should have seen this place before I gave God a helping hand."

In August 1989 the explosion of a nearby underground Con Edison steam pipe spewed roaring clouds of asbestos into the air with a blast so intense that it took three lives, injured many, displaced residents from their homes, and forced us out of the Synagogue for months. (See Chapter 11.) The explosion inflicted such extensive damage to the Biblical Garden that we had no choice but to uproot the plantings. Once again, the lot was bare.

With faith, and the advice and assistance of our members Donald King and Naomi and Ben Saltzman, we replanted the garden and installed benches along the walks, making it a serene neighborhood spot for rest and reflection. Gramercy Park is a community that cherishes and fiercely protects its trees and plants, and residents and visitors appreciate the beauty of our

Synagogue's two vest-pocket gardens, each with a different character—one somber, dedicated to lives lost, the other bright and colorful, a witness to life renewed.

When I retired in 1994, and in celebration of the 40th anniversary of the founding of the congregation, a plaque was dedicated in the Biblical Garden in honor of Phyllis and me and the founding members of The Brotherhood Synagogue. On it is inscribed the opening verse of the sublime 24th Psalm, "The earth is the Lord's and the fullness thereof."

AUXILIARY GROUPS

Every rabbi knows that it is impossible to run a congregation without the assistance and ideas of volunteers. The Torah relates: when the Holy Ark was built in the wilderness, no one person was permitted to work alone; it had to be a collective effort.

Auxiliary groups have become an integral part of synagogue life, giving members an opportunity to contribute their talents, skills, and experience, as well as being a source of suggestions for programs and activities. Equally important, by working together on the various projects developed by these groups, members come to know each other and often form close friendships.

Sisterhood has always worked very hard and contributed generously to the congregation. I often called it "the strong right arm" of the rabbi. In our early years the Women's Auxiliary, as Sisterhood was called then, was in charge of the weekly Oneg Shabbats; provided Religious School scholarships; arranged holiday programs, theater parties, and fund-raising events; planned joint bazaars with the Women's Society of the Village Church; collected toys and clothing for needy and hospitalized children;

assigned the Friday night candle blessings; and decorated the succah.

The Men's Club arranged Sunday brunches and lecture series on Jewish culture and history, and it presented a prayer book as a gift to the Bar Mitzvah boys, just as Sisterhood did for the Bat Mitzvah students. One of the major Men's Club projects was to sponsor a professional recording, "Sermon in Jewish Music," featuring Cantor Leib Mirkovic and our choir, with my commentary preceding each selection.

By the 1980s separate congregational groups for men and women were no longer so popular. Synagogues and fraternal groups saw a diminution in their membership rosters, and conditions in the city discouraged people from attending evening activities. While the Men's Club soon ceased to function, a number of longtime Sisterhood members were determined to continue this important group. They changed the meeting time to Sunday afternoons and revitalized the programming. Lectures on current issues, theater parties to Yiddish plays, folk dancing, brunches, and social gatherings attracted a new generation of members, and Sisterhood has remained an active organization. In the 1990s a Women's Havurah was formed, and it has been successful with supper meetings and innovative activities.

In the 1950s we had a popular Young Adult League, but its format and style were not in tune with 1960s culture. On the other hand, our Bet Kafe, the first Jewish coffeehouse, attracted large gatherings to its poetry readings and folk music sessions. In the 1980s and early 1990s we organized several singles groups, each of which flourished for a short time and then faded away.

Several times, in both Greenwich Village and Gramercy Park, my wife and I tried to organize a Couples' Club for younger members, but somehow the idea never took hold. However, our efforts did afford us an opportunity to become better acquainted with many talented young people, a number of whom became active in the congregation.

To some extent the development and expansion of auxiliary groups in our Synagogue may have been limited by the fact that we have been an independent congregation and did not have available the professional resources of the national congregational organizations. Nevertheless, our membership includes many young couples as well as single men and women of all ages who attend services regularly, enroll in adult education classes, participate actively on committees and serve on the Board.

A friend once wrote, "Participation in the building of a Temple to the Lord is the greatest and most rewarding mitzvah."

The Police Call for Help

When the New York City Police Academy, just half a block away, received a bomb threat and had to evacuate its building, the officials asked if they could send the recruits over to the Synagogue for a few hours. Soon hundreds of young men and women marched into the sanctuary, for most of them their first time in a synagogue. We explained some aspects of Jewish life, showed them religious vestments, and tried to calm their anxiety. Later, when Academy instructors asked them to write about this experience, some of the young people candidly revealed their misconceptions and apprehensions: "When I was in the Synagogue all of my prejudices and misbeliefs left me," said one recruit. Another confessed: "To see the Jewish faith, its people and practice close up, diminished my fear of the Jew." One recruit wrote that he realized "that they [the Jews] are a people with pride and substance just like me." Others acknowledged, "It was quite an honor to finally enter a synagogue."

11

"The People's Synagogue"

*"It is not enough for a synagogue to be a
place of worship and a seat of education. It
must also be a center for community service."*

RABBI SIDNEY E. GOLDSTEIN

Once it became known that The Brotherhood Synagogue had acquired and restored a landmark building in the famed Gramercy Park historic district, we were inundated by requests to use our facilities.

We did our best to accommodate groups such as block associations, residents of nearby apartment houses, neighborhood civic groups, and a plethora of Jewish organizations, all of which constantly need space for meetings and programs. Moreover, we offered the best possible financial arrangements for eleemosynary institutions—"no charge," for fundamentally we are all doing the same work. Houses of worship ought not be in the rental business. Furthermore, it has been my experience that most civic organizations make generous voluntary contributions to cover expenses.

A variety of support groups were welcomed: families of Alzheimer patients, families of depressives, Holocaust survivor groups such as Second Generation and Hidden Children, and study groups for recovering Jewish addicts. A chapter of

Alcoholics Anonymous (AA) continues to hold weekly meetings in our building. One of the AA members wrote, "The door opened to us began, for many, a new life of hope and the support so necessary for a continued life of sobriety."

Because I was active in many Jewish and ecumenical organizations, it was natural that they would meet in our building from time to time. Here plans were made to rescue Ethiopian Jews, to reach out to communities around the world searching for their Jewish roots, to develop relationships between Christian denominations and the Jewish community, to teach Jewish educators, to understand problems facing Israel, and to foster better relations between blacks and Jews. Several programs were particularly exciting: a meeting and a luncheon for 75 African-American and Jewish clergy; dialogues between black and Jewish teenagers; model Passover Seders arranged by the Anti-Defamation League (ADL) as part of its "World of Difference" initiative to promote understanding and friendship among Jewish, African-American, and Hispanic congregations.

One Seder stands out in my mind. I had passed the *afikomen* (a symbolic piece of broken matzah) to one of the African-American ministers to hide, according to the custom. When it came time for the children to look for it, two youngsters in our congregation crawled up on his lap begging him to tell them where it was hidden. The children knew that he knew where the *afikomen* was hidden. If they could find it, they would get a prize. I'll never forget his kind face and loving arms embracing the children.

While remaining nonpartisan, our Synagogue encouraged political awareness by conducting open discussions with Concerned Citizens Speak, an active neighborhood civic group, featuring mayors, police commissioners, and other high-ranking officials.

Members of Congress periodically hold "town meetings" here, and for fifteen years we arranged annual pre-election forums initiated by my son, Herbert, and chaired by him for many years. They gained such a fine reputation that for city and local candidates for public office the forums became known as "the place to be."

Periodically we hosted the community Thanksgiving Eve service in cooperation with the committee of local clergy. In keeping with our efforts to assist the needy, the building became a central drop-off location for contributions of clothing and food.

One December day I received a call from the president of the Lexington East Twenties Society (LETS) with a pressing problem: because Christmas and New Year's Day would fall on Fridays that year, senior citizen centers and other agencies would be closed, with the result that needy elderly people who depended on the hot meals they served would have nothing to eat for two three-day holiday weekends; there would also be no deliveries to the homebound. Could their clients pick up their food packages at the Synagogue on those two Fridays?

We were more than willing to help, but first I had to explain that we could not handle nonkosher food in our building. LETS agreed to order kosher packages, and I called a kosher caterer, who agreed to prepare 375 dinners each of the two weekends. To solve the problem of delivery of the meals-on-wheels, our always resourceful Executive Director, Phillip Rothman, called on our members. The response was immediate. They not only came but brought their cars. It was a real *mitzvah* and opened our eyes to the impoverished and often squalid conditions in which many people were living, just a few blocks from elegant Gramercy Park.

Groups visiting sites of Jewish interest in the city often included us on their itinerary. Others, such as ORT (Organization for Rehabilitation Through Training) and Hadassah, met here regularly. The Synagogue also became a regular stop on walking tours of the neighborhood. The more who came, the more pleased I was. Whenever possible, I tried to greet each group personally, to relate not only the history of the building but also the philosophy of the congregation.

One year, prior to a United Nations session on disarmament, we opened our doors for a rally attended by several hundred people who had come to hear Grandfather David Monongye, a 100-year-old Hopi Indian elder, and the Venerable Fujii, a Japanese monk, express the hope of the prophet Micah that nations will learn war no more. On another occasion we also made our building available to the Office of Tibet and the New York Association of New Americans for a solemn Oriental peace and brotherhood presentation, with personal representatives of the Dalai Lama in attendance. As the shrill tones of horns were sounded, I couldn't help but shout, "Next year in Tibet!"

A columnist for *New York Press*, a local publication, writing about "the best" places in the city for various activities, cited The Brotherhood Synagogue as "the best place to think," calling it

> a sanctuary in which to collect our thoughts. Going to the chapel will elicit peace anytime of the workday or weekend. All denominations are invited. There is little light, the place is clean, the air is somehow cleaner than outside and nobody bothers you. Before you enter, however, check in at the office so they don't think you're ripping them off. Hey, this is the city.

THE RUSSIANS ARE COMING

So great is the injunction in Jewish law to redeem captives (*pidyon shevu-im*), that it supersedes even the requirements to feed and clothe the poor. After the end of World War II, caring for the enormous number of refugees and displaced persons (DPs) led to the establishment of special agencies to "receive, resettle, and retrain." For over two decades our congregation was very much involved in this *mitzvah*.

Of the hundreds of thousands of DPs, 200,000 were Jewish. In 1946 the United Service for New Americans (USNA) was organized to assist immigrants to the United States. In 1948 Congress passed the Displaced Persons Act, allowing DPs to immigrate to America, and a year later the New York Association for New Americans (NYANA) was founded, with a staff of 590 from the USNA. For more than a decade (1984–1995) I was honored to serve on NYANA's Board of Directors with a superb professional staff and volunteers deeply committed to putting into practice the values of justice, compassion, and freedom.

NYANA helped resettle 38,000 Jewish refugees from Greece, Hungary, Egypt, Rumania, Cuba, Czechoslovakia, Poland, the Soviet Union, Syria, Iran, Ethiopia, and Afghanistan. By 1972, at the behest of the American government, NYANA was also assisting non-Jewish refugees from Uganda, Vietnam, and Cambodia, including "boat people," and cooperated wholeheartedly with the Tibetan–U.S. Resettlement Project. No other resettlement organization in this country has had such extensive experience.

But it is probably the resettlement of Russian Jews for which NYANA is best-known. For years the Jewish world had been clamoring for the release of Soviet Jews who wished to emigrate and live unhampered by the restrictions and discrimination of a society that had brutalized the Jewish community. The teaching of Hebrew was considered a crime, and to identify oneself as a Jew meant a willingness to endanger one's life.

Our congregation participated in the annual Solidarity Sunday marches on behalf of Soviet Jews, and several children in our Religious School "twinned" with a Soviet Jewish boy or girl, whose name was then recited during our worship service so that the child could symbolically have a Bar or Bat Mitzvah.

In 1969 Russia issued 13,000 exit visas. Of the 11,000 men, women, and children who decided to come to the United States, about half chose New York as their destination. Of these, 95 percent were assisted by NYANA. The flow peaked in 1979 with the arrival of 14,000 Soviet immigrants in New York.

Ten years later, when restrictions eased under the leadership of Mikhail Gorbachev, 40,000 Soviet Jews left their native land and about half arrived in New York, where NYANA, with funding from United Jewish Appeal–Federation, managed their resettlement. NYANA representatives greeted the newcomers at the airport, provided temporary housing, set up English language and American history classes, arranged for health care, offered vocational training or retraining and job placement, obtained scholarships, and even taught the skills needed to manage daily life in New York. Above all, NYANA enabled the new Americans to maintain their dignity.

Locally, our Synagogue, together with other congregations in the neighborhood, organized a program to welcome the new arrivals, arranging periodic visits to nearby hotels where many of the newcomers were first housed, so that their initial contact with the New York Jewish community would be pleasant and joyful.

For Jewish immigrants NYANA developed an extensive acculturation program. In 1975, when Edna Rosenman, then NYANA's
Director of Community Services, was planning workshops about
Jewish holidays and festivals, she turned to our Synagogue, located just four blocks from NYANA, for assistance. She was also
aware, she explained later, of our reputation as a warm and welcoming congregation, traditionally oriented but not dogmatic in
approach. We offered to hold the workshops in our Synagogue,
for the quintessential element of our work as a congregation is
that the ideal of religious brotherhood obliges us not simply to
live and let live, but also to *help* live.

From then on, and for a number of years, groups of several hundred new Americans from the Soviet Union, Iran, and Eastern
Europe visited our sanctuary several times a year. For most, it was
their first time in a synagogue, the first time they could see, hold,
and caress a Torah and kiss its mantle. Tears flowed, but these
were tears of joy and relief that they no longer had to be afraid
to express their Judaism publicly.

With Russian and Farsi translators at my side, I greeted our visitors and explained the beauty of our heritage and traditions. I
usually began with a brief history of our building—the role of the
Quakers in helping slaves find freedom during the Civil War, and
decades later assisting refugees after World War II—and pointed
out that the two congregations that have worshipped in the
building, one Quaker, one Jewish, have always been guided by a
desire to bring hope and help to people of diverse backgrounds,
just as NYANA does.

The workshops focused on the customs and practices of the
Sabbath, the High Holydays, and the festivals and holidays.
Together parents and children joyfully made *Kiddush* and recited
the *motzi* (blessing over the bread), listened to the sounds of the

shofar, decorated our outdoor succah, lit the Chanukah Menorah, heard the story of deliverance at Purim, tasted the Passover matzah and recounted the epic story of the Exodus from Egypt, and recited the Ten Commandments on Shavuoth. At one program children of our Religious School mingled with our guests and made them feel at home. Following each workshop, NYANA arranged a party, and the spirit was so *lebedik* (lively) that I invariably joined the circle of dancers.

One Soviet Jewish family became part of our congregation and was befriended by our members. They often thanked us for restoring their spirit for life and making them feel like "normal people" again. When a brother, suffering from a life-threatening heart condition, followed them to New York a few years later, members of our congregation helped arrange his care.

It was a privilege to work with outstanding Jewish communal professionals, in particular NYANA's Executive Vice President, Mark Handelman, and Mrs. Rosenman, and the truly dedicated and caring officers and Board, who presented me with NYANA's Distinguished Service Award for "helping countless Jewish refugees return to the faith of their people."

Perhaps I myself did not fully recognize the impact the workshop project had on others until I read excerpts from a sermon to his New England congregation by the Reverend Thomas Damrosch, who had spent seven months in our Synagogue as a student intern from the General Theological Seminary. He recalled a particular experience:

> That year at The Brotherhood Synagogue, in New York City, I met a group of people to whom deliverance from persecution and hardship had very immediate meaning. We were visited by a group of nearly a hundred new Jewish immigrants to this country. Some had just arrived from the Soviet Union, the rest from Iran. We ate and drank

together in the Harvest Booth, the succah, in the front yard, in public, without fear of persecution. Inside the Synagogue, the Ark was opened, and weeping women and men touched the sacred scrolls of the Torah as free people. It was a unique experience to be there as a Christian.... At least for that moment, all of us had a glimpse of the possibility of a true humanity.

REACHING OUT TO THE DEVELOPMENTALLY DISABLED

A Hasidic grandfather, the renowned Rabbi Shneur Zalman, chided his son for being so immersed in his Judaic studies that he was unaware that his child had fallen out of his crib and was crying. The grandfather remonstrated; "To be engrossed in learning and meditation is indeed very lofty. Yet one should never be insensitive to the cries of a child."

Thirty years ago in Greenwich Village The Brotherhood Synagogue established a special program of religious education for mentally retarded children. After we moved to Gramercy Park, we learned that there were several residences in the neighborhood for working adults with developmental disabilities. Although many residents were Jewish, they had very little contact with Jewish life. Realizing that here was a need we should meet, we initiated a special program where they could learn about Jewish traditions, celebrate the holidays, and socialize. Our staff called them the "SPEC" group (special education class), and they often invited non-Jewish fellow residents to join with them. The needs of an adult group were naturally different, but the principle was the same—God's house should be open to everyone.

One of our first decisions was to offer the men and women in the program membership in the Synagogue, for we recognized their desire to feel part of a congregation. "By giving members of your community an opportunity to know people with disabilities, you are performing a fine job of community education," said Dr. I. Joseph Harris, then Associate Commissioner for Mental Retardation Services in New York City. "You are dispelling myths and quelling fears, fears often born of lack of exposure to people who are different." One year when our congregation sponsored a fund-raising breakfast for the United Jewish Appeal, I suggested that we invite the SPEC group. Some members of the planning committee were leery, concerned that the class might become restless and talkative and disturb guests at nearby tables. But I insisted. As I had anticipated, they not only were attentive and courteous, but made a most generous contribution—a clear demonstration of how dignity begets dignity.

On a bus tour to places of Jewish interest in New York City, led by our Trustee Dr. Sam Brown, a popular tour guide, the group was warmly received at each stop. If it was a synagogue, someone was sure to ask whether that congregation had a special class for "people like us." We soon realized that our program was unique.

Thanks to the generosity of a number of our congregants, the class regularly enjoyed festive Chanukah parties, with good kosher deli and gifts, as well as lovely model Passover Seders. We also tutored those who wished to prepare for an adult Bar or Bat Mitzvah and provided a Kiddush in their honor. The group participated in a Sabbath service once or twice a year, their roles assigned by their teacher, Kenneth Fried; they loved it and came up to the altar smiling and happy. One young man especially enjoyed delivering a speech and proved to be very articulate and quite poetic in his remarks.

Two brothers in this program decided to celebrate their Bar Mitzvah together. Since their family was part of the congregation, we were particularly anxious that everything go smoothly, and it did. Each recited his portion to the best of his ability. Then, unexpectedly, the younger brother turned to me and asked permission to deliver a short speech. There was a murmur of anticipation as I introduced him. Slowly, he began: "I hope that I can do good things for the Jewish people as did my great, great, great, great, great grandfather, the Baal Shem Tov." Then he sat down. It was very quiet; then the handkerchiefs came out.

At a symposium on programs for the developmentally disabled, where The Brotherhood Synagogue received an award for outstanding achievement, one of the speakers was the renowned civil rights leader Bayard Rustin. A Quaker himself, Mr. Rustin was pleased that our congregation had acquired the 20th Street Friends Meeting House, where he had often worshipped.

These were trail-blazing initiatives. The effect of our work lives on as parents still reflect on the times when their young children attended classes and always felt so much at ease. When I retired, a mother wrote to me that she appreciated what we did for the youngsters then, and for her own adult son now. "There was always space," she reminisced, "and an invitation for participating in holidays and the Sabbath, plus a Sunday School program for these men and women."

Another parent, who had enrolled her daughter in our original class in the 1960s, noted that our program was "instituted at a time when very few people or organizations were including anyone who was 'different'" and that "the religious training these children received stayed with them for many years."

SHELTERING THE HOMELESS

At the close of the nineteenth-century when a fire broke out in the eastern European city of Brisk, seat of famed Rabbi Chaim

Soloveitchik, destroying a number of homes, the Rabbi not only invited the homeless residents to sleep in the synagogue until their houses could be rebuilt, but he joined them each night. "As long as there are homeless," he said, "I want to share their anguish and deprivation."

In twentieth-century New York the number of homeless men, women, and children had increased to alarming proportions by the early 1980s. No matter what the city administration did to expand the number of shelters, it was never sufficient. To confront this emergency, Mayor Edward I. Koch exhorted religious institutions to consider providing mini-shelters that could house five to ten homeless guests each night. A number of churches were already involved in such efforts, but glaringly absent were synagogues. It was not that Jewish congregations were insensitive to the plight of the poor and needy or unmindful of the concept of charity. Quite the contrary. The very word *tzedakah* (charity, righteousness) is ingrained in the Jewish soul; but somehow the concept of providing on-site shelters in synagogues had not yet taken hold.

In January 1983 Mayor Koch, himself a Jew, strongly reprimanded the Jewish community because not a single synagogue had enlisted in the shelter program. A few days later the Mayor repeated this charge at a special meeting of The New York Board of Rabbis, challenging our synagogues to get involved. His plea pained me and filled me with a sense of guilt. I looked around the room and understood my colleagues' hesitation—they were reluctant to make a commitment without advance approval from their Boards; but I could not sit quietly in that hushed and charged atmosphere without responding. I raised my hand and said, "The Brotherhood Synagogue will open its doors to the homeless." The moment I sat down, I too realized that I had a formidable task ahead to convince our Board of Trustees to support my decision.

At an emergency meeting of our Executive Committee I acknowledged that yes, I had offered the facilities of our Synagogue, but I had done so in hope that other neighborhood congregations would join with us. The Executive Committee was not totally opposed to the idea but would have preferred prior evaluation of three major issues: liability, health, and maintenance. For example, the only place the shelter could be set up was in the community room, where Religious School classes and other programs took place. How would the parents react? Would there be a problem of contagion? Would our neighbors protest a shelter on Gramercy Park? I couldn't object to any of these questions, but I argued that if churches could establish shelters, why not synagogues? They must have had the same concerns.

I marshaled my arguments for undertaking this project. "Housing," I asserted, "is a human right." A Hasidic statement proclaims that "a community which has no synagogue and no shelter for the poor must first provide for the poor." Besides, our Synagogue had a reputation as a pioneering congregation and here we had an opportunity to set an example. Quietly, I turned my heart to Heaven and pleaded; "Lord, caring for the homeless is also Your responsibility. I want to do *Your* will, so please do mine and help pass this motion!"

We posed all our questions to the Partnership for the Homeless, a nonprofit coalition of faith communities founded in 1982 by Peter Smith. Their experience had been that shelters for small groups in houses of worship provide a much more comfortable, beneficial, and safer setting than the large and impersonal armories that house several hundred people a night. Their practical suggestions and reassurance alleviated many of our anxieties.

Our President, Dr. Gerald J. Friedman, proposed that, since I had already offered the use of our building, we should consider ways to fulfill this commitment. The matter then went to the full Board of Trustees, which, in spite of some reservations, overwhelmingly endorsed my proposal. In fact, one winter when severe and bitter cold weather set in early, a Board member who had initially voted against a shelter chastised our staff for not arranging to open it sooner.

We opened our shelter in February 1983 and since then have welcomed eight to ten guests three nights a week during the winter months, providing food, friendly conversation, and a warm night's rest. Our guests are carefully screened by a social service agency, and the city arranges transportation, folding cots, and linens. Volunteers serve a light supper and early breakfast and stay overnight with one of the Synagogue's sextons. The project's overall coordinator, Wally Dobelis, is a caring, sensible man who knows how to make our guests feel welcome and comfortable.

Mayor Koch attended the formal opening of our shelter, which was reported in the *New York Times*, and he jokingly tossed a quarter onto a cot to test how tightly the sheets were fitted. We received a high grade. Once again The Brotherhood Synagogue had led the way. Soon after, two other rabbis, one in Queens and one in Brooklyn, also offered to participate in the program.

We were dismayed to learn the background of some of the guests. One was a college professor who had lost his job. There was a noncommissioned Naval Reserve officer, and his wife, whose monthly stipend was inadequate to support them. Interestingly, several guests returned after their lives had stabilized and volunteered their services as a way of thanking us for helping them in a time of need.

Some would argue that the state and the city have the primary responsibility to provide shelter for the homeless, but I believe that a house of worship should not expect government to do what it is not willing to do. As Isaiah proclaimed, to feed the hungry, clothe the naked, and shelter the homeless are among our most fundamental religious obligations.

The reaction of the community was very positive. Sister Josephine Tsuei, the President of nearby Cabrini Medical Center, wrote, "God bless you for your leadership in promoting brotherhood among men."

Even more important is the example we set for our children. A young man donated some Bar Mitzvah gift money "to help out." When a child asked why cots were being set up and was told about the shelter, he reflected, "I'm really proud to be a member of a synagogue that does this to help homeless people."

CULTURE AND THE ARTS

As civilization developed, people turned to music and art for new dimensions in their harsh lives, as has been clearly revealed by archeological discoveries of primitive musical instruments, delicate pottery, sculptured figures, and graceful drawings of animals on the walls of caves. King David was a singer and a harpist; Miriam led the women of Israel in dance and song after the crossing of the Red Sea, rejoicing with timbrels; cornets were sounded to herald major events and to muster able-bodied men in times of crisis; and music accompanied the worship services in the ancient Temple.

The Lord Himself was the great Architect who specified the designs of the Tabernacle in the wilderness and the Temple in

Jerusalem, using the finest materials, precious stones and metals. "Worship the Lord in the beauty of holiness," exhorted the Psalmist. Bezalel and Oholieb, gifted artists chosen for this sacred task by the Lord, supervised the artisans who crafted the holy vessels and vestments.

Because I believe that music is a universal language of brotherhood by which heart speaks to heart and soul to soul, The Brotherhood Synagogue has always made our sanctuary available for music. As Rabbi Nachman of Bratzlev declared, "Nature is saturated with melody, heaven and earth are full of song."

As with music so with art. The artist is one to whom all experiences are revelation. The rabbis of old often alluded to the overwhelming power of the artist, even going so far as to consider artists superior to prophets, for while a prophet perceives emanations of God's glory and power only intermittently, an artist is inspired by a continuous awareness of the power of creativity.

Presenting cultural programs was in keeping with our outreach efforts, observed Roslyn Statsinger, who chaired our art shows for several years, to educate the community not just about our religious traditions but also about our artistic heritage.

One of the important programs after our coming to Gramercy Park was a series of art shows, exhibiting paintings, drawings, prints, sculpture, and Judaica by leading contemporary artists such as Larry Rivers, Will Barnet, Roy Lichtenstein, and Robert Rauschenberg, as well as works by the noted Jewish artists Chaim Gross and Rafael Soyer. The first show, organized by Rema Freiberger, was held in 1976 and was so well received that it became a major event for several years.

Each show was a gala occasion and required a year of preparation, and each one was hung so beautifully that it transformed our community room into an elegant art gallery. The last art show, in 1991, was chaired once again by Mrs. Statsinger, with her husband, Irving, a past President of our congregation. The art was of the highest quality, attracting a constant stream of visitors, and proceeds helped defray the costs of renovating our building and meeting our mortgage obligations.

A question raised repeatedly is whether nonsacred music is appropriate in a synagogue. Rabbinic opinions vary, from a more restrictive approach to a more permissive viewpoint. However, one has to use judgment and always ask a number of specific questions about the program before approving an event sponsored by an outside group.

Because of the excellent acoustics in our sanctuary, community orchestras, bands, and choral groups asked if we could provide space and rehearsal time. In return, they would present concerts in our building—always including Jewish music. We tried to oblige when our schedule permitted. Over time the Synagogue has been home to the Dessoff Choirs, the Goodman Chamber Choir, the Shirah Choir, and later the Gramercy Brass.

To express its gratitude, the Gramercy Brass, under the baton of John Henry Lambert, Jr., son of Salvation Army friends, has regaled the community with a Thanksgiving holiday concert in the sanctuary. In celebration of Israel's 40th anniversary of independence, the famed Boys Choir of Harlem sang with the Shirah Choir at a program co-sponsored by the Manhattan Borough President, David N. Dinkins, and Ambassador Moshe Yegar, Consul General of Israel.

One year, in honor of Jewish Music Month, our congregational choir and 50 members from New York area choirs gave a concert of Jewish liturgical works seldom heard in this country. Other groups that have performed here include the Jewish People's

Philharmonic Chorus, with programs of Yiddish songs, and the Jewish Choir of Finland.

Other fine musical programs were arranged by the Sisterhood, and The Doctors' Orchestral Society. Among our most successful community events were free Sunday afternoon concerts held under the auspices of Friends of Young Musicians, an organization founded to provide concert experience for exceptionally gifted young artists. Cantorial concerts were always popular. Cantor Abraham Wolkin frequently performed with his choir. For many years our longtime Cantor, Leib Mirkovic, and later Cantor Herman Diamond, and I presented an annual "Sermon in Jewish Music." We would select a theme, which the Cantor presented in song while I explained how the music illustrated the significance of the written words.

Among our members was the renowned film director and producer Joseph Green, who made the first Yiddish talking movies, starring Molly Picon among others. Produced on location in Poland between 1935 and 1938, just prior to the German invasion, his four films document and preserve the way of life in Eastern Europe for a Jewish population of several million, most of whom perished in the Holocaust. Mr. Green made the films available to our Synagogue for Yiddish film festivals that drew hundreds to our building.

Another celebrated filmmaker to share his work with our Synagogue was Harry Rasky, a member of our congregation in Greenwich Village, who had won an Academy Award for his documentary on Marc Chagall. In 1991 Mr. Rasky came to New York from his home in Canada for a screening of his film "To Mend the World," shown in our sanctuary as part of an evening commemorating Yom Hashoah (Holocaust Remembrance Day). The event was co-sponsored by our neighbor the National Arts Club.

When our congregation was located in Greenwich Village, we co-sponsored the Greenwich Mews Theatre, housed in our building. That tradition continued on Gramercy Park with readings of plays on Jewish themes by our member Nomi Rubel; and it was in our sanctuary that the great Yiddish actress Ida Kaminska gave her final performance.

Synagogues are also educational institutions. Our adult classes offered a wide range of subjects, from Hebrew and Yiddish language courses to studies in Bible, Talmud, Jewish history, and literature. In the 1980s we initiated scholars-in-residence programs with outstanding educators such as Dr. Abraham I. Katsh, President Emeritus of Dropsie University in Philadelphia, and Professor Norman Redlich, one of our members, former Dean of the New York University School of Law. In addition, I frequently invited to the pulpit distinguished speakers of many backgrounds and faiths—ambassadors, bishops, college professors, public officials, university presidents, and other personalities, in the fields of religion, government, international affairs, medicine, education, science, and the arts.

The Library Committee, chaired for many years by Phyllis Block, organized a Jewish book fair and a popular series of "Meet the Author" talks, presenting well-known literary figures, as well as prominent writers in our own congregation.

For several years The Brotherhood Synagogue has welcomed the family and devotees of Sholom Aleichem to the annual *yahrzeit* (anniversary of death) reading of his will and humorous stories. This program is particularly fitting since his grandson, Dr. Sherwin Kaufman, and his family have been members of our Synagogue since our early years.

The Brotherhood Synagogue is blessed with a beautiful historic building, and its beauty is greatly enhanced by service to the community. "It is important to work to keep life within our landmarks," said Gene Norman, a former Chairman of the Landmarks Preservation Commission, in addressing our congregation. This is exactly what our Synagogue has sought to accomplish.

EXPLOSION ENDANGERS SYNAGOGUE

In the summer my family and I usually enjoy a late afternoon stroll on Shabbat, but Saturday, August 19, 1989, was a drizzly, cloudy day, so we decided to stay in. About 6:30 P.M. we were startled by a tremendous blast, and then from our windows we saw huge clouds of dark smoke billowing into the air near the corner of 20th Street and Third Avenue, almost obliterating a 20-story apartment house (No. 32 Gramercy Park South), just a block away from our home. "My God! Oh my God!" I exclaimed. Fearful that the building, just a few doors east of our Synagogue (No. 28) was about to collapse, we rushed down to the street, as did everyone else. No one knew what had happened, but the continuous roaring sound was terrifying and unnerving. There was also fear of a gas main explosion. The police quickly cordoned off the streets and evacuated people from their homes. With dozens of rescue vehicles arriving, their sirens screaming, the area seemed like a battlefield.

At the same time we were very anxious about my elderly mother-in-law, who lived with a home attendant just a few floors below us. As it turned out, they had left the apartment moments after the blast and fled to safety several blocks away, but we didn't know that, so Herbert ran back into the building to try to find his grandmother. We said the evening prayers out on the street, thinking of our family and the safety of the community. I looked around for members of the congregation living in No. 32 and wanted to rush over to the Synagogue, which was only about 50 feet from the site of the explosion; but there was no way I could get there since the police would not permit pedestrians on the street, not even the Rabbi.

Four hours later people in our apartment house were allowed to return home. As soon as we walked in, the phone rang. It was Phyllis's mother's aide calling from a nearby hospital. Mom was obviously frightened, not knowing where we were, but otherwise all right, and we were able to bring her home that night.

Eventually we learned that a Con Edison steam pipe running along East 20th Street had ruptured, killing a young mother napping in her apartment and two Con Edison workers. Had the weather been pleasant, the sidewalk cafe directly across the street from No. 32 would have been busy and the death toll might well have been higher. Miraculously, the doorman's life was spared because he had just stepped away to discard something into the trash basket on the corner.

Rabbi Daniel Alder, who had just begun his service with the congregation, my son, and I went over to the emergency shelter set up in the gym at the nearby Police Academy, going from aisle to aisle looking for our members and neighbors and offering whatever help and solace we could. The next day we heard that one of our members, who owned a dress shop in No. 32, had been trapped inside with a saleswoman for what seemed to them like an eternity before they were able to race out to safety.

When we went into the Synagogue the next morning, we were relieved to find no outward signs of damage. All week, as the media focused on the neighborhood, members, friends, and public officials called or stopped by the Synagogue to offer assistance. The staff and I worked in the office for the rest of the week while the street was being repaired.

At noon on Friday, with no advance warning, city officials arrived and gave us two hours to evacuate the Synagogue because of asbestos contamination in the immediate vicinity. Some apartment houses, businesses, and our Synagogue would have to be closed indefinitely until the asbestos could be abated and interiors and exteriors cleaned and washed.

The High Holydays were now less than a month away, but our immediate concern was where to worship in the interim. There was no time to notify our members and make arrangements for the coming Shabbat, which upset me terribly because this would probably be the first time that we would not worship together as a congregation. I promised myself that the following week we would be reunited.

Our neighbors were also given only a couple of hours to pack a few possessions, leave their homes, and move into the Gramercy Park Hotel and other facilities Con Edison had rented for them. I brought important Synagogue records and files to my home, and, after ensuring the safety of the Torahs, I paused to say a prayer of thanks to God that we had been spared.

The community was furious and bitter at the revelations about the presence of asbestos and fearful of its potential danger. Fortunately, the Synagogue had been closed at the time of the explosion, and tests indicated that the interior had not been contaminated.

Within a few days workers began erecting scaffolding around No. 32, two nearby smaller apartment houses, and the Synagogue, and they wrapped the buildings in white plastic. It was an eerie sight—workers wearing protective spacesuit-type garb and masks crawling over the buildings and literally washing every inch of walls and windows. The plants and soil in our two gardens had to be sacrificed, but thankfully the Wall of Memory in the Garden of Remembrance was saved. For months the Gramercy Park neighborhood was characterized around the city as "asbestos alley," and people were reluctant, even afraid, to come into the area.

Nearby synagogues, churches, and schools called to offer us space for services, classes, and meetings. Their support and concern helped us maintain a semblance of normal operations during this traumatic period. A Bar Mitzvah scheduled for the end of September was moved to nearby East End Temple, and a memorial service took place in The Village Temple on East 12th Street.

Our immediate problems now were to decide where to conduct High Holyday services, find a suitable location for a September wedding, and arrange classroom space for the Religious School.

The wedding had been scheduled to take place in our sanctuary, with a reception at the Gramercy Park Hotel, but 20th Street was now closed to pedestrians and traffic and the abatement process would obviously not be completed in time. The families were understandably distraught and asked if the ceremony could possibly be held in Gramercy Park itself. I explained that weddings in the Park were not permitted, but the family pleaded with me to speak directly to the Chairwoman of the Park Trustees, Mrs. Constance Gibson. I was skeptical but promised to do so. I called, she listened, and even before I had a chance to finish, she responded, "Of course!" Everyone was relieved and elated. Con Edison and the Police Department assisted with the arrangements, and even the weather was perfect. The musicians set up their instruments; the Synagogue provided the *chuppa* and chairs; three rabbis officiated as passersby peered through the Park fence. When the ceremony was over, Con Edison staff posed the bride and groom in hard hats.

The work of the congregation continued in a suite at the hotel, where we could keep appointments, and in a trailer on 21st Street, complete with telephones, typewriters, and copiers. For the first two weeks our office had been operating from my apartment. Rabbi Alder, Phillip Rothman, and our staff were extremely good-natured and efficient throughout the crisis. Everyone pitched in and neighbors even cared for our terrified Synagogue cat, Kinneret. Rabbi Alder and I provided counseling for residents evacuated from their apartments, and our sextons offered to help them with errands and chores. In a story about the explosion and its aftermath the *New York Times* referred to us as the "Friendship" Synagogue, and when you come to think of it, it was not such a serious error!

Our Synagogue and Calvary Church co-sponsored a service of prayer and thanksgiving, gathering in the church sanctuary to remember the two workers and young mother who had lost their lives and to pray for the recovery of the injured, grateful that our community had not suffered a greater disaster.

Meantime, we had asked Con Edison to inquire if the facilities of Baruch College of the City University of New York might be available to us for the High Holydays. The location was perfect— on East 23rd Street, three blocks from our Synagogue; the college would be closed on Rosh Hashanah and Yom Kippur in any event, and the main auditorium seated 1,300. I told one of Con Edison's representatives, "Be sure to mention my name to the President of Baruch, Dr. Joel Segall." The college staff did everything, and more, to accommodate our needs.

As I prepared my sermons and looked ahead to the High Holydays, I thought back to our year of wandering after we left Greenwich Village. Our activities were now spread out all over the Gramercy Park neighborhood: Board meetings at Calvary Church;

Sisterhood meetings and adult education classes at the Salvation Army residence; Religious School at the Jack and Jill School and Friends Seminary; Shabbat services alternating between East End Temple and Town and Village Synagogue. It was a challenge just to keep our members informed where programs and services would be held each week.

It would be three months before the City Department of Environmental Protection permitted the congregation to return to our building. Although we rejoiced in coming home, we had mingled emotions, since our neighbors were still living in temporary quarters and had lost many of their possessions. Some of our congregants, especially Religious School parents, were still worried about asbestos in the area and contamination in our building. Even though we resumed worship services and our office reopened, we continued to hold classes elsewhere until the interior of the Synagogue could be thoroughly cleaned and painted.

At the end of the year we held a *chanukat ha-bayit* service (rededication of the house) to give praise to God, whose mercy had brought us home again, and to express appreciation to the community for its concern and enormous assistance. Nevertheless, it would be almost a year before life in the neighborhood returned to normal.

Thanks to the skillful and persistent negotiations of Arthur Abbey, a Synagogue officer and attorney, Con Edison settled our claim against the company and we looked optimistically to the future. Some months later I read an article describing the restoration of an old, historic home that precisely reflected our feelings about our Synagogue: it stated that when people have renovated a building with love and care, they become bound heart and soul to the site. In the words of the Talmud, "It is a joy to live in one's house."

A MENORAH IN THE PARK

How a Chanukah Menorah was erected in Gramercy Park is a good illustration of the Talmudic adage, "What the mind cannot resolve, time eventually does."

As we planned our move to Gramercy Park, we were aware that the presence of a synagogue would undoubtedly bring changes to a community that had had little contact with the traditions of Jewish life. In 1654 Peter Stuyvesant, the Dutch governor of New Amsterdam who owned the land on which the Park and contiguous neighborhoods were established, reluctantly admitted to the colony 23 Sephardic Jews from Brazil, but only after being ordered to do so by his employer, the Dutch West India Company, and without granting them all of the rights other residents enjoyed.

Neither he nor Samuel Ruggles, who developed Gramercy Park in 1831, could have predicted the growing number of Jewish families in the area in the mid-twentieth century and the arrival of a synagogue that would attract thousands of people throughout the year to the neighborhood, making it a hub of Jewish life.

With good intentions, some people advised us to avoid any overt display of our heritage, but we rejected that approach because it was based on fear and timidity and was unworthy of democratic ideals. Always mindful that whatever we planned should be done in a dignified manner, we affixed a mezuzah on the front doorpost and a Menorah to the façade, placed a granite cornerstone engraved with Hebrew words in our Garden of Remembrance, and each fall set up a large colorful succah in our courtyard.

After our move to the community, I made a formal request to Mrs. Gibson, Chairwoman of the Park Trustees, for permission to display a large Chanukah Menorah inside the Park. I called attention to the fact that many members of our congregation lived around the Park and that there was a large Jewish population in the community. I had the full support of the Reverend Thomas F. Pike, who concurred that, since there was a long-established tradition of setting up a Christmas tree in the Park, a Chanukah Menorah was an excellent idea that would enhance the beauty and significance of the holiday season.

But it was not to be. This was not a church–state issue since Gramercy Park is a private property, and no disrespect toward us was intended. But the Trustees regarded the Christmas tree as cultural, and not religious, and a Chanukah Menorah as religious, not cultural. They suggested that perhaps a secular symbol might be more acceptable, but I rejected this proposal. After all, what would I have chosen, a large wooden *dreidel* (top) or a papier-mâché *latke* (pancake)?

I decided to bide my time, but whenever I renewed my request, Mrs. Gibson's answer was always the same. Yet in so many other ways she was flexible and always a great friend and admirer of our Synagogue—arranging for us to assemble our Torah procession in the Park when we moved into the building; opening the Park to our worshippers on Yom Kippur afternoon; and allowing us to conduct a wedding in the Park during the steam pipe explosion crisis. A horticulturist herself, she especially loved our succah and gardens.

Fifteen years later, however, the outlook would be different. There had been elections to fill three vacancies among the five Park Trustees. Two of the new Trustees were Jewish, one of them an officer of our congregation and also a lot owner on the Park. There had also been changes in the leadership of the Gramercy Neighborhood Associates (GNA), established in 1912 and one of the city's oldest volunteer civic organizations, promoting the well-being of the area as a whole but with no authority in the administration of the Park itself. The new GNA president, James D. Dougherty, felt very keenly about having a Chanukah Menorah in Gramercy Park and submitted a proposal to the Trustees, now chaired by Mrs. Sharen Benenson. Encouraged by his conversations with them, Mr. Dougherty urged me to broach the subject once again, confident that this time my request would be approved. And it was. He informed me that the GNA would pay for a Chanukah Menorah, just as it does for the Christmas tree. What a thoughtful and generous offer!

"The Brotherhood Synagogue has been a good neighbor and citizen of the Gramercy area for many years," he stated, "and we are delighted to be able to say 'Thank you.'" The selection of the Menorah was left up to the Synagogue, and we invited one of our members, M. Milton Glass's son, Elliott, an architect, and a director of the GNA, to assist us.

And so on November 28, 1994, twenty years after our move to the neighborhood, I lit the first light on the first Chanukah Menorah in 163-year-old Gramercy Park. I called the occasion, just a few months after my retirement, "a dream come true," a demonstration of "the unique respect and understanding the people of Gramercy Park have for one another that is at the heart of what makes New York City so great." All our neighbors were then invited to join us for a party at the Synagogue.

The Chanukah lighting ceremony and celebration are now established events, and Gramercy Park is a spiritually richer community today. As we gaze at the lights of the Menorah and the Christmas tree, how apt are Shakespeare's words. "How far that little candle throws his beams! So shines a good deed in a naughty world."

Boyhood Classmates Meet Again

One day someone mentioned to me that the President of Baruch College, Dr. Joel Segall, had also grown up in Bridgeport, Connecticut, my home town. I decided to get in touch with him and we made a date for lunch. We found out that we had lived in the same neighborhood as children and had even attended the same after-school cheder (daily religious school classes).

At one point in the conversation Dr. Segall mentioned that he had had a paper route and delivered Yiddish newspapers in the neighborhood. "My parents subscribed to the Forward," I told him. "Then I was the one who delivered your paper every day. Every few weeks I would come into the homes of my customers for payment. I must have been in your house many times." I looked at him astonished. He even asked me about some of my cousins whom he remembered from our younger years.

Now, some 50 years later, we found ourselves at the helm of two institutions three blocks from each other, in New York's Gramercy Park community, one a college president, the other a rabbi.

12

Black Jewish Communities

*"When the Lord brought back the exiles that returned
to Zion, we were like dreamers, Our mouths were
filled with laughter, and our tongues with song."*

PSALM 126

THEY HAVE COME HOME

On May 25 and 26, 1991, the glory of the God of Israel did not fail the remnant of the Beta Israel (House of Israel) Ethiopian community who had been languishing for months in the capital at Addis Ababa, waiting to flee a life of oppression for freedom in Israel. Even though the mission had to be carried out on Shabbat, the chief rabbis gave it their full approval, because for *pikkuah nefesh*, the saving of life, the laws of the Torah may be suspended. More than 14,000 Ethiopian Jews were airlifted to Israel that weekend in a remarkably planned 36-hour heroic rescue effort code-named "Operation Solomon," the fulfillment of their age-old dream.

For the Jewish people everywhere it was a moment in which history dramatically unfolded in our presence. With eyes bathed in tears of joy, we watched this dignified and beautiful community come home. For many Ethiopian Jews who had fled the barren desolation of their villages it was the climax of long, dangerous treks across mountains and deserts, exacerbated by the scourge of famine and disease, which took the lives of many family members. Now they sat quietly in the cargo bays of the huge planes, as their priests intoned God's ancient promise, "I will take you unto Me on the wings of an eagle," and implored God with a prayer, "Redeem us speedily for the sake of Thy name." They arrived in Israel with just the clothing on their backs, many without shoes, and some nursing newborns delivered in flight.

Kol ha-kovod, "All praise," to those who planned and executed the operation so meticulously and with such great compassion, caring for the elderly, the sick, the infants. The government of the United States has earned the abiding gratitude of the Jewish people for its vigorous support and intense diplomatic negotiations that resulted in this dramatic and humanitarian airlift, and for an earlier mission, "Operation Moses," during 1984–1985 when some 8,000 Ethiopian Jewish refugees in Sudan were flown to Israel. Israel demonstrated to the world that selfless humanitarian efforts could not only save lives but offer the promise of a better future for our children in generations to come. We pray that those who remain in Ethiopia will soon be reunited with their families in Israel.

For me these rescue efforts were the climax of over 40 years of preaching, imploring, writing, and educating the congregation and community on behalf of Ethiopian Jews. But I do have one regret: I wish I could have been at the airport in Addis Ababa or Israel and been more personally involved in their arrival. Every time I see the photographs of giant aircraft ferrying our people from Africa to the glistening land of promise, my heart swells with joy.

How enormously proud I am of the efforts of members of The Brotherhood Synagogue on behalf of this ancient community.

From our earliest years as a congregation I urged support for the American Pro-Falasha Committee, which subsequently merged with Beta Israel, an Ethiopian-based agency, and the congregation always responded. My brother, Rabbi A. Allen Block, along with Professor Martin Warmbrand, one of our members, and with Leonard Benari, a supporter of African culture, and others helped plead the cause of this isolated and virtually unknown community of Jews.

Even now members of our congregation have made it an assignment on their trips to Israel to visit absorption centers where Ethiopian families reside as well as schools for new immigrants. I was deeply touched by a letter from the director of a community youth agency in the north who told me the story of a couple from our Synagogue who visited his facilities and noticed Ethiopian Jewish youngsters among the residents. Remembering what they had learned about them in our congregation and impressed by the work of this agency in helping them, they made a generous contribution in my honor. Others have from time to time brought me priceless pieces of sculpture and other traditional artifacts fashioned by Ethiopian artisans. I have been so moved by their kindness and their understanding of the problems facing this community as the people strive to adapt to life in Israel and plan for the future.

Many scholars believe the Ethiopian Jews are descendants of Menelek, the son of King Solomon and the Queen of Sheba, who was dispatched to Ethiopia to govern under Solomonic rule. Other historians contend that these Jews, once numbering over half a million, trace their lineage to one of the ten lost tribes, Dan, which may have migrated to Ethiopia after the destruction of the kingdom of Israel in 721 B.C.E. Their Hebraic influence upon the land was strong, their adherents increased in number, and they translated the Pentateuch (the Five Books of Moses) into Geez, the ancient Ethiopian language. However, by the fourth century C.E., with the rise of Christianity, their power waned and their glory faded.

Called "strangers," or "Falashim," they were forced to live in primitive villages in remote mountainous regions in the north, where they struggled to eke out a meager existence from inhospitable farmlands. They were discovered in 1867 by a French Jewish scholar, Professor Joseph Halevi, who encouraged his student, Jacques Faitlovich, to live among the people and learn their ways. It soon became all too evident to him that this Ethiopian community knew virtually nothing of Jewish history, Talmudic discourse, or rabbinic law. Their observance of Jewish laws and customs was limited to those written down in the Pentateuch.

Years would pass before Dr. Faitlovich succeeded in persuading world Jewish organizations to aid their impoverished and beleaguered brethren. Turmoil in the land caused by the Italian war resulted in an upheaval of the Falasha community, many of whom fled to eastern and southern areas of Ethiopia. During the 1930s and 1940s the American Pro-Falasha Committee, either alone or in conjunction with the Beta Israel Committee in Ethiopia, worked to provide the kind of support and assistance these forgotten communities needed if they were to survive. This project became part of an international Jewish community effort that lasted for half a century.

In 1974 Dr. Graenum Berger, a distinguished communal administrator who had headed a leading agency of the Federation of Jewish Philanthropies of New York, convened a meeting in Chicago to bring the plight of Ethiopian Jews to the attention of world Jewry. He founded the American Association for Ethiopian Jews (AAEJ), an advocacy organization committed to sounding the alarm that their ranks were being rapidly decimated by Ethiopia's government-sanctioned anti-Semitism, economic deprivation, and the civil war ravaging the country. The earliest meetings of the AAEJ were held in The Brotherhood Synagogue.

Dr. Berger did not hesitate to speak out and warned the world about the potential genocide facing Ethiopian Jews. They had to be rescued at once, he would assert again and again, and he pleaded with Israel to develop a plan for a massive *aliyah* (immigration to Israel), while simultaneously sending supplies to the many villages that lacked sufficient food to sustain their people. But the major Jewish organizations would not listen, and some even refused to allow him to speak at their conventions. Nevertheless, he persevered and would not be silenced. As an early member of the Board of Directors of the AAEJ, I was aware of the enormous obstacles we had to overcome, not only because of our very limited funds but from the failure of both Israeli government officials and American Jewish leaders to consider saving Ethiopian Jews as a major obligation. On one occasion I sat down at a quiet meeting with an Israeli diplomat and the head of an influential American Jewish organization to explain the urgency of the situation, which, if not resolved soon, might have global repercussions. When asked why the AAEJ was so critical of Israel's slow response, I repeatedly indicated that this was an emergency. Time was of the essence. There is a time for quiet diplomacy and a time for aggressive pressure; now, I insisted, when Jews were suffering, it was imperative to act.

Meanwhile, the AAEJ was ransoming a few Ethiopian Jews at a time, finding often circuitous ways to transport them to Israel. At my urging, members of The Brotherhood Synagogue contributed thousands of dollars to this operation, one of very few synagogues to do so at that time.

Whenever I met or heard of travelers who had returned from a visit to Ethiopia, I invited them to bring the latest news to our congregation, and we participated in every effort to raise funds on behalf of our endangered brethren. Our Religious School children studied about this community and contributed to its support, and they are still doing so on behalf of the Ethiopian Jewish children growing up in Israel.

The Jewish world is indebted to Graenum Berger and his wife, Emma, and to their successors at AAEJ for championing the cause of Ethiopian Jews to the world. Without their years of tireless advocacy, this community might well have disappeared.

In October 1976 our Synagogue Board fulfilled Dr. Berger's request to send a Sefer Torah to the Jewish community in Ambober, in northern Ethiopia. It would be the first time that they would possess a Torah scroll written on parchment; they had been reading from Bibles printed in Geez.

The Torah I selected had been stitched together from sections of parchments, most likely from Torahs that had been rescued and restored after the Holocaust. Such a Torah, I felt, with its parchments of different textures and scripts of various styles, would represent a bond between Ethiopian and world Jewry.

When this Torah arrived in Ethiopia, it was temporarily placed in a synagogue in the capital, Addis Ababa, because one wall of the Ambober synagogue, a circular structure of stone and straw, had collapsed a few weeks before. A corrugated tin roof capped by a bent Star of David protected the bare interior of the Ambober synagogue. There was no cabinet, such as a Holy Ark, in which to place the Torah, nor a lectern or table from which to read. Happily, the synagogue was rebuilt and rededicated, and "our" Torah was brought up from the capital and presented to the

Kesim (elder priests) as hundreds of people gathered for the annual Segged celebration, which for Ethiopian Jews commemorates the rebuilding of the second Temple in Jerusalem.

Other gifts from our congregation soon followed: boxes of *talleisim* (prayer shawls), *tefillin*, skullcaps, and religious books and supplies. Imagine how excited we were, some months later, to recognize in a magazine article on Ethiopian Jewry, "our" Torah, with its distinctive embroidered mantle, being carried in a religious procession by one of the *Kesim*. When at last this community prepared for its exodus, the priests carried this Torah, which found a place of honor in the Holy Ark at an absorption center in Israel. Did not our rabbis say, "Even a Torah has to have *mazal* (luck)"?

Seventeen years later, in 1993, in response to an appeal by Barbara Ribakove Gordon, founder of the North American Conference on Ethiopian Jewry (NACOEJ), we sent a second Torah, this one to a new community in Beersheba, Israel. This gift was made possible by the generosity of Dr. Leo Koven and his wife, Joan, a second-generation family in our Synagogue, who personally brought it to Israel and presented it in memory of the doctor's parents, Max and Sophie Koven, early members of our congregation. The Kovens reported that the presentation ceremony was a unique and festive event led by the *Kesim* in their new synagogue and attended by Israeli officials. NACOEJ takes a vital role in helping meet educational, health, and social needs of Ethiopian Jews while enabling them to preserve their cultural heritage.

No one underestimated the problems of integrating thousands of unskilled newcomers unfamiliar with modern life and hygiene. As happy as they were to be in Israel, they were uncertain and apprehensive about how they would be accepted, and feared rejection. Sadly, they have not been recognized by all rabbinic bodies as bona fide Jews. Former Sephardic Chief Rabbi Obadia Yosef recommended that they go through a ceremony of "renewal of the covenant," which would make them fully recognized as Jews in the State of Israel. But even this simple requirement raised fears among them about their place in Israeli society. The young people are bright and learn quickly, and they serve honorably and valiantly in the Israeli armed forces, but their life is often stressful and at times seemingly hopeless. The poverty rate among these immigrants is high and government absorption efforts have not always been adequate for their special needs. Yet, in spite of the many hurdles they face, in my mind they represent one of the finest elements in the country, worthy of continued assistance from the world Jewish community.

Having accomplished its major mission, the AAEJ dissolved at the end of 1994, but many of its members are supporting programs and activities sponsored by the newly formed Israel Association for Ethiopian Jews (IAEJ).

I am delighted to have been dubbed one of the "grandfathers" of the movement on behalf of Ethiopian Jewry. For its active role in the historic redemption of our people from Ethiopia, a Certificate of Honor was presented to The Brotherhood Synagogue by UJA–Federation. Even more gratifying are the sentiments of Mr. Yona Bogale, a representative of Ethiopian Jewry, addressed to our congregation: "May I express deepest thanks from the entire community for the wonderful gifts which will further contribute to bridge the gap between the Falashas and the Jewish people of the world."

Ethiopian Jews express their faith and their gratitude to the Almighty in this ancient prayer:

Thou art blessed. O Lord,
  be merciful to me.
By day be Thou my shepherd,
  and my guardian at night.
When I walk be my guide,
  when I sit be my Guardian.
When I call Thee,
  keep Thou not silent.

BLACK JEWS IN AMERICA

The north end of Bridgeport, Connecticut, where I lived as a child, was home primarily to Europeans of many backgrounds, with a sprinkling of black families. When on one occasion a black child visited our Talmud Torah (religious school) to enroll in Hebrew classes, I looked forward to making friends with him. But he and his parents moved away, and I lost track of him.

Years later, when I came to New York City to begin my rabbinic studies, my interest was piqued in hearing about a community of Black Jews in Harlem, the Commandment Keepers Congregation, then located at West 128th Street and Lenox Avenue, now at 1 West 123rd Street. Perhaps I could find a clue as to what happened to the family I had met in Bridgeport. But it was not to be.

One Saturday morning in the spring of 1952, I attended services at Commandment Keepers and found them most inspiring. I remember leaving the synagogue exhilarated by the fervor of the worshippers and their prayers, the songs they sang, and the sermonic message of their leader, Rabbi Wentworth Arthur Matthew. The periodic responses of "Hallelujah!" and "Amen" during the sermon added to the joyful mood of the service. When I went there again, I took along members of my family and fellow rabbinic students.

In most congregations, when the Torah is taken out of the Holy Ark, the people sing a Hebrew melody of praise to God during the procession of the Torah scroll around the synagogue. In Rabbi Matthew's synagogue, however, theirs was not the traditional melody of *L'cha*, "Thine O Lord, is the greatness, power, glory..."; rather, they chose a song with a stirring cadence, which in time became a favorite anthem of mine: "We are marching to Zion, beautiful, beautiful Zion. We are marching onward to Zion, the beautiful city of God." I caught myself humming it often.

Shortly after my visit, an article by Harry C. Schnur about the Black Jews of Harlem appeared in the *Congress Weekly*, a publication of the American Jewish Congress. He had attended services at the synagogue about the same time as I had, but his impressions were quite different, to say the least, and his comments disturbed me: he carped about the deviation from the usual traditions and noted errors in Hebrew; he criticized the choir and spoke pejoratively about the rabbi's sermon.

I could not let his complaints go unanswered, and I sent off a "letter to the editor," challenging a number of the author's opinions. "So what if the Hebrew pronunciation of these Black Jews was not so perfect? Whose Hebrew is?" I wrote. So what if their choir is not a professional choral group? Surely the warmth and earnestness of their rendition echo in the heart, and that is where it counts. Would the writer label other Jewish services that do not conform to his upbringing as having "Christian overtones"? Nor did I appreciate his evaluation of the rabbi's sermon, as a "long and rambling discourse."

What the author did, it seemed to me, was to visit a congregation of Black Jews with a predetermined opinion that this synagogue was more a showcase for the curious than a genuine house of worship for the faithful. If, as Mr. Schnur implied, there was a question about whether Rabbi Matthew or his people were authentic Jews, then, I stated, this matter should be brought to rabbinical bodies for adjudication. If they *are* Jews, they should be accepted, encouraged, and assisted by synagogue, rabbinic, and communal organizations.

The writer referred to the congregants as suffering a "double handicap," being both black and Jewish. I countered that rather than being a burden, Judaism has always been a guide to a higher standard of conduct and to a more spiritual life. Rather than being handicapped, Black Jews had a double blessing. Didn't Moses himself marry a Cushite, and Cushites were people of color?

Urged by friends to channel my anger toward a constructive effort on behalf of the Black Jewish community, I wrote to 100 prominent American rabbis throughout the country—Orthodox, Conservative, Reform, and Reconstructionist. I sent them a covering letter with a copy of Mr. Schnur's article and my response to it and asked the rabbis for their comments. I received 35 to 40 replies. Their views varied widely. Some argued that Black Jews were not authentic Jews but a cult seeking to identify with the historic past of the Jewish people. Others stressed that Judaism is color-blind and that it is our responsibility to work with our brothers and sisters in that community. "Let us hope," said one rabbi, "that what Moses did in marrying Zipporah… would be seen as a norm rather than an exception." Reading the diverse responses of the rabbis, I understood that I seemed to be concerned more with Jewish humanity than with Jewish sociology. Nevertheless, I realized that I should research more thoroughly the background and roots of the Black Jewish community in America.

Currently, there is no generally accepted theory as to how, when, and where the Black Jewish community began to take root on American soil, whether by immigration, intermarriage, or conversion. One theory holds that at the time of the Exodus from Egypt (circa 1350 B.C.E.) other Israelites fled westward across the Sahara Desert, in the opposite direction of Moses, and ultimately settled on the west coast of Africa; that during their long journey, they came in contact with the Ashanti tribes of North Africa, whom they taught traditions of their Hebrew forebears. In his book *Hebrewisms of West Africa* (The Dial Press, 1930), Joseph J. Williams claims that eventually this contact between the Israelites and Ashantis led to cultural, religious, and racial integration.

Centuries later, descendants of these ancient Israelites may have been among the slaves brought from West Africa to the West Indies. Were they the ancestors of the Black Jews in America? Or, as time passed, perhaps their descendants were among the slaves eventually transported to the American colonies. Unfortunately there is little scholarly documentation on the subject.

The number of Black Jews in the United States in the antebellum period is also highly speculative. However, by the 1920s some black nationalists were turning toward Judaism under the inspiration of a few charismatic leaders, including Arnold Ford and Wentworth A. Matthew, both of whom had been influenced by Marcus Garvey and his movement to return to Africa.

In some Black Jewish circles there is a desire to shift the focus away from being adherents of Judaism, the "white man's religion," to being "Israelites." Another group, calling themselves "Black Hebrews," claims in effect that theirs is the true faith of the biblical patriarchs, who, they contend, were born in Africa, the continent they consider the cradle of world civilization. "Fair-skinned" Jews are viewed as interlopers, Edomites, who usurped the role of God's chosen people and are to be rejected and spurned.

On the other hand, others in the Black Jewish community share the sentiments of one of their leaders: "I am a Jew," wrote Cantor Eliezer Brooks, "and this is the most important thing to me. I just want the opportunity to be an active Jew, in Torah, in song and in dance to be serving the God of Israel and the Jewish people."[1]

In 1919 Rabbi Matthew, who had been born in Ghana, founded Commandment Keepers Synagogue in Harlem. By the time I met him, he was referring to himself as Chief Rabbi of Black Jews of the Western Hemisphere. Whether he earned the title or assumed it is uncertain, but no other leader commanded the respect of the Black Jewish community and was highly regarded by the King of Ethiopia. He also instructed and ordained many Black Jews for leadership positions, among them Rabbi Small, his close associate for many years, and Rabbi Albert Moses of Congregation Mount Horeb in the Bronx, whose rabbinic staff included many whom Rabbi Matthew had ordained. Eliezer Brooks was called upon to serve as cantor at the Commandment Keepers Congregation in Harlem, while Rabbi Hailu Paris and Cantor Otto Brown served in the Bronx with Rabbi Moses for many years.

I saw in Rabbi Matthew a self-confident man who possessed great inner strength, with a powerful voice that revealed the persuasiveness of a born leader. His piercing, penetrating eyes captured everyone's attention, and with a large white *tallis* wrapped around his broad frame, he cut a striking figure. I would often characterize him as a lion of Judah. We developed a friendship

---

1. Two books, The Black Jews of Harlem by Howard M. Brotz (Schocken Books, 1970), and Black Jews in America by Graenum Berger (Federation of Jewish Philanthropies of New York, 1978), discuss the history of this community.

and I visited his congregation often, trying to help and encourage them as much as I could. I invited Rabbi Matthew and his rabbinic staff to my wedding, and his remarks at the reception were one of the highlights of the day. Members of his synagogue often came to worship with my congregation, where they knew they would always be warmly received.

Just how many Black Jews are there today? The answer is open to debate: Some estimate from 3,000 in the United States to 300,000 in the Western Hemisphere. The fact is that we have no accurate figures. I would say the number is greater than 3,000 and considerably less than 300,000. In many cases congregations of Black Jews have called themselves "Israelites" by virtue of their commitment to the God of Abraham, Isaac, and Jacob. They do not regard the *mikveh* (immersion in water) and *tipas dam* (symbolic circumcision) as essential so long as their hearts feel an attachment to Jewish history and traditions. On the other hand, many Black Jews have undergone conversion according to *Halakhah,* among them the large family and congregants of Rabbi Abel Respes, who founded Congregation Adat Beyt Mosheh in Philadelphia in 1951 and later moved to Hammonton, in southern New Jersey. Some years later Rabbi Respes visited the Land of Israel.

Within the Jewish community, inquiries about Black Jews are usually channeled to me. Lately I have been receiving a number of calls from documentary filmmakers and students writing theses about Black Jews.

Early in our history The Brotherhood Synagogue began to work with Black Jewish young men and women, encouraging them to *daven* (pray) with us and participate in our services. We lent support to the formation of a program called *Hatzaad Harishon*, or "First Step," with the assistance of Canadian Jewish educator

Yaakov Gladstone, Zionist youth organizations, and the Federation of Jewish Philanthropies, to teach Black Jewish teenagers Hebrew, Jewish history, and Jewish culture. Although various problems led the group to disband after a few years, it nevertheless served as a good introduction for these young men and women to the mainstream Jewish world, both here and in Israel, and many went on to greater involvement and achievement in Jewish education and communal service.

Since 1963 our Synagogue has had the privilege of hearing Cantor Brooks, a certified cantor and a rabbi, who has sung and spoken to our congregation so frequently that I often find myself informally introducing him as *chazan sheni*, our second cantor. We have invited rabbis from the Black Jewish community to preach from our pulpit. In 1964 Cantor Otto Brown, who had studied at the Cantorial Institute of Yeshiva University, sang at our summer Sabbath services, assisted by the fine young vocalist Constance Thompson.

Another strong and articulate voice in the Black Jewish community has been Rabbi Hailu Paris, currently the leader of Mt. Horeb congregation in the Bronx, who has often been a guest speaker in our Synagogue. Born in Addis Ababa, he left Ethiopia in 1936 when it was being overrun by Italian fascists. Reared in America— I knew his mother—he studied in Israel, was ordained by Rabbi Matthew, and holds a Bachelor's degree from City College and a Master's degree from Yeshiva University. "The Black Jew's problem," he stated, "is not anti-Semitism, but rather how to maintain his Jewishness." The passing of charismatic leaders like Rabbi Matthew and Rabbi Respes was a great loss for Black Jewish life. "Matthew," Rabbi Paris once commented, "was from the old school. He had strong religious beliefs, he was structured. My generation lost its religious roots."

Today Black Jewish worshippers are joining synagogues all over the country. Year by year the number of adherents grows. A few have affiliated with the Lubavitcher movement. However, congregations whose members are mainly Black Jews continue to function primarily in New York City and Westchester (such as Beth Ha-Tefilah Ethiopian Hebrew Congregation in Mount Vernon, led by Rabbi Yhoshua Ben Yohonatan). But there is no one overall congregational group to which they belong, nor are their rabbis affiliated with the major rabbinic organizations.

Few people are aware that there have been civic leaders and government officials within the Black Jewish community, including a former Deputy New York City Police Commissioner, a former Deputy Commissioner of the Transit Police, and the executive director of an important community organization. In addition, there have been well-known Black Jewish personalities such as the late entertainer Sammy Davis, Jr.; Julius Lester, the author and commentator; Reuben Greenberg, the police chief of a large Southern city; the late Sarah Harvin, lecturer and hostess of a television program; and William Pinkney, the only black man to sail solo around the world. He and his wife, Ina, had been members of The Brotherhood Synagogue when they lived in New York. Before he set sail, he affixed a mezuzah to his boat, and I had a chance to give him a *bracha* (blessing).

There was a time when leaders of the Black Jewish community and I traveled together around New York City to share our experiences. In 1969 newspapers in this country and abroad carried a full-page article about Black Jews and the work of our Synagogue in assisting them, as well as my observations and suggestions for integrating our two communities. It was only natural, therefore, that a number of Jews of African-American descent would be attracted to The Brotherhood Synagogue. Indeed, over the years

Jews of many cultural and racial backgrounds have attended our services: a former Japanese Shinto priest who converted to Judaism, a Mexican Jew from Xhalapa, a young woman convert from the Dominican Republic. Dr. Ephraim Isaac, an Ethiopian Jew with a Yemenite father, who is the Director of the Institute of Semitic Studies at Princeton University, told me that in Ethiopia an American Jew had given him the name of The Brotherhood Synagogue as one to visit when he came to the United States. Later, when Professor Isaac was studying for his Ph.D. at Harvard, he and I served together on the Board of the American Association of Ethiopian Jews.

When informing our Synagogue Board of Trustees of new membership applications, I made it a practice not to mention race. We have welcomed many Black Jews into membership in our congregation, among them Mrs. Alice Horton and her son, Herman (Mordechai), whom I trained for his Bar Mitzvah and whose marriage it was my joy to perform. At one point we had as members five generations of a family, the Harvins, who were longtime and regular worshippers.

Color is no barrier to being selected for a leadership role. We probably were the first synagogue in the United States to have a member of the Black Jewish community as president of the congregation, Vertella Valentine Gadsden. Born in Kingston, Jamaica, the daughter of the founder of Beth B'nai Israel congregation in Harlem, she grew up in New York City where her parents were known as the "kosher Jews of Harlem." As a young girl she was an outstanding student at the West Side Institutional Synagogue. She has also brought her professional skills and management experience to our congregation as Chairman of the Board of Trustees and Sisterhood President.

Black Jews have much to teach us. When confrontations between blacks and whites erupt in cities across America, members of Black Jewish congregations could serve as a bridge if only they had a cadre of strong secular and rabbinic leaders. I have long maintained that who better than they could reach out to people in a time of mistrust, hostility, and anti-Semitism whenever these occur in the black community.

The wider Jewish community must find a way to help groom their bright young men and women for positions of leadership. For years I urged some to enter accredited rabbinical schools and study with outstanding scholars. Their talented vocalists could become *chazanim,* (cantors), and their capable young people trained as Jewish educators and administrators; but first, we must provide scholarships for youngsters whose parents lament that they cannot afford the tuition at Jewish day schools.

It is time—and long overdue—to integrate Black Jews into the activities of the mainstream American Jewish community. Our pulpits should proclaim the mandate of racial equality and religious brotherhood enunciated by the prophet Amos: "Are ye not as the children of the Ethiopians unto Me, O Children of Israel? saith the Lord."

What are we waiting for?

From Panama to New York

One day my wife and I visited a member of the congregation at her home and recognized some pieces of framed folk art as unmistakably of Panamanian origin. "What is your interest in Panama?" I asked. It seemed that she and her family had lived in Europe and found refuge in Panama at the onset of World War II. I mentioned that when I was in the Army I had been stationed there, at Cristobal-Colón on the Atlantic side of the Canal Zone. A few weeks later she came to my office with a photograph showing soldiers and sailors at a Sunday morning coffee klatch at a Jewish Welfare Board facility in Colón. Her mother had been one of the hostesses. This was the same photograph my parents had seen in the Yiddish Forward. From the caption they learned where I was stationed.

I remembered that my friend Cantor Eliezer Brooks had spoken about Panama. The next time I saw him I asked, "Eliezer, didn't you also live in Panama during the war?" "Yes," he said, "I was working for a bus company as a driver and taking personnel from a number of Army posts to and from the city." "Were you a driver of a small jitney?" I asked. "We called them 'Chivas,'" he replied, and recited all the stops along the route. He knew them all and he knew them well. The bus held 12 to 15 people and the fare was 10 cents. "Did you sing to your passengers?" I asked. "Sure," he said, "I was known as the singing driver. I grew up and was educated in Panama and went to a Canal Zone school. Later I came to the United States, and shortly afterwards I went to study for the cantorate."

It's a small world. Here is a leader in the Black Jewish community who has sung for our congregation many times. I wonder how often I may have been a passenger on his bus. Then we were unknown to each other, but now we're friends and colleagues.

13

Christian–Jewish Relations:
A Personal Perspective

*"We must work toward educational development and
communication among peoples to reduce the abrasive
effects of differences. Differences, as we have learned
in the pluralistic experience of America, can be a
source of enrichment rather than a threat."*

RABBI MARC H. TANENBAUM

In the fall of 1996 seven clergymen were honored at a dinner at the historic National Arts Club for outstanding service to the Gramercy Park area community, all of us recipients of the Interfaith Humanitarian Award given by a neighborhood organization, Concerned Citizens Speak: two Roman Catholic priests, two Protestant ministers, an Armenian Archbishop, and two rabbis, I among them. The smiles, laughter, embraces and good-natured bantering belied the age-old dictum of "dislike for the unlike," used to justify the belief that different religions can never coexist harmoniously. For my wife and me, it was another one of the fine programs we have enjoyed over the years with friends of all faiths.

In the Ten Commandments the first word is *anochi* ("I"), and the last word, *ray-eh-cha* ("neighbor/friend"). God is saying to us, "I will always be your best friend." If we succeed in enlarging our circle of friends, then God is pleased, but if we permit enmity to prevail, God feels alienated from His world.

Perhaps, then, a first step toward achieving brotherhood and friendship is for people to learn to laugh and celebrate together, and the way to such an idyllic goal is to begin on a person-to-person level. One day as I was walking with my friend Joe, we greeted a genial local delivery truck driver whose name is also Joe, and for a few moments we stood "kibitzing" (joking) together. Later I said to my friend, "More lasting good will and feelings of brotherhood can sometimes be expressed in moments like this than in elaborate programs."

Why has it taken centuries to develop cordial relations between Christians and Jews?

FROM PERSECUTION TO FRIENDSHIP

I have always been anguished by almost 2,000 years of constant and unending attacks against us by Church leaders who, until very recently, taught and maintained that the Jewish people must eternally bear the guilt of having committed deicide. For centuries Popes promulgated severely restrictive decrees that limited the occupations, trades, and professions that Jews could enter and the neighborhoods where they could live. Jews were compelled to wear special apparel and were not permitted to engage Christian women for household duties.

We have been reviled and subjected to the most heinous and ignominious acts and false accusations because we would not accept the teachings of the Church. No wonder that many Jews, especially in lands under ecclesiastical rule, feared entering a church and tried to avoid walking past a church; they dared not build a synagogue too close to a church; nor did they make overtures of friendship toward Christians.

Church-sanctioned anti-Semitism drove a wedge between Jews and non-Jews. Zealous Church leaders and malevolent monarchs expelled Jews from lands where they had lived for centuries. Other Jews were sacrificed on the flaming pyres of the Inquisition, in bloody massacres carried out by the Crusaders on their way to Jerusalem, and at the hands of raging mobs who terrorized Russian Jews during the pogroms at the turn of the twentieth century. As the seventeenth-century French philosopher Blaise Pascal wrote, "Men never do evil so completely and cheerfully as when they do it from religious conviction."

Paradoxically, there were periods when the people manifested such animosity toward the Jews that safety of the Jews had to be secured under the watchful eyes of the Popes. Conversely, there were eras when Popes were bitterly antagonistic while the people were protective of the Jewish population.

Was there an innate desire on the part of the Church to glorify its philosophy of faith over the legitimacy of other religions? Were the Jewish people considered a threat to the primacy of the Church? Or was it a misinterpretation of the concept of chosenness that was the basis of the hostility?

The concept of the Jewish people as *am segula* (God's "beloved treasure") does not in any way connote favoritism. It refers principally to everyone's obligation to serve God and all humanity. When the Ten Commandments were offered to the world, it was the Jewish people alone who accepted them. As the popular old saying goes:

How odd of God, to choose the Jews.

'Tis not so odd, for the Jews chose God.

I once saw a documentary film on Christian iconology and beliefs, which focused on the drama of Jesus crucified at Calvary. The narrator's description of the scene was gripping and foreboding. The accusations of Jewish participation in the crucifixion so disturbed and upset me that my mind reconfirmed what my heart had long understood, that the New Testament is replete with anti-Jewish overtones that can be used for anti-Semitic purposes.

I remember as a youngster listening to Father Charles Coughlin spouting forth his regular Sunday afternoon diatribe of hate on the radio. Sometimes I had the dreadful feeling that all of us were sitting on a soon-to-explode powder keg. The dominant symbol of Christianity, the cross, conjured up centuries of persecution and bloodshed, and I found myself turning away in fear when I saw a priest or a nun.

Many years later, the winter after our congregation moved to Gramercy Park, we received a letter from a passerby who was incensed that our outdoor bulletin board wished "A Merry Christmas to our Christian neighbors." "I was shocked to see in front of a synagogue a Christian slogan 'Merry Christmas.' This slogan meant to me, because I am coming from Vienna, Austria, the order of the German Gestapo to kill Jews and to burn their synagogues on the day they lit their green tannenbaum." She concluded, "I think it is a betrayal to Jewish people to put that slogan in front of a Jewish synagogue." On the other hand, when our Synagogue shared a joint sanctuary with the Village Presbyterian Church, the Minister and I used to exchange greetings at each other's holidays through bulletin board messages, and everyone commended us. I do, however, understand the pain and bitterness of others.

Rabbi Moshe Leib of Sassov once related a conversation he heard between two peasants. One asked, "Tell me, Ivan, my friend, do you love me?" The other replied, "I love you very much." "Ivan, do you know what pains me?" "How can I know what pains you?" "Ivan, if you cannot feel what pains me," remonstrated the first, "how can you say you love me?" It was not until late in this century that Christian leaders, secular and religious, fully acknowledged the extent of the suffering and pain the Church had inflicted on the Jewish people, in whose tradition Jesus was born and reared.

Some years ago, following numerous acts of vandalism and arson affecting synagogues and Jewish day schools in New York City, I received a letter from Rev. Dr. Benjamin Minifie, Rector of Grace Church (Episcopal) in Greenwich Village: "I am ashamed of and I deplore anti-Semitism and I am always embarrassed by it. It is utterly contrary to all my beliefs and convictions as a Christian. I shall always believe that you and I stand in a succession of a common heritage and tradition, and I have always so taught throughout my ministry."

If the first step toward religious brotherhood is to promote friendship, the second step is to develop a feeling of empathy toward other faiths and acknowledge that there is really only one God. While there are many roads that lead to the summa of belief, who among us can say "my way" is ultimately the best and only way?

It would promote greater understanding if professors of religion, and even clergy, would cease alluding to a Jewish "God of Law" in contrast to a Christian "God of Love." Rather, they might teach that centuries before Jesus lived, Hebrew scriptures proclaimed the highest moral precepts, such as "Thou shall not hate thy brother in thy heart"; "Thou shall not take vengeance nor bear any grudge, but thou shall love thy neighbor as thyself"; "Execute justice for the fatherless and the widow and love the stranger in giving him food and raiment"; "If thine enemy is hungry, thou shall surely feed him; if he be thirsty, thou shall give him water to drink." These were principles enunciated in the Hebrew scriptures that Jesus studied and that were a source of inspiration to him.

Despite the travails and agony that Christendom heaped upon the Jewish people, great voices in Judaism have nevertheless long recognized the power and influence of Christianity on world history. Moses Maimonides stated in his work *Yad ha-Hazaka ("The Strong Hand")*: "The teachings of him of Nazareth [Jesus] and of the man of Ishmael [Mohammed] who rose after him help to bring to perfection all mankind."

THE ROAD TO BROTHERHOOD

When I was ordained in 1953, two expressions were current in religious circles: "brotherhood" and "interfaith." They were soon superseded by "dialogue," a more formal interchange of ideas among leaders of the various faith communities. For myself, I viewed dialogue sessions less as an occasion to discuss theology than as a chance to develop warm relationships among ourselves. A leading rabbi, Arthur Hertzberg, challenged us: "*What are we going to do together* that there be less hatred and less violence; *what are we going to do together* so that more poor people are not poor?" In the same vein, the noted Christian preacher Dr. Harry Emerson Fosdick observed, "The best way to get together across dividing lines is *to work together* on common tasks," precisely the philosophy of The Brotherhood Synagogue.

My long association with Rev. Dr. Jesse William Stitt gave me a rare opportunity to develop a deep bond with a Christian clergyman. Our friendship and shared experiences repeatedly proved to me that people are people, no matter what their religion or the hour they gather in worship. Their quest is identical, for love, harmony, justice, and truth.

Dr. Stitt would often relate that, after attending a synagogue service, one of his parishioners commented on the similarity of the Psalms to prayers in the Church liturgy. Dr. Stitt replied, "And where did you think the Church got them from?"

To encourage feelings of friendship, I frequently invited clergy of other faiths and races to address our congregation. Our members in particular appreciated Dr. Stitt's sermons, and whenever he included a Yiddish or Hebrew word or phrase, they loved him more dearly. My association with the Village Church also offered me an unusual milieu to learn more about Christianity and the common elements of our religious beliefs. I wish every rabbi could enjoy the close professional and personal relationship I developed with Dr. Stitt and other priests and ministers. They have broadened my outlook and given new dimensions to my work. As I have often stated, every rabbi should have a minister and every minister should have a rabbi with whom to share the fruits of our common labors.

There are many opportunities for clergy to build good will in a community. Let me cite two examples. One summer I helped parishioners of a small church in a New Hampshire town where I was vacationing. I was a frequent guest at the hotel thanks to the graciousness of the proprietors, who were members of my congregation. The minister of the church was away and there was no one to conduct Sunday services. I was asked if I could help out.

No problem. I was familiar with the order of the worship service as a result of my years of association with Rev. Dr. Stitt. The parishioners read the liturgical passages, and I read the universal prayers. Since I had just returned from the march on Washington where Rev. Dr. Martin Luther King, Jr. had delivered his impassioned "I Have a Dream" speech, I chose that experience for my sermonic message.

One Friday night following Sabbath services someone called my attention to a group of marchers and musicians passing in front of our Synagogue. It was the weekend of the Orthodox Easter, and members of the local Greek Orthodox Church were circling the Gramercy Park neighborhood in remembrance of Good Friday. Standing at the front door of the Synagogue, I lifted my hand as a sign of greeting, and it was reciprocated. The following year we anticipated the procession and exchanged the greeting of *Shalom*. Once, when their observance fell during Passover, the priest called out in Hebrew, *Chag Same-ach*, ("Happy Holiday to you"). Some of my congregants chastised me when I greeted the marchers, recalling that in Europe during the Middle Ages Jews were ordered off the streets on Good Friday and feared for their lives if they ventured outdoors. But others praised my overtures of friendship. I knew what *I* had to do. This is New York—a different time, a different place, and a different attitude.

Unfortunately, in many lands ancient enmities continue to cause untold suffering and anguish. Far too often religious fanaticism beguiles us into false reasoning that *we* have all the saints in our corner and others have all the sinners. It requires constant effort to build bonds of mutual respect; sadly, it sometimes takes but a misguided act by a single individual to tear them apart. Our task is to teach each generation that we are all the children of God.

AFTER THE HOLOCAUST: REMORSE AND REPENTANCE

With the end of World War II, the nations, both Allies and the Axis, tabulated their losses: forty million lives, among them six million Jewish souls—a million and a half of them children—put to death simply because they were Jewish. Never before had such horrific acts of genocide been recorded in the annals of history. Deep in shock and bereavement, world leaders were asking, "What went wrong?"

There is no doubt that religion had failed the world. Too many religious leaders lacked the moral strength and courage to challenge the forces of evil and condemn the Nazis as they systematically sent millions of Jews and others to the crematoria. When I visited churches and cathedrals in Germany in 1960, I repeatedly wondered: "Of what value are all the symbols and ceremonies, beautiful altars and sanctuaries when so little was done to save the victims? Where were the voices preaching the word of God?"

Given the power and influence of the Vatican, many still charge the papal hierarchy with being negligently (some even say deliberately) silent during World War II, even though many convents, monasteries, and schools did shelter refugees and some Church officials provided false identification papers to facilitate their escape. Our Synagogue's first cantor, Leib Mirkovic, was among those who owed their lives to clergy, who also hid Torah scrolls and sacred synagogue treasures.

Nevertheless, in the face of unimaginable barbarities, the Roman Catholic Church seemed to have maintained a policy of neutrality, assuming a public stance, at least, of quiet witness to the systematic annihilation of millions of people, Catholics and Protestants as well as Jews. To these charges, the Church contended that for the Holy See to have spoken out forcefully and publicly at the time might have been futile and harmful and would have unleashed more repressive brutalities and endangered Christian institutions.

For myself, I cannot accept this as justification of the Church's silence. Where was the Church on *Kristallnacht*, November 9–10, 1938, when all the synagogues in Germany were set ablaze, when Jewish businesses were vandalized and Jews were forced to wear a yellow star, making them an easy target for taunts and beatings? Did religious leaders forget the affirmation, "I am my brother's keeper"?

Three years after the war the Protestant World Council of Churches confessed, "We have failed to fight with all our strength the age-old disorder which anti-Semitism represents. The churches in the past have helped to foster an image of the Jews as the sole enemies of Christ which has contributed to anti-Semitism in the secular world."

In the years after the *Shoah* (Holocaust) Christian leaders of all denominations organized forums and conferences to confront the horrors and to plan ways to educate their followers so that such wanton extermination of human lives could never recur. It took an assemblage of crimson-robed Cardinals, convened by a compassionate Pope John XXIII, as late as 1960 to finally abrogate the accusations of deicide against the Jewish people and to accept the concept that God's covenant with Israel is still valid. In his short reign Pope John convened the Second Vatican Council to examine the Church's doctrine of faith vis-à-vis other faith communities. His edicts were hailed as reflecting a spirit of *aggiornamento*, opening a window of friendship. On one occasion, upon hearing the phrase *pro perfidis Judaeis* ("unbelieving Jews") recited as part of the Good Friday liturgy, Pope John XXIII immediately halted the service and ordered that phrase eliminated.

These historic meetings of the Vatican Council resulted in a commitment of the Catholic Church to revise "the teachings of contempt" that had made Jews pariahs in the eyes of the world. In an extraordinary 1965 document, *Nostra Aetate* ("In Our Time"), the Church acknowledged its Jewish roots and the Covenant between God and "Abraham's stock" as well as its "common patrimony with the Jews." The Church therefore "deplores the hatred, persecutions, and displays of anti-Semitism directed against the Jews at any time and from any source."

It took almost 50 years after the defeat of the Nazi regime for other European political and religious leaders to admit publicly their complicity, their sins of omission, and their responsibility that led to the deaths of millions of Jews. A "Declaration of the Evangelical Lutheran Church in America to the Jewish Community" denounced the theological anti-Semitism of Martin Luther and acknowledged the "catastrophes" that befell Jews "in places where the Lutheran churches were strongly represented." Now the Lutheran organization expressed a desire for "increasing cooperation and understanding" with the Jewish community.

In the spring of 1995, in an emotional address to members of the Israeli Knesset, many of whom were Holocaust survivors, the President of Lithuania, Algirdas Brazauskas, stated that he [bowed] "his head to the memory of the more than 200,000 Jews of Lithuania who were killed."

On the occasion of the 50th anniversary of the liberation of Auschwitz, both German and Polish bishops expressed contrition and acceptance of responsibility: "Today the fact is weighing heavily on our minds that there were but individual initiatives to help persecuted Jews" during the time of the Third Reich.

Polish bishops admitted that while "many Poles reacted with heroic courage and sacrifice, risking their lives and that of their families,... there were also those who were capable of actions unworthy of being called Christian." Future generations must be educated "in the spirit of mutual respect, tolerance, and love."

Similar thoughts were expressed by the Dutch Roman Catholic Bishops Conference: "A tradition of theological and church anti-Semitism contributed to the climate which allowed the Holocaust to take place."

In October 1997, following a visit to the United States Holocaust Memorial Museum in Washington, D.C., Ecumenical Patriarch Bartholomew I, the spiritual leader of 250 million Eastern Orthodox Christians worldwide, declared: "The bitter truth for so many Christians of that terrible time was that they could not connect the message of their faith to their actions in the world."

National soul-searching has been particularly intense in France, where the anti-Semitism of the Dreyfus affair a century ago still resonates. After World War II many high-ranking French officials accused of being responsible for crimes against humanity were sheltered by some church groups and even by the government for decades until a few were eventually tracked down, imprisoned, and brought to trial in the 1990s—old men, but still unrepentant.

Addressing the Jewish community of France in March 1997, Jacques Chirac, President of the Republic, reiterated the "official acknowledgement" he had made shortly after his election a year and a half before, admitting "the French government's responsibility for the arrest, deportation and death of thousands upon thousands of Jews" during the "dark years" of the Nazi occupation of France.

On the eve of Rosh Hashanah, in 1997, French bishops met in the Paris suburb of Drancy, from which thousands of Jews had been deported, and issued a candid "Declaration of Repentance" for the silence of the French Catholic Church during the Holocaust.

Following are excerpts from a statement by Archbishop Olivier de Berranger of St.-Denis:

> The time has come for the church to submit its own history, during this period [the Holocaust] in particular, to a critical reading, without hesitating to acknowledge the sins committed by its sons....
>
> It is important to admit the primary role, if not direct, then indirect, played by the constantly repeated anti-Jewish stereotypes wrongly perpetuated among Christians in the historical process that led to the Holocaust.
>
> In the face of the persecution of Jews... silence was the rule, and words in favor of the victims the exception.
>
> Today we confess that silence was a mistake. We beg for the pardon of God, and we ask the Jewish people to hear this word of repentance.

The current Pope, Polish-born John Paul II, who lived through the Nazi era, has been exceedingly sensitive to the pain and anguish inflicted upon the Jews by the Polish people during the Holocaust and has sought to offer contrition. He has visited concentration camp sites and arranged for a concert in the Vatican in memory of victims of the Holocaust to which the Grand Rabbi of Rome was invited and seated next to the Pope. In 1986 the Pope himself went to the Great Synagogue of Rome, the first such papal visit.

Just a month after the French bishops' pronouncement, Pope John Paul II, addressing 60 theologians of various Christian

292 A Rabbi and His Dream

denominations rejected anti-Semitism as "totally unjustifiable and absolutely condemnable," calling it a "pagan" refutation of the essence of the Christian doctrine. He admitted that "In the Christian world—I do not say on the part of the Church as such— the wrong and unjust interpretations of the New Testament relating to the Jewish people and their presumed guilt circulated for too long, contributing to feeling of hostility toward these people... next to those Christians who did everything to save the persecuted at the risk of their own lives, the spiritual resistance of many was not that which humanity expected from the disciples of Christ."

These themes were reiterated in "We Remember: A Reflection on the 'Shoah,'" released in Rome in March 1998 by the Vatican Commission for Religious Relations with the Jews. Accompanying the document was a letter to Cardinal Edward Idris Cassidy, president of the Commission, from Pope John Paul II. The 10-page document took eleven years to produce.

Responses in the Jewish community to the document ranged from gratitude and appreciation to too little too late. I still pose the question: in spite of all the Church's explanations and justifications, if the Pope is regarded by his flock as God's spokesman on earth teaching and proclaiming a message of justice and love, did not the Vatican have a moral obligation to denounce publicly, even if it would result in pain and sacrifice, the unspeakable crimes of the Nazi regime against the Jewish people and all victims of persecution? Many in the Jewish community still seek further explanation for the Church's public silence during the Holocaust as well as during the centuries of persecution and anti-Semitism it had tolerated.

BUILDING BRIDGES OF UNDERSTANDING

When I was studying for the rabbinate, I proposed and helped organize a meeting at Union Theological Seminary to bring Christian seminarians and rabbinical students together to dispel misunderstandings between communities and to foster friendships. Some 35 years later this idea was developed into a structured program at meetings of a special committee of Jewish and Episcopal clergy and leaders of the Anti-Defamation League and General Theological Seminary (Episcopal) in New York City. The committee, of which I was also a member, was chaired by Dr. Lee Belford, Professor of Religion at New York University, who had also encouraged the promotion of dialogue among seminary students.

We were extremely fortunate to have as his successor the Reverend Dr. James A. Carpenter, Professor of Theology at the General Theological Seminary, a brilliant scholar and committed advocate of religious cooperation, who sought to increase the knowledge and understanding of Judaism among students for the Episcopal priesthood.

Strengthened by the committee's support, and with the full consent of the Trustees and faculty of the General Theological Seminary, in 1986 Dr. Carpenter established the Center for Jewish–Christian Studies and Relations. Included in its mission was an innovative program which would provide men and women studying for the Episcopal priesthood with the option of fulfilling part of the Seminary's field placement requirement in a synagogue. The seminarians would thus have a unique opportunity to explore the roots of their Christian heritage and to see the world through Jewish eyes, with the hope that, as ordained ministers, they would be able to impart to their congregations and communities the insights they had gained about Judaism and Jewish life. I was so excited about the goals and direction of the Center that I immediately offered The Brotherhood Synagogue as a participating congregation.

The students who enrolled in this program were required to spend ten hours a week at a synagogue, including attendance at Sabbath and festival services and life-cycle ceremonies, to keep a journal about their experiences, and to meet regularly with Dr. Carpenter. Formal and informal discussions with the rabbis and staff, as well as with members of the congregation, would also enable the seminarians to better understand the heart and mind of the Jewish people.

Since 1987 our congregation has been privileged to work with an especially fine group of men and women—many preparing for the ministry as second or even third careers—and we have been enriched by their insight and talents, even as, by their own admission, they feel they have learned more about the foundations of their own faith and heritage. Some of the seminarians taught adult education classes, one sang in our lay choir, and all were invited to give a sermon on a Shabbat. Our members were very enthusiastic and welcoming, often inviting the students to their homes for Shabbat and holiday dinners.

In evaluating their experiences and impressions, some interns were captivated by the reverence, joy, and delight in the Torah; others appreciated the sanctity of the Sabbath and holidays, with their emphasis on family observances; several cited a better understanding of the centrality of Israel in Jewish life. One seminarian wrote about our Synagogue: "We have experienced their [the Jewish people's] biblically rooted and renowned hospitality. We have seen their strong sense of community, which powerfully binds the living and the dead into one great people. We have experienced in their worship and their life the abiding faithfulness of God." Another reflected; "I have worshipped as my spiritual forebears did while, at the same time, experiencing living Judaism."

At the end of the placement period the congregation presented each seminarian with the gift of a *Chumash* (Five Books of Moses). One young woman was especially appreciative of this gift because she had been "wondering how I would continue the *parasha* (weekly Torah portion) readings—in some way continue to *daven* and journey with you."

When students graduated, my wife and I attended the ceremony at the Seminary, rejoicing with them as part of our congregational family. One year when it appeared we might not have a seminarian assigned to our Synagogue, I jestingly said to Dr. Carpenter; "Have you ever seen an adult congregation cry? That's what will happen if you can't send us an intern this year."

The Center sponsored other programs as well: scholarly lectures, discussions and forums on theological and communal issues, and an annual *Kristallnacht* worship service organized by the students and held in the Seminary's main chapel. There was an ongoing dialogue between students at General Theological Seminary and at Hebrew Union College–Jewish Institute of Religion, as well as joint courses with the two schools.

In 1993, the year before Dr. Carpenter and I both retired, the Hebrew Union College–Jewish Institute of Religion, from which I was ordained, bestowed upon him the honorary degree of Doctor of Humane Letters, citing his "courageous religious leadership [that] has served to build bridges of understanding between Christians and Jews." By coincidence, just a week before, on commencement day at General Theological Seminary, I had marched in the colorful academic procession with trumpets sounding and banners waving, the first rabbi to whom the Seminary awarded the honorary degree of Doctor of Divinity. I was recognized for my years of service to the community, for "ground-breaking work with the Center for Jewish–Christian Studies and Relations" and a "passionate belief in the kinship of all humankind." It was one of the proudest moments of my career and a splendid way to mark my 40th anniversary of ordination.

I invited Dr. Carpenter to speak at a Friday night service, as he had on other occasions, and there we stood together, in academic garb, two good friends and colleagues, reminiscing about the major changes we had witnessed in religious life, yet aware of the many challenges ahead for the next generation of clergy.

A NEW SPIRIT

Forty-five years ago priests rarely entered synagogues. Today they are in the front ranks of every major interreligious community endeavor, as, ever since the Second Vatican Council, the Catholic Church has made a special effort to reach out to the Jewish community. I remember seeing several young priests attending Saturday morning services at a synagogue in Jerusalem and praying with fervor, and a young priest at a Sabbath eve service. And why not?

In 1969, soon after the Vatican called upon Roman Catholics to work with their Jewish brothers and sisters, 80 students and their teachers from a neighborhood parochial school visited The Brotherhood Synagogue. Although we had been in Greenwich Village for a long time, this was the first visit from a Catholic group.

About that time, one of the oldest Catholic churches in the city, a few blocks from our Synagogue, was repairing its façade. I happened to walk by one day with one of my congregants, who pointed out to me a New Testament verse engraved high above the pediment: "We preach Christ crucified, unto the Jews a stumbling block, and unto the Greeks foolishness." Later I suggested to the pastor that this might be a propitious time to consider replacing it with a verse that would reflect the new spirit emanating from the Vatican. He was not at all receptive, so I took my suggestion to the Archdiocese. Again, to no avail.

While the Jewish community recognizes that people of good will welcome changing attitudes in the Christian world, the average person still looks to the local minister, priest, or rabbi for guidance. Ultimately, the attitude toward religious brotherhood will be determined not by edicts from national and international religious leaders but at the local level by what is taught—or not taught—in schools, in all houses of worship, and particularly in the home. How vital it is, therefore, to educate young people, our future clergy, leaders, and teachers, about the faiths and beliefs of others in historically accurate and sensitive ways so that they can have a positive influence on their parishioners and on future generations. As Rabbi Leon Klenicki, Director of the Department of Interfaith Affairs of the Anti-Defamation League, expressed it, there has to be a "sharing of spirituality," an acceptance of the many paths taken as we all search the way to God.

I believe that the clergy and community leaders—indeed all of us—must speak out unequivocally and teach and preach that racial and religious hatred have no place in this world.

All of us must therefore applaud the efforts of the Rochester Board of Rabbis, the Jewish Community Federation, and that city's Roman Catholic Diocese, which in May 1996 entered into an agreement to work together "in ways that can have profound effects on the daily lives not only of their two peoples but of all who live in the region." Their aim was to combat and respond publicly to "all forms" of racism and religious intolerance, to promote frequent communications between their groups, and to strive to enlighten and become more sensitive to each other in areas of particular concern.

This move follows directly in the spirit of the Covenant of Brotherhood between the Village Presbyterian Church and The Brotherhood Synagogue in 1954 and should be duplicated in every community.

I believe that religious leaders have an obligation to speak in the name of God, who wants us to respect and love one another. Apathy and inaction will only swell the ranks of demagogues who will prey on the uneducated and uninformed and incite yet another cycle of fear, persecution, and terrorism.

May the day come speedily when we can say to one another, as did the Friar in Lessing's *Nathan the Wise*:

Nathan, you are a Christian.

Yes, I swear

You are a Christian—better never lived.

And Nathan responded to the Friar:

Indeed, the very thing that
    makes me seem
Christian to you, makes you a
    Jew to me.

A Bracha for a President

At a luncheon for the then exiled President of Haiti, Jean-Bertrand Aristide, there were speakers from Catholic and Protestant groups as well as the African-American and Hispanic communities. As the representative of The New York Board of Rabbis, I was invited to say a few words on behalf of the Jewish community. After each speaker finished his remarks, President Aristide rose to say "Thank you." When it was my turn, I concluded with the traditional priestly bracha, the benediction, in Hebrew, and the President again rose, stretched out his hand to me, and said in Hebrew, "Toda Raba" (thank you). What a gracious gesture, I thought, for the President to have acquired a few Hebrew phrases.

In his own remarks he shared his feelings about the pursuit of justice and peace, speaking first in English and then in his native Creole. "Now," he said, "I would like to direct a few words to our Jewish friends here." For two or three minutes he spoke in flawless Hebrew. The Jewish guests were flabbergasted. I could hardly restrain myself and, as the President finished his talk, I jumped up, took the microphone, and expressed in Hebrew our profoundest good wishes to him and his people. Only later did I learn that President Aristide, a Catholic priest, had spent two years studying in Jerusalem.

14

A Lifetime of Service

"To be a Jew means to bear a serious responsibility
not only to our own community but also to humanity."

ALBERT EINSTEIN

"Go out and change the world." This was the challenge whispered to me by Rabbi Nelson Glueck, President of the Hebrew Union College–Jewish Institute of Religion, as he placed his hands on my shoulders when I was ordained. It is not easy to repair a fractured society, however. According to legend, Satan complained to the Almighty about the greatness preordained for the saintly Levi Yitzhak even before his birth. "Don't worry," the Lord reassured Satan. "I am making him a rabbi! He will be so busy with his duties he won't have the time to bring order to the world."

A rabbi's work, particularly in America today, is multifaceted. We are expected to be preachers and teachers but, willingly or unwittingly, we get involved in many aspects of congregational and community affairs. Then there comes a day when we wake up to realize that, in addition to being teachers and counselors, we have become directors of programming, journalists, archivists, publicists, fund-raisers, and on and on.

While I have always considered my duties as being principally to serve the needs of my congregation, I also felt that a rabbi must become involved in the larger congregation of Israel, here and abroad, and be active in both the Jewish and non-Jewish world.

When our congregation was founded and the media reported our unique partnership with the Village Presbyterian Church, many organizations invited the Minister and me to tell our story. Even though I was extremely busy nurturing a fledgling congregation, I recognized the importance of conveying our message to a wider circle, and one way to achieve that was to be active in communal affairs. Such involvement would also provide an opportunity to learn more about the issues facing the broader Jewish community and problems of concern to our immediate neighborhood. Therefore, over the 40 years of my rabbinate I accepted invitations to serve on boards in religious as well as civic communities, and the experiences have been rewarding for the intellectual growth they offered and the friendships I made. Obviously, I was not involved in all these organizations all the time; my rabbinic duties and obligations always took precedence. Yet there were certain groups whose philosophy and activities complemented the work I was doing.

SERVICE TO THE JEWISH COMMUNITY

Immediately following my ordination I joined the CENTRAL CONFERENCE OF AMERICAN RABBIS (CCAR) to continue my association with my colleagues from both the New York and Cincinnati schools of HUC-JIR. The student body at the time represented a broad range of religious observances, and I accepted that diversity as a source of strength. One day one of my colleagues remarked, "Irving, you're such a traditionalist, so what are you doing here?" I answered, "I enjoy the camaraderie, which reflects Dr. Wise's universal approach."

Simultaneously I applied for membership in THE NEW YORK BOARD OF RABBIS (NYBR). With 800 members, it is the largest representative body of Orthodox, Conservative, Reform, and Reconstructionist rabbis in the world. Founded by six New York area rabbis in 1881 and originally called The New York Board of Jewish Ministers, its goal was to confront spiritual and moral malaise as it affected Jewish lives and to foster the well-being of the entire community. Before long, the NYBR called on me to deliver invocations and benedictions at civic and religious functions and to represent the Board before city agencies on issues such as drugs, violence, youth, and intergroup relations. In time I was elected to the Board of Governors and asked to host NYBR radio and television programs that would relate the principles and practices of Judaism to problems of the day.

For ten years, in the 1970s and 1980s, I broadcast over WHN, then a popular music station, and was given a very unusual format to provide spiritual commentaries to songs performed by some of the leading country music singers. I must have done something right, because my programs helped win an award for the station. My Sunday morning radio talk show, *Contact*, also on WHN, covered a wide range of subjects from Hadassah to Hollywood, from Jewish war veterans to justice in the courts, and was carried by affiliate stations across the country. Discussions on gambling and health were especially popular.

And so it went. Because of my activities with the Black Jewish community, the NYBR asked me to chair its Interfaith Committee and develop programs that would build bridges of friendship with Catholic, Protestant, and Muslim leaders, along with African-

American, Hispanic, and Jewish clergy. Our mission was to narrow the widening gap of mistrust, to conduct genuine dialogue in areas of disagreement, to share our heritage with each other, to deepen respect for each group's contributions to society, and to enable our congregations to know one another through exchanges of pulpits and visits to each other's houses of worship.

The Brotherhood Synagogue welcomed Bishop Norman Quick, President of the Protestant Council of New York, along with a group of his church officers and members with their families, to a Friday night Shabbat dinner, and he addressed our congregation at services. A few weeks later Bishop Quick reciprocated, and we chartered a bus to take a delegation of our members to his church in Harlem, where I spoke to a very receptive gathering.

Among the highlights of my committee's efforts were a visit of a number of officers and Board members from The New York Board of Rabbis to the Islamic Cultural Center in Manhattan; a gathering at The Brotherhood Synagogue of 75 prominent clergy from the African-American and Jewish communities; a conference on civility; panel discussions and joint press conferences to respond to problems and crises and to demonstrate how all clergy reject the use of violence to resolve disputes.

We also instituted a pre-Thanksgiving luncheon, which has since become an annual program attended by clergy of many faiths. In 1992 the Reverend Jesse Jackson accepted the Board's invitation to speak at the luncheon, an event viewed as a major breakthrough in Black–Jewish relations.

Perhaps I am somewhat of an anomaly to my colleagues at the NYBR. The Reform consider me a traditionalist while the Orthodox think I'm liberal. No matter; I respect all the members of the Board because, in spite of our disparate backgrounds, we work together and speak out of a desire for Jewish unity. While I am aware that numerous Jewish organizations, local and national, issue statements on behalf of their constituent members, and that is good, but it is not good enough. The New York Board of Rabbis speaks on Jewish issues with a unified voice, and that is even more significant. This is what I have been preaching throughout my career.

There is a sign on the desk of Rabbi Gilbert S. Rosenthal, the Executive Vice President of the NYBR, that reads, "Much good can be accomplished if you don't care who gets the credit." Nevertheless, I must admit that in 1986 I felt very proud and honored to be named the first recipient of the Rabbi Israel and Libby Mowshowitz Award presented to a rabbi "for advancing the positive image of Judaism in the community through cultural programs, humanitarian service, philanthropic endeavors, and interreligious activities."

FIGHTING ADDICTIONS

As we search the world for places where we can fulfill the *mitzvah* of *Tikkun olam* (repairing the world), we must endeavor to view circumstances and actions as God sees them. Just as God provided clothing for Adam and Eve, arranged the burial of Moses, and brings healing to the sick and comfort to the bereaved, we too are obligated to carry out the same *mitzvot,* not only for the Jewish community but for the non-Jewish world as well.

My association with UNITED JEWISH APPEAL (UJA) dates back to 1946–1947, when, as a senior at the University of Connecticut, I served as a chairman of the first UJA drive on our campus. After returning from Israel and before I entered rabbinical school, UJA invited me to travel and discuss my experiences in the Haganah. Later, in the early years of our congregation, we were cited as an example of the zeal a synagogue must demonstrate to conduct a successful UJA campaign.

But it was as Co-chairman of the UJA-FEDERATION'S TASK FORCE ON ADDICTIONS in the Jewish Community that I had an opportunity to make an important contribution. One morning I received a call from Rabbi Isaac N. Trainin, Director of the Commission on Synagogue Relations of the Federation of Jewish Philanthropies. "Irving, you've got to help us. I want you to co-chair our Task Force on Addictions with Dr. Louis Linn, a distinguished psychiatrist."

Dr. Linn and others had been contending that alcoholism, drugs, and gambling had long afflicted the Jewish community, but too little was being done to confront the situation. Dr. Linn keenly felt, and I concurred, that while "we must search for the Jewish component in addiction, we cannot eliminate all recreational behavior simply because it might result in the disease of a minority. Nevertheless, addiction to whatever activity or substance must be met head-on."

It was our feeling that the problems resulting from addictions cross boundaries and afflict traditional as well as nonobservant Jewish families. We recommended that synagogue religious schools introduce drug prevention programs at a very early age and continue them according to the students' level of comprehension, and that family orientation sessions follow up on the information presented to the students. We also advocated that rabbinical schools include courses or lectures on addictions, that rabbinic organizations be made aware of counseling programs in their communities, and that religious leaders avail themselves of the professional resources of agencies such as the JACS Foundation (Jewish Alcoholics, Chemically Dependent Persons and Significant Others) to provide guidance and programming suggestions. We also recognized that many in the Jewish community might seek help more readily if they knew that there were support groups in local synagogues. The Brotherhood Synagogue, for example, has long hosted a weekly meeting of Alcoholics Anonymous, and its members have often commended us for being understanding, and welcoming, and willing to help them in their struggle.

The Task Force on Addictions and UJA–Federation published a pamphlet entitled "Open the Synagogue Doors," urging congregations to sponsor support groups. The time was long overdue. In it we stated that "the conventional wisdom that Jews never drink to excess or depend on drugs or gamble compulsively is a myth that has led Jewish addicts and their families to deny the problem and avoid seeking help. It has closed most synagogue doors to vital rehabilitative self-help programs."

In 1986 the Task Force held its first national conference, in conjunction with which a 379-page book entitled *Addictions in the Jewish Community*, edited by Dr. Stephen Jay Levy and Dr. Sheila B. Blume, was published by the Commission on Synagogue Relations. When the Task Force began its deliberations, only thirteen synagogues took up the challenge to open their doors to support groups. Subsequently there would be more than three times that many.

When I completed my term on the Task Force, I was satisfied that Dr. Linn and I had achieved something worthwhile for the Jewish and general communities. In a talk to Jewish communal workers I stated: "Substance abuse need no longer be a blight on the pages of our historic record as a people. We can give renewed hope to those whose way of life simply means that they are crying out to us for help." In 1987 the Commission on Synagogue Relations of UJA–Federation presented me with its *Tzedakah* (righteousness) Award for "conspicuous devotion and adherence to the practice of justice and lovingkindness." I appreciated the respect of my colleagues, and especially their friendship.

RESETTLING NEW AMERICANS

For over ten years, from 1984 to 1995, I served on the Board of Directors of THE NEW YORK ASSOCIATION FOR NEW AMERICANS (NYANA), the largest refugee resettlement agency in the country and a model for similar organizations. Not only did NYANA resettle thousands of Russian immigrants, but it opened its heart and doors to refugees from countries in Southeast Asia, Ethiopia, Tibet, and other lands where people were fleeing terror and oppression. Founded in 1949, NYANA has helped half a million strangers to a new land find apartments and jobs, learn English, enroll their children in school, start their own businesses, and become American citizens. "Enabling [newcomers] to become independent is the cornerstone of NYANA's resettlement philosophy," explained Mark Handelman, the agency's Executive Vice President.

I am very proud that The Brotherhood Synagogue was able to host hundreds of immigrants in our sanctuary and introduce them to the customs and practices of Jewish life, an experience that most of them had been denied as they were growing up. To witness Jewish men, women, and children lovingly touch the Torahs was to reveal the power of religious freedom that we so often take for granted. (See Chapter 11.)

On one occasion I offered a commentary at the conclusion of a NYANA Board meeting, under the agenda item "good and welfare," relating the agency's work to the philosophy of Judaism. It was so well received that from then on almost every Board meeting concluded with a brief spiritual message. I was so pleased when Board members, many of them prominent leaders in the Jewish community, told me they stayed to the very end of the meetings just to hear these commentaries. Their enthusiasm only served to confirm my conviction that all Jewish organizations should introduce moments of spiritual education into their deliberations.

ANTI-DEFAMATION LEAGUE

Because of my interreligious efforts I was named to the Regional Board and the Executive Board of the New York Chapter of the Anti-Defamation League of B'nai B'rith (ADL), whose mission is to fight bigotry, racism, and anti-Semitism, to help the victims of prejudice find justice, to research and publish information about neo-Nazi and other hate groups, and to alert law enforcement agencies and the Department of Justice when necessary.

One of the programs initiated by the ADL, The World of Difference Institute, was aimed at breaking down racial and ethnic stereotypes and prejudices. Since the episode of the exodus from Egypt is replete with universal themes, the Institute organizes model Passover Seders to highlight the shared struggle for human rights. The Brotherhood Synagogue hosted a number of these Seders, attended by leaders of the Hispanic community and of the Bridge Street A.M.E.(African Methodist Episcopal) Church, as well as clergy and lay leaders of various other denominations. And there is nothing quite like an inspired church choir singing gospel melodies based on themes from the Passover Haggadah.

SETTLING DISPUTES

The JEWISH CONCILIATION BOARD OF AMERICA tried to resolve interpersonal family and business disputes within the Jewish community without recourse to the secular court system, but with the legal and moral power to adjudicate the disputes brought before its three-judge panel: a rabbi, who acted as chief judge, a businessman, and an attorney. I frequently served on the panel in the 1960s and found each session exciting and rewarding because it brought *shalom bayit* (domestic peace). I remember a case in which the litigants were a mother and son, and when the decision had been handed down and the hearing was over, the son abruptly turned away from his mother and walked toward the door. I called him back and suggested that he remember the love between a mother and son and the sacrifices a parent makes for a child. Understanding exactly what I meant, the son hugged his mother and they walked out together with smiles.

THE JOINT PASSOVER ASSOCIATION

I like to serve an organization that is dedicated to fulfilling the *mitzvot* of Jewish life. The Joint Passover Association (JPA) does just that, enabling those with very limited resources to observe Passover in accordance with tradition and in dignity. Through cash grants the JPA helps thousands of Jewish people provide for their needs during the festival week. As the clients talk with the volunteer counselors, their other problems often emerge, and they are referred to community agencies for assistance. With costs rising each year, more and more New Yorkers come to rely on the support of the Jewish community through the Joint

Passover Association. Children in our Religious School have also participated by filling jars with "pennies for Passover."

THE AMERICAN JEWISH CONGRESS

In my early years as a rabbi I was active in the American Jewish Congress (AJC), founded by Rabbi Stephen Samuel Wise. This organization is always in the forefront of support for Israel, combatting anti-Semitic and anti-Israel attitudes, fighting for human rights, speaking out against prejudice wherever it might be directed, and fostering Jewish education.

When I was in rabbinical school, a request came from the AJC for a student to teach classes on Judaism in people's homes. I volunteered. Many of the families lived in the then new Stuyvesant Town and Peter Cooper Village developments between East 14th and 23rd Streets, and we would sit in a circle on the floor discussing Judaism. Three decades later, after The Brotherhood Synagogue had moved to Gramercy Park, a number of people told me, "Rabbi Block, I remember when you were a rabbinical student and led discussions in my living room."

UNITED ISRAEL WORLD UNION

Founded in 1943 by journalist David Horowitz, the son of a Swedish cantor, the United Israel World Union, whose motto is "One God, one law for all humanity," seeks to bring into Jewish life people in various parts of the world who claim to be followers of the Mosaic laws. Thanks to his efforts, men and women who refer to themselves as B'nai Noah (children of Noah), who love the God of Israel, the Bible, and the land of Israel, have been given an opportunity to study about Judaism. Over the years The Brotherhood Synagogue has helped by sending prayer books and religious articles—even lending a Torah to a community in Vera Cruz, Mexico—and by hosting many annual meetings of the United Israel World Union. Mr. Horowitz, a past president of the United Nations Press Association and, at age 95, the longest active correspondent at the U.N.—having come in 1947 to cover the debate on Palestine—continues to encourage men and women, wherever they may live, who wish to study the faith of Judaism.

CHAPLAINCIES

The role of the chaplain is to convey a sense of spirituality and hope and to view ethical issues from a religious perspective. As a war veteran, I serve three organizations: The Jewish War Veterans of America (JWV), the 369th Veterans Association, and the American Veterans of Israel (AVI).

I have had the privilege of serving twice as National Chaplain of the JEWISH WAR VETERANS, the oldest veterans' organization in the country, established in 1896 as the Hebrew Union Veterans Association. Seeking to provide a structure for Jewish efforts to share in the responsibility of safeguarding and protecting America and its values, the JWV has rightfully earned the accolade, "The patriotic voice of American Jewry."

When our congregation left our Greenwich Village sanctuary, members of local JWV posts responded to my request to serve as honor guards when the Torahs were carried out. A year later it was my great joy to summon the JWV to serve once again, but this time to help carry the Torahs into our new Gramercy Park home.

In the summer of 1983 while I was attending the JWV national convention in Atlanta, a group of JWV members were riding on a city bus when a passenger began shouting invectives against the Jewish people. The bus driver, who was black, pulled the brake, turned to the man, and said, "In my bus, I don't permit any bigotry." There was a short exchange between the driver and the hate-filled passenger, and the driver radioed the police. The following day, JWV members and their families agreed to appear in court on behalf of the city, and the racist was sentenced to 60 days in jail.

The JWV invited the driver and his wife to attend the convention's concluding dinner and presented him with a token of appreciation for his courage and determination. The driver related that as a young boy he had watched a passenger harangue an elderly black man, demanding that he give up his seat. The elderly gentleman left with tears in his eyes, and the young boy never forgot that incident.

Before I left Atlanta, I attended a Sunday morning service at the Ebenezer Baptist Church, where the Reverend Dr. Martin Luther King, Jr. and his father had been preachers. There were many visitors, and my presence as the National Chaplain of the Jewish War Veterans was recognized. Twenty years earlier I had marched three or four ranks behind Dr. King in Washington, D.C., and had stood just a few feet away from him as he delivered his majestic "I Have a Dream" speech.

A past Commander of the New York County JWV, Emanuel Goldstein, introduced me to the 369TH VETERANS ASSOCIATION, an organization of mainly black former servicemen and women, founded in 1953 by veterans who had served with the 369th anti-aircraft artillery during World War II. The Association is an outgrowth of the all-black 15th Infantry Regiment, which distinguished itself in service with the French army in World War I.

The 369th, which raises funds to develop housing for low-income residents and provides scholarships for inner-city children, was seeking a Jewish chaplain to join the Catholic and Protestant chaplains. I couldn't refuse my good friend Manny Goldstein. I was deeply impressed by the members' devotion both to the highest ideals of American life and to their cultural heritage, and I participated in many of their programs, among them an annual gospel concert to commemorate Dr. King's birthday and a parade on Fifth Avenue in May.

I have encouraged the JWV and the 369th to invite each other to march and to send delegations to each other's events, such as the 369th's parade and the Salute to Israel parade. One year I was asked to help find a solution to an awkward situation when both parades were scheduled for the same Sunday afternoon in May. For reasons of religious observance and to avoid a conflict with the annual Yom Hashoah (Holocaust Remembrance Day) observance, the Jewish community asked the officers of the 369th if it would be possible to reschedule their parade. They graciously agreed to do so out of respect for the Holocaust survivors, and a delegation from the 369th marched in the Salute to Israel parade, where their participation was acknowledged and honored. I was very proud to wear my two chaplain's caps that day.

The third veterans' organization to which I belong is the American Veterans of Israel (AVI), consisting of some 4,500 American and Canadian men and women volunteers in Israel's War of Independence. It is affiliated with the world MAHAL (*Mitnadvei Chutz La-Aretz*), foreign volunteers in Israel's battles for statehood. The mission of the AVI is to educate each generation about the heroic role played by men and women from other countries, Jews and non-Jews alike, and to assist disabled veterans and personnel in the Israeli armed forces.

No matter what their members' color or creed, each of these veterans' organizations is made up of brave and loyal Americans, and I am proud to have been invited to serve with them.

There were other significant chaplaincies. In 1964 I was appointed Grand Chaplain of the FREE AND ACCEPTED MASONS of the State of New York. Freemasonry is a fraternity whose rituals, based on the construction of King Solomon's Temple, draw on symbolism and metaphor and refer to God as the Supreme Architect. It teaches that the corollary to the fatherhood of God is the brotherhood of man.

Masonry has been a tradition in both my family and my wife's family, and I was "raised" as a Master Mason in 1953, at Maimonides Lodge #743 in the 6th Manhattan district. When Masons meet for the first time, they ask one another, "From whence do you hail?" a question meant not only to find out the name and location of each other's lodge, but to share a sense of pride in their common goals: providing young people with academic scholarships, opportunities for community service, and summer camping; advancing medical research; and developing housing for retirees.

When I became Grand Chaplain, I promised myself to accomplish something tangible and meaningful, not hold the position in title only. I soon found my cause. The beautiful Masonic Home in Utica, New York, had a chapel for Christian services but no designated room for Jewish worshippers. One of my cousins, Harry Simon, a high-ranking Mason, and I drove to Utica to present our case directly to the Superintendent of the Home, and by the time we left we had a commitment that arrangements would be made for both a Jewish chapel and a meditation room for nondenominational prayer. Some months later I received blueprints, and before long the Jewish chapel was dedicated.

Another chaplaincy that occupied me for a brief period was a prison assignment administered by The New York Board of Rabbis for Jewish inmates in state institutions. During the first six months of 1974 I went twice a week to the Federal House of Detention for Men, in lower Manhattan. Although I was preoccupied with our congregation's search for a new home at the time, I thought it would do me a world of good to take on an entirely different activity such as this for a few months.

The warden offered me the option of meeting with the prisoners either in the visiting area of the cell blocks or in the officers' social room. I opted for the cell blocks because I could then meet prisoners of other faiths as well, who might wish to sit down and talk with a rabbi. I also visited those confined to maximum security areas.

The first time I arrived at the cell blocks, I was greeted by a self-appointed committee of Jewish inmates, who explained they wanted to be sure I would be as fully respected as the other chaplains. After I learned that the prisoners enjoyed receiving little gifts, especially greeting cards, I always made sure to bring along a pocketful of cards-for-all-occasions. They were eagerly snapped up and became a bridge in my developing a rapport with the men.

In one of my discussions with the warden, I emphasized the need to make kosher food available, but he claimed that doing so would impose too much work for his staff. They had already rejected a proposal by a group of prisoners who contended that their religion required them to have a thick steak every morning and a bottle of Dewar's! Today kosher food is generally available in prisons upon request. During my tenure I was able to arrange through The New York Board of Rabbis for two kosher, traditional Passover Seders at the prison, the second of which received unusual television coverage, showing the Seder in progress, with comments by the warden.

Among the inmates was a young Jewish Frenchman awaiting sentencing for possession of drugs. He confided to me that somebody had surreptitiously tossed something into his locker at the railroad station. The warden explained it differently, saying that the young man was being charged with having stashed a large cache of drugs in the locker. The inmate asked me to bring him a French/Hebrew prayer book, which I did. A few weeks later when my wife picked up the morning paper, she asked me, "What was the name of that Frenchman you've been visiting?" When I answered, she said; "You won't find him there next time you go. He was part of a group that just broke out of prison." To this day I wonder what happened to him and my prayer book.

SERVICE TO THE CITY AND STATE

Some city and state agencies have clergy advisory boards, one of which was at the HOME TERM COURT (now Family Court), under Judge Anna Moskowitz Kross, who later became Commissioner of Correction. A growing number of children were involved in acts of delinquency, but not enough counselors were available to spend time with them and their families. The Court turned to clergy, among other trained volunteers, to meet with these families and then advise the Court about their needs.

One year Mayor Robert F. Wagner summoned 100 members of the clergy of various faiths to study and discuss with him difficulties facing young people. We divided into subcommittees to examine topics such as delinquency, street gang clashes, and criminal acts. Somehow I was assigned to the subcommittee dealing with pornography and the salacious magazines youngsters could readily purchase. That posed a dilemma. I had to look through these magazines, but I didn't want to be seen buying them, so I made it a point to do so out of the neighborhood or to send someone else to buy them for me. Eventually the deliberations of this advisory group led to the formation of the New York City Youth Board.

As our congregation became even better known, I was invited to give invocations at the opening of the City Council, the State Assembly, the State Senate, and at citywide public events.

After our move to Gramercy Park I was named to COMMUNITY BOARD 6, which represents our area. The meetings and discussions were interesting, but many of the issues were unfamiliar to me, and the sessions often contentious. While I appreciated the opportunity to meet civic leaders, I asked to be excused after my one-year term because of my pressing schedule at the Synagogue. I also think I was just not temperamentally suited for this kind of Board.

There are strong opinions pro and con on the question of landmarking houses of worship. Landmarking preserves the heritage of the past, but I also recognize the position of religious institutions for which landmark status might cause a financial hardship. It does impose certain restrictions on a congregation with regard to renovations, for example, that might prove more costly than anticipated, or make it difficult to alter physical facilities in order to expand community services.

Since 1986 I have been serving on the Advisory Committee of "Common Bond," a publication issued by the NEW YORK LANDMARKS CONSERVANCY, a private, not-for-profit organization founded in 1973 to protect and preserve architecturally significant buildings. The Conservancy provides assistance for the renovation of historic properties and educates the public on the importance of historic preservation. "Common Bond" is a technical assistance newsletter published three times a year by the Sacred Sites department and focuses on historic houses of worship in New York State.

OUT AND ABOUT IN THE COMMUNITY

An organization called THE OPEN CONGREGATION, whose members include laity and clergy of various faiths, is dedicated to assisting houses of worship to become accessible. Because of our congregation's growing reputation for efforts in that direction, I was invited to serve on its Board.

When we were renovating our building prior to moving in, I urged our Board and officers to install an elevator, because I was aware that the second-floor sanctuary might be inaccessible to a number of our members. Unfortunately, it would be ten years before it was installed, along with an outdoor ramp leading into the building. In the interim we all learned just how necessary it is to make houses of worship accessible not only to the physically challenged but also to those who are visually handicapped or hearing-impaired. Our Synagogue now has large-print prayer books available and an improved sound system. In addition we have prayer books in Braille, which we acquired during the years we had a blind cantor, Stephen Cassell. (See Chapter 10.)

The Open Congregation shares office space with DISABLED AND ALONE/LIFE SERVICES FOR THE HANDICAPPED, which was founded in 1988 by Leslie Park, former Executive Director of United Cerebral Palsy of New York City, in response to a heart-wrenching question: "Who will care for our disabled family members after we pass away?" As advances in medical care have lengthened the life span of people with disabilities, aging parents are even more concerned about the future of their mature handicapped children. Disabled and Alone tries to answer that question by providing long-range financial planning advice, "customized" service, and a "personalized" program for each client, as well as family counseling and social services. The men and women on Mr. Park's Board, some of them parents of disabled children, give enormous amounts of their time and expertise and are truly doing God's work. That is why I willingly accepted the invitation to serve with them.

For ten years (1957-1966) I was a member of the Board of RELIGION IN AMERICAN LIFE (RIAL), a national organization sponsored by a number of faith groups "to help increase the membership, vitality and outreach of congregations in all faith traditions… and to help increase the number of people affiliated with houses of worship." Its placards and slogans became familiar to riders of nationwide transit systems as a result of effective campaigns prepared by the Ad Council of New York as a community service to assist RIAL in developing visual materials that would attract attention and encourage regular attendance at houses of worship. I hope that in some measure we did succeed.

About a year after our Synagogue was founded, I was invited to become a charter member of the newly formed KIWANIS CLUB of Greenwich Village, a fraternal group dedicated to the betterment of the community and fellowship among its members. By regulation, no business or profession could be represented by more than two members. I was one of the two clergymen; the other was the Reverend Allison Grant of Grace Church School. Every year the Kiwanis Club honored a civic leader, and in 1961 Rev. Dr. Stitt and I were chosen "Men of the Year." The photographic portrait of both of us that accompanied the award hangs proudly in my home and in the Synagogue, a reminder of enduring friendship.

One day a colleague, Rabbi Moshay P. Mann, phoned me to ask if I would be interested in taking his place on the Board of Trustees of the VICTOR E. PERLEY FUND, an organization that was unfamiliar to me then but which I came to regard very highly. Victor Perley believed in the concept of citizenship, and he was intensely committed to improving the lives of young people and giving them opportunities for personal development and educational advancement. (One young man went on to become a federal judge.) After Mr. Perley's death, his estate established a fund which, among other things, provided individual scholarships and support for several long-established settlement houses in Manhattan.

When Rabbi Mann decided to retire, he was asked to nominate his successor and called upon me. I accepted, and it has been heartening to have had a role in the distribution of hundreds of thousands of dollars to benefit young New Yorkers. When I myself retired after more than two decades as a Perley Fund trustee, I too was invited to name my successor and chose my son, Herbert, because of his experience and involvement with city and state youth agencies. I hear from other trustees that he is already making his mark in their deliberations.

Let me now return to the challenge I faced at my ordination: to go out and change the world. I hope I have, at least in some small measure, made life in my community less harsh, a little brighter, and a little better, and perhaps I was able to change people's outlook with regard to other faiths.

I worked with men and women of all backgrounds, acquired friends, and opened my mind to new ways of approaching problems and issues. My service on the various Boards also enabled me to introduce traditions of Jewish life to those not of our faith, and to demonstrate how the principles of Judaism can be applied to contemporary issues. In the words of Hillel as recorded in *Ethics of the Fathers*: "If I am not for myself, who will be for me? And if I am only for myself, what am I? And if not now, when?"

The Rabbi as Storyteller

A number of years ago I was introduced to Pastor John Gensel of St. Peter's Lutheran Church in Manhattan, known as the Pastor to the jazz community, and through him I made the acquaintance of his good friend Eddie Bonnemere, a fine jazz musician and composer. On one occasion I had the pleasure of hearing him play one of his own compositions, entitled "There Is a God." When I related to Mr. Bonnemere a Hasidic story with a similar theme, he suggested that I participate with him in the installation service of Pastor Gensel. Mr. Bonnemere would conduct his ensemble and I would narrate the story.

Our collaboration was so successful that we repeated it several times, including on stage at Lincoln Center on March 1, 1981, during a concert of his music. I related the tale of Rabbi Levi Yitzhak of Berdichev who, one Friday afternoon in the midst of the hustle and bustle of preparations for the Shabbat, instructed his sexton to summon all the town folk to the center of the village for an important announcement that could not wait. When the sexton implored the Rabbi to postpone it until after the Shabbat, the Rabbi insisted that the announcement had to be made immediately. Out of respect, the people gathered expectantly in the town square; the Rabbi mounted a platform and slowly and loudly declared, "I, Levi Yitzhak, son of Sarah, do hereby announce and proclaim the greatest news of all time: There is a God in the world!" At that moment, as I stood on the stage wrapped in a large tallis, my arms outstretched, the drums rolled and the choir sang out joyfully the refrain: "There is a God in the world!"

15

Israel as I See It

"We extend our hand to all neighboring states and their peoples in an offer of peace and good neighborliness, and appeal to them to establish bonds of cooperation and mutual help with the sovereign Jewish people settled in its own land. The State of Israel is prepared to do its share in common effort for the advancement of the entire Middle East."

DECLARATION OF THE ESTABLISHMENT OF THE
STATE OF ISRAEL, MAY 14, 1948—5 IYAR, 5708

No subject grips me and consumes my mind and spirit with a flaming passion more than the State of Israel, the land and its people. For four decades I devoted my Rosh Hashanah morning sermon to the issues and problems confronting the Jewish State.

When I was a young boy in *cheder*, I went around with a Jewish National Fund blue box, knocking on doors to solicit money to send to Eretz Israel to purchase land, plant trees, and build highways. I believed then, as I do now, that the Land of Israel is mine, too. Having served in the Haganah defense forces in 1947–1948, I know first-hand the terrible price that was paid with Jewish blood. The Jewish community fought with its principal weapon, the spirit of faith; *ein breira*, there is no alternative, but to fight and survive.

No one can prognosticate the future; that is left solely to God. Nor in matters of security should we decide what the Israeli government and the Israeli people ought to do. It is their lives, their security, and their future that are at stake. Ours is the commitment to help.

WHO OWNS THE LAND?

What a beautiful land it is—diversified, compact, her hills like the undulating humps of her camels; her slopes filled with vineyards, orchards, honey, and grazing flocks, so that the mountainsides seem to melt away; her vibrant cities and towns a contrast between ancient architecture and modern construction. The desert is blooming once again; farmers grow fruit and vegetables, and universities are centers for the arts, science, and culture.

The quintessential question is who owns the land. Who is entitled to the land—the Jews, whose ancestry, heritage, and possession date back to the time of Abraham, around 1800 B.C.E., or the Arabs, who controlled the region during the reign of caliphs for four centuries, from 634 C.E., when Muslim armies invaded the country? After that, Palestine fell to the Crusaders, the Tartars, Mongols, Mamelukes, and Turks. In 1922 the League of Nations entrusted Palestine to Great Britain as a mandatory power following the dismantling of the Ottoman Empire after World War I. The British mandate was terminated on May 14, 1948, when Israel proclaimed its independence.

It is my firm belief that the Land of Israel belongs to the Jewish people by historic right, by League of Nations mandate and United Nations decision, by purchase of hundreds of thousands of acres through the Jewish National Fund, by the sweat and tears of its pioneers, by the blood and lives of its defenders. It belongs to the Jewish people who, from the destruction of the Second Temple by the Romans in 70 C.E. and Bar Kochba's revolt in 135 C.E., have lived in hope and dreamed messianic visions, yearning and praying for the day when they could return to the land bequeathed by God to their ancestors. Did not Moses implore God: "Look forth from Thy holy habitation, from heaven, and bless Thy people Israel, in the land which Thou hast given us, as Thou didst swear unto our fathers, a land flowing with milk and honey" (Deuteronomy 26:15).

Rashi, the eleventh-century supreme commentator on the Bible, quotes Rabbi Isaac to explain why the Torah begins with the story of creation rather than the exodus from Egypt:

For if the nations of the world should say to Israel, "You are robbers, because you have seized by force the lands of the seven nations" [Canaan], they [Israel] could say to them, "The entire world belongs to the Holy One, Blessed be He, He created it and gave it to whomever it was right in His eyes. Of His own will He gave it to them [nations of the world] and of His own will He took it from them [nations of the world] and gave it to us [the Jewish people]."

If ever there was a people of whom it could be said that its attachment to its land is from time immemorial, it is the Jewish people and the Land of Israel.

Whereas the once mighty Canaanites, Phoenicians, Philistines, and Assyrians have vanished, Israel alone still exists, in a land holy and sublime, as Isaiah described it centuries later, "an eternal excellency, a joy of man's generations."

THE MYSTIQUE OF ZIONISM AND MESSIANISM

Zionism is derived from the word *Tzion*, one of the original names of Jerusalem and the name of the hill where King Solomon built the great Temple. To me, the four letters *tzaddik, yud, vav, nun,* which spell the word *Tzion* in Hebrew, represent *tzaddik, Adonoy, v'ne-eman*—The Lord is righteous and just. Zionism refers not merely to the restoration of territory, but also to the spiritual qualities of that land where, in the Messianic era, all nations will congregate and worship one God and live in brotherhood and peace. Said the historian Joseph Klausner, "The Messianic idea is the most glistening jewel in the glorious crown of Judaism."

For centuries the question was: when should the Jewish people begin to rebuild the land of their ancestors? A people scattered, dispersed abroad in many lands, did not have the leadership and the ability to mobilize its strength. Yet the spark of hope was never extinguished. In every house of worship, wherever our brothers and sisters congregated, regardless of the conditions in which they lived, they prayed for the day when the Jewish people could return to Zion. But a truncated nation does not easily replenish itself, and the few attempts to gather the dispersed were futile. Nevertheless, the amazing and miraculous fact, defying all previous national experiences, is that the Jews clung to their visions and dreams, and we endured to witness the fulfillment of biblical prophecy.

There are some Jews who literally await the coming of the Messiah with great fervor. For them no attempt to restore our ancient homeland and achieve a lasting peace can succeed until the Messiah comes. How can there be harmony except in a utopian era? Modern Zionism, however, rejected the concept of waiting and asserted that the Jewish people will be the Messiahs, bringing renewal and redemption. Ahad Ha-am, the nineteenth-century Hebrew essayist, predicted that Zionism would resolve not only the political homelessness of the Jewish people but even more, the spiritual yearnings of Judaism.

Martin Buber said that the Jewish people must build a moral and ethical state but could do so only in the freedom of their own country, where they could then engage in the full and uninhibited development of Judaism, its culture, language, and civilization, free from persecution and oppression. We do not want the land for the Jews alone, he stated, we want it rather for the benefit of all mankind.

Zionism is certainly not racism. Those who introduced and voted for such a resolution at the United Nations in 1975 did not understand, or rather, did not *want* to understand and respect the philosophy of a Jewish state: her right to live in peace and security with her neighbors and to be considered a member of the family of nations. Is anti-Zionism anti-Semitic? A noted Christian leader responded, "Not necessarily, but almost always."

In any event, whether one believes that the Messiah will be an individual or represents a visionary era, if Israel is morally strong, the Jewish people might conceivably be the heralds of a Messianic era.

ISRAELI–ARAB CONFLICTS

Confrontation between Arabs and Jews is not a new issue. Hostilities date back to the time of Muhammad in the seventh century c.e. when he attempted to forcibly convert the world to his new philosophy, particularly the Jews who lived in Arabia. Although there were intermittent periods—the Golden Age of Spain, for example—when Jews and Arabs lived together peacefully and prominent Jews such as Maimonides held high positions in Arab kingdoms, their underlying relationship was marked by centuries of warfare waged against Jewish communities. The clash between Arabs and Jews in the Middle East since the beginning of the twentieth century has been, I have always felt, less about acquisition of land than to thwart the Western influences and democratic ideas the Arabs feared would undermine their culture.

Some contend that Great Britain, the mandatory power, should have briefed Arab leaders more fully about the plans set forth in the pivotal Balfour Declaration of 1917, when Lord Balfour, then British Foreign Secretary, wrote to Lord Rothschild, head of British Jewry, stating the British government's support for "the establishment in Palestine of a national home for the Jewish people" and promising "to use their best endeavors to facilitate the achievement of this object." At the same time, the text indicated that it should be "clearly understood that nothing shall be done which may prejudice the civil and religious rights of the existing non-Jewish community."

Some Arab leaders did accept the intent of the Balfour Declaration. In 1919 Emir Feisel, Sherif of Mecca, wrote the following to Professor Felix Frankfurter: "We feel that the Arabs and Jews are cousins in race, having suffered similar oppression at the hands of powers stronger than themselves.... We Arabs, especially the educated among us, look with the deepest sympathy on the Zionist movement.... We wish the Jews a most hearty welcome home."

However, in 1921, the naming of Haj Amin al-Husseini—a man known for his hatred of the Jews—as *Mufti* (chief religious leader) of the Supreme Muslim Council proved disastrous. During his rule Arab leaders in Palestine instigated riots and launched murderous assaults against the *yishuv* (Jewish settlements)—such as in Jaffa, Rehovot, and Hadera in 1921; in Hebron in 1929, and in attacks from 1936 to 1939 in which hundreds of Jews were slaughtered.

During World War II, Arab leaders, for the greater part, lent their support to the Axis powers and not to the Allies.

As I reflect on the "ifs" of history, I wonder: If Great Britain had consulted with the Arabs in advance, would that have made a difference? If the British had earnestly tried to bring Arab and Jewish leaders together, would that effort have succeeded? Could conflict have been averted or mitigated and hundreds of thousands of lives, Arab and Jewish, been spared?

As Jews around the world vowed to reestablish a Jewish state in their ancient homeland, Arabs vowed to destroy it. The revelations of the fate of six million Jews during the Holocaust and the plight of thousands of surviving refugees languishing in displaced persons camps gave added urgency to the United Nations vote of November 29, 1947, to partition Palestine into two states, one to belong to the Jewish people and the other to the Arabs. The Jews accepted it, the Arabs did not. I can never forget dancing in joy in the streets of Jerusalem that day. Three days later Arabs attacked and burned Jewish stores in Jerusalem in midday. Within a few days I was recruited for the Haganah and assigned to the defense of Jerusalem.

When the Declaration of Independence of the State of Israel was signed on May 14, 1948, Israel reached out to her Arab neighbors in friendship, pleading with them to remain and live together with the Jewish people in peace and cooperation. This overture was immediately rejected and five Arab armies invaded Israel on the very day she came into being, boasting that Israel could readily be pushed into the sea; their anger intensified as Israel became stronger, but the hand of the Almighty prevailed. Many Arab inhabitants of the villages around the areas of combat fled to Jordan and adjacent Arab lands; the Arabs who remained became Israeli citizens.

In 1949 the first President of the State of Israel, Chaim Weizmann, stated, "The world will judge the Jewish state by its treatment of the Arabs." To this day there are many Arab-Israeli citizens (both Muslim and Christian) living in Israel. While their young sons and daughters are not required to serve in the Israeli armed forces, they participate in the political process and elect representatives to the Knesset.

I view the events as more than merely Arab-Jewish confrontations, however; I see them in the context of an ongoing effort by the Arab people to regain the hegemony of the Middle Ages when the Muslims captured the Iberian Peninsula and moved north across the Pyrenees into France to invade Europe and to dethrone their rival, Christianity. My fear is that this goal may still drive the Arab world and that the conflict will not remain localized in the Middle East. The Israelis know that their country is a buffer to Arab expansion. A strong Israel is absolutely essential for the security of Western civilization.

PEACE BETWEEN JEWISH AND MUSLIM COMMUNITIES

The world has failed to recognize the magnitude of the difficulties and perils that have always confronted Israel in her quest for peace. Israel as a nation has seldom experienced a sense of confidence in the words of her Arab neighbors. Two groups in particular, the Islamic Jihad and Hamas, have incited the Arab population to resort to violence and to destroy anything (and anyone) Jewish. Both groups have openly stated their avowed intentions to crush Israel and set up an Islamic state. The Palestine Liberation Organization had earlier declared that it would never recognize Israel's statehood, not even if the PLO were to set up its own independent state in the West Bank, nor would it ever allow Israel to live in peace. Libyan President Col. Muammar Qaddafi has stated: "Let the Jews choose another part of the world for their homeland. We do not want Jews living in Arab lands."

There is such fervor in the declaration of a holy war (*Jihad*) against Israel that it has almost become a religious tenet. The Hamas Manifesto has proclaimed that Jews have no political or historic roots in Palestine, that it is forbidden for anyone to concede any part of the land to them, and it decrees, "Kill them wherever you find them." But, according to Talmudic sages, "To hate Israel is to hate God. To rise against Israel is to rise against God. And to help Israel is to help God."

Some problems are seemingly intractable, and the Arab–Israeli conflict is certainly among them. Even though Israel is currently at peace with two of its neighbors, Egypt and Jordan, I believe it will require time and yet another generation to reach a peace agreement. But I also believe that, with patience, the day will come when genuine peace will be achieved, and what a glorious era that would be.

One of the main tasks facing Arab and Jewish young people is to learn how to channel their bitterness and enmity into friendship and cooperation. On one of my visits to Israel, my guide shared with me the comment of an Arab woman, "What do the Arab leaders want of us? We do not want war. I want my husband to go to work. I want him to come home in the evening and sit at the table and eat the food I prepared for him, and I want the children to grow up healthy and strong."

Imagine what a beautiful, fertile crescent there would be if Arab states and Israel shared their skills on ventures for the advancement of agriculture, medicine, industry, and the arts. Efforts in that direction are continually being developed by several organizations that sponsor a variety of joint Jewish–Arab activities, from sports and art to education and community service, for people of all ages and walks of life. One boy, Ahmed, admitted; "I was convinced that Jews hate us and I was happy to discover how nice they are to us and how well-behaved they are." Allen, 11 years old, confessed; "I thought Arab kids wore different clothes and ate weird food, but I discovered they are just like us."

On the other hand, members of my congregation shared with me a story about their visit to a similar community, where, during a cordial discussion, there was a jolting moment of candor when the head of an Arab school forthrightly stated that regrettably the Arab mentality and its vision of Arab nationalism would never accept Israel on equal terms. To those who assert that if only the current Arab–Israeli conflict can be resolved there might some day be true and lasting peace in the Middle East, I reply that it will not happen as long as extremists continue to preach hatred of each other.

LAND FOR PEACE?

Ask leading rabbinic authorities for a Talmudic interpretation of the *halakhic* question as to whether Israel can offer a territorial compromise if that leads to peace, and you will get varying answers. Some insist that whatever areas of the Holy Land have fallen into Israel's hands must forevermore remain the property of the Jewish people; others, equally committed, believe that whatever leads to a real and lasting peace should be explored. Two former Chief Rabbis, one Ashkenazic and the other Sephardic, issued a joint ruling forbidding territorial concessions, while another former Sephardic Chief Rabbi contends that the importance of saving lives supersedes the value of territory. Nevertheless, many fear that in time such a peace could potentially weaken Israel piece by piece.

- Would Jewish settlements in Judea and Samaria have to be dismantled and Jewish settlers removed?
- Would any plan include Jerusalem? Would that holy city once again be divided?

We have been taught by Rabbi Shimon Bar-Yochai that the Holy One gave the Jewish people three precious gifts—Torah, the Land of Israel and the world to come—and that all three can be acquired only through struggle and pain. How often the kings, subjected to constant invasion by their neighbors, would cry out, in the words of the Psalmist, "I am for peace and thus do I speak, while they are for war." Therefore, the monarchs were counseled to follow the dictum, "If you want peace, prepare for war." And so it is even today. Someone wryly described Israel's situation this way: Israel is a great country located in a bad neighborhood.

The projected visit by His Holiness Pope John Paul II to Jerusalem in the year 2000 has renewed Christian interest in the 4,000-year history of the city. It has long been considered by our rabbis as the spiritual center of the world; its name, Ir-Shalom, means "City of Peace." Anyone who has ever walked its streets must surely have had a feeling of *déjà vu*, of having been there before. So much of the world population is attached to Jerusalem by religious traditions: here the binding of Isaac took place; Jacob stopped here on his way to Mesopotamia and dreamed his famous dream of the ladder ascending to Heaven; David captured the city from the Jebusites; King Solomon built the magnificent

Temple on one of the city's seven hills. Holy to Christians is a site called Calvary, where the crucifixion took place; Muslim tradition ascribes that from the site of the Dome of the Rock Muhammad ascended to heaven.

An old legend tells of two brothers who lived on the sides of one of the hills of Jerusalem. One brother was a family man, the other a bachelor. Each was concerned about the welfare of the other and, unbeknown to each other, at nighttime each carried sacks of grain across the hill to help the other. One night they chanced to meet and understood the depth of their feelings. Heaven ordained that place as the site where the Temple would be built.

History has not granted this city a halcyon existence. Revered by the Jewish people as God's holiest place, it was to be sacked by the Babylonians, occupied by the Persians, conquered by the Greeks, torched by the Romans, attacked by the Crusaders, occupied by the Mamelukes, won by the Turks, captured by the British, and made an enclave by the United Nations. No place has been more fought over, anguished over, prayed for, or dreamed about than the city of Jerusalem.

What is it that makes Jerusalem so exciting? Is it the amalgam of cultures, customs, and garb, the blend of antiquity and modernity? Is it the diversity of a thousand and one languages reverberating in the hills? Some people say that we associate Haifa with commerce, Tel Aviv with lively entertainment, and Jerusalem with study, faith, and the search for the meaning of life. It is not only a city of hills and ridges, streets and buildings, but a place where people have left their hearts and their hopes for humanity. Thus we are bidden by the Psalmist, "... see the good of Jerusalem all the days of thy life."

Cities have souls, and few have captured my heart and soul as has the city of Jerusalem. I can still feel the thrill when first I saw Jerusalem, and how reverently I walked upon its soil. Something happens to me whenever I am in Jerusalem. There is a sense of inclusiveness. I remember seeing a little girl, beautifully dressed for the Shabbat, playing hopscotch by herself inside the walls of the Old City, and asking myself whether she was aware that she was playing at the center of the universe. There is no city like it. No wonder the Talmud comments, "The Holy One said: I will not enter the heavenly Jerusalem until I can enter the earthly Jerusalem."

The most challenging problem facing Israel on the world scene is whether Jerusalem will remain the undivided capital of Israel. The words of Prime Minister David Ben-Gurion in 1949 are still pertinent today:

> Jerusalem is the very heart of the State of Israel. We are proud that Jerusalem became holy to other religions, and we will certainly make all the necessary arrangements to ensure that adherents of other religions will be able to satisfy their religious needs in Jerusalem.... But we cannot conceive of the possibility that the United Nations should attempt to tear out Jerusalem from the State of Israel, or to strike at the sovereignty of Israel in her Eternal Capital.

Half a century later the State of Israel continues to grant autonomy to religious authorities of all denominations over their holy sites in Jerusalem and provides funds for their maintenance and renovations. Truly, this remarkable city is already international.

Ultimately, Israel's salvation will be hastened not by diplomatic negotiation, but rather by her commitment and adherence to the prophetic messages of righteousness, justice, and truth. If I were a member of the Knesset and obliged to cast a vote as to whether we should exchange land for peace, I would be guided by the midrashic tale of an encounter between the prophet Elijah and a farmer. The farmer was struggling with a profound question: "Which shall I love more, the Torah of Israel or the people of Israel?" The prophet answered the question by posing another question: "Which would you choose?" "The Torah," responded the farmer. "No," said the prophet, "if there be no people, who will study the Torah?" Applying this reasoning to the present conflict, reluctant as I may be to part with any of the land, I would nonetheless cast my vote in that direction, for what is of prime importance is the survival of our people in an Israel at peace. The unfortunate reality is that, given current Arab attitudes as expressed in their speeches and press, even this sacrifice would be no guarantee of peace. And therein lies the dilemma.

THE SPIRIT OF THE LAND

There is no vision for Israel the people without Israel the land. Yes, I know we existed for 2,000 years without a Jewish homeland, but do you really call dispersion, exile, persecution, discrimination, banishment, the Inquisition, and the Holocaust the kind of existence to be perpetuated? Rabbi Abraham Joshua Heschel once said: "When I go to Israel every stone and every tree is a reminder of hard labor and glory, of prophets and psalmists, loyalty and holiness. The Jews go to Israel not only for physical security for themselves and their children; they go to Israel for renewal."

Despite all its woes and problems, Israel is a country where enduring greatness is measured not by material things but by the gifts of the human spirit. I want a strong Israel—strong spiritually, socially, economically, and militarily—a great Israel, left in peace, flowing with the milk and honey of kindness and compassion.

One Friday afternoon in Jerusalem I sat on the steps of an outdoor promenade in the Talpiot section, where in 1947 I had been interrogated by the British looking for the perpetrators of a bomb blast. And now here I was, 40 years later, before Shabbat, listening to a concert by high school students while before me lay a sweeping panorama of old and new Jerusalem that had to be the most beautiful sight upon which I have ever laid my eyes. Surely heaven and earth must meet there. Many times since, I have reflected on the scene of the young, bare-headed musicians led by a teacher who wore a yarmulke. To me, the allegory was striking: the young men and women playing their instruments represent the nations of the world; the conductor is Israel, faithfully following the score, the Bible, creating harmony out of dissonance.

At the same time that Israel cherishes the heritage of the past, it has moved forward in areas of cultural and scientific achievement. According to UNESCO, Israel ranks second in the world in the number of books published per capita. It leads the world in the number of scientists and engineers working in research and development. Just as the nations of the world came to Joseph in Egypt at a time of severe famine, so they come to Israel today to benefit from her scientific expertise. Israel is a major producer and exporter of life-saving medical equipment used in the most advanced hospitals in the world. Tens of thousands of students from many countries, with or without diplomatic relations with Israel, have come to learn to farm and to fight disease and hunger. Israel is a leader in developing the uses of solar energy, and it has been lauded as "a world Internet superpower." But if there is no peace and the attention and resources of the country are diverted to warfare, yet another generation will suffer the consequences, ancient enmities will persist, and the future will be bleak for Israel, her people, and the world.

I can never forget a conversation with a minister in the lobby of the King David Hotel in Jerusalem. He was seated alone, and I thought I recognized him as someone from New York. Although it turned out we had not met before, I took the opportunity to ask how he was enjoying Israel. He enumerated several of the holy sites he had visited, and when I asked if he planned to visit Tel Aviv, Haifa, and some of the kibbutzim near Jerusalem, he answered curtly, "I did not come here to see political Zionism." What a contrast to the attitude of my good friends Rev. Dr. Jesse W. Stitt and Rev. Dr. Carl Hermann Voss, ardent Christian Zionists who loved Israel and understood her as the fulfillment of God's plan for the ingathering of His people from the four corners of the earth.

One Shabbat morning in Jerusalem, after services, I was invited to the home of then Chief Rabbi Isaac Halevy Herzog, father of the late President Chaim Herzog. The Rabbi related that a visitor on his way to Egypt to meet with President Nasser had asked whether the Rabbi had a message for Mr. Nasser. "Yes," said Rabbi Herzog, "take a look in the book of Isaiah, Chapter 19:24:

In that day shall Israel be the third with Egypt and Assyria, a blessing in the midst of the earth."

RELIGION AND POLITICS

Few issues in Jewish life in recent years have generated such emotional and passionate discussions as the question, *Mi Yehudi*? Who is a Jew? particularly as it relates to Israel's Law of Return, which grants every Jew the right to take up residence and automatically become a citizen of the State of Israel. Why then the outcry over clarifying the status of who is a Jew by the Chief Rabbinate of Israel?

According to Jewish legal law (*Halakhah*) a Jew is one who is either born of a Jewish mother or has formally accepted the faith of Judaism. Although early Judaism may have developed along patrilineal lines, by the time of Ezra and Nehemiah, in about 546 B.C.E., the sages had stipulated that the line of descent be matrilineal, since it is universally accepted that a child's mother is recognized more readily than its father.

As for embracing the faith of Judaism, the rabbis developed a procedure for conversion to Judaism: application (expression of sincerity of intent), preparation (study), examination by a Bet Din (religious court), and solemnization. Over the years the Chief Rabbinate of Israel has called attention to deviations in the process of conversion, particularly on the part of some liberal rabbis, such as not requiring *mikveh* (immersion in water) and circumcision, and accepting patrilineal descent. The Orthodox rabbinate fears that differing standards will cause confusion and division in the household of Israel.

The problem is further aggravated by the fact that even when a Bet Din of Reform, Conservative, or Reconstructionist rabbis adheres strictly to the *halakhic* requirements, and many do, the Orthodox rabbinate of Israel refuses to recognize the validity of their conversions because it does not accept their status as rabbis. It claims exclusive authority in this area. What is desperately needed is a willingness to work out a solution whereby the requirements for conversion are standardized and acceptable to all. There is no reason why this cannot be achieved in an atmosphere of mutual respect. It will not be easy, but then nothing of supreme value is easily attainable.

While I have high respect for the Orthodox rabbinate, I have long believed that there should be no religious political parties, for in politics elected officials are often required to make concessions, solicit deals, and sometimes bend truth for the sake of compromise. Religious leaders and organizations ought not to be involved in political wrangling.

I would much rather see the rabbinate put emphasis on instructing the people on the laws, judgments, and statues of Torah and on the spirit and words of our prophets. If the Orthodox rabbinate in Israel demands total supervision over life-cycle events, let its leaders at least stop denigrating rabbis from other branches of Judaism, and let them decry the frequent lack of civility in speech. Let them instruct their followers to cease throwing stones on Shabbat, an action that only desecrates the very day they want to sanctify, and let them seek ways to accommodate all who wish to worship at the Western Wall and not turn them away in anger and tears. It is extremely important for the rabbinate to maintain the dignity that befits servants of the Lord.

I surely do not want Israel to be just another Levantine state displaying her flag at the United Nations. When I left Jerusalem in 1948, I returned to America convinced that the land, which has been the cradle of religious civilization, now had new spiritual tasks to perform, to become, as in ancient days, a beacon of morality, ethics, and humanity, with a concern and love for all people.

I pray that the future of the land of Israel will be based upon the precepts of the Torah and teachings of the prophets. I pray that Israel will be a leader among nations in providing food for the hungry, care for the displaced, shelter for the homeless, healing for the sick, and rehabilitation for the downtrodden. I pray that Israel will forever represent all that is noble in both the principle and application of people's humanity toward each other.

I believe that if the people of Israel live righteously, the nations of the world will learn to live righteously.

I believe that if Israel is strong and has peace, the nations of the world will attain peace.

I believe with Theodor Herzl, father of the modern State of Israel, who prophesied in his book *The Jewish State* that "the world will be freer by our liberty, richer by our wealth, greater by our greatness."

Because I am a Jew I believe that *"Am Israel Chai."* Israel *lives.* Israel *must* live. Israel *will* live.

As Israel celebrates her 50th anniversary of independence, let us proclaim the traditional blessing recited on a special occasion:

Baruch ata Adoshem, Elokeinu melech ha-olam, shehecheyanu, vekiy-manu, vehigianu lazman hazeh.

Blessed art Thou, O Lord our God, King of the universe, who has kept us in life, sustained us and enabled us to reach this season.

Even the Trees Are Jewish

When I was working on a kibbutz in the Galilee in the summer of 1947, a father came from the United States to implore his son to return home. An older son was also in Palestine and therefore none of the children was at home. The three of us—the father, the younger son, and I—had lunch together in the kibbutz outdoor cafe, where the fish served were selected on order from our own ponds.

After lunch we sat on a small patch of coarse grass and the young man said, "Dad, look at this grass." Then he pointed to the mountains in the distance, "Dad, look at those mountains!" His father responded hastily, "If you come back, I'll give you all the mountains you wish—the White Mountains, the Green Mountains, the Allegheny Mountains." His son continued, "Look at those trees, Dad!" We gazed at the scrawny trees, hardly anything to boast about, and his father replied, "I'll give you the Endless Mountains and all the trees of the Catskills if that's what you want." His son countered: "Dad, you don't understand. This is our grass, these are our mountains, and these are our trees—they belong to the Jewish people."

16

Summing Up

"Brotherhood—Still the Hope of the World."

IRVING J. BLOCK

No one book, especially one that combines memoir and history, can adequately portray a person's emotional and psychological reaction to problems and situations, for there is no way to predict the issues that will confront us in life; I have always sought to rely on my principles and my ideals.

One's philosophy of life is like the rudder of a ship steering through the currents of daily living. I have also been guided by a series of moral and ethical beacons that have enabled me to proceed toward goals, both defined and undefined, and to decide and respond to a host of important matters in my personal life and in my rabbinic career.

I cannot pinpoint the exact moment when I decided to become a rabbi. I struggled with that decision all through my college years, my war experiences, and even into the early months of rabbinical school. For some the rabbinate is a calling, for others it is a conviction; for me it is essentially a commitment of service to God. Perhaps there was an inner voice of conscience that probed, "Yisrael ben Pesach, where art thou?" and I responded, *"Hineni."* Here I am.

Here is what I believe with all my heart, the guidelines on which my rabbinate is based: There is but one God, and no matter what one's faith, color, creed, or background, the image of God is imprinted on all of us. We are all born with equal promise of God's love, and no one has an advantage over another. Every individual is unique, and none is like any other. As Jews, our mission in life is to teach by precept and example that there is a God in the world, and therefore we are obligated to respect each individual and promote a climate of understanding so that we may all live in dignity.

I believe with the Hasidim that each human being possesses a divine spark, and that to live in harmony requires us to bring these sparks together. My rabbinic career has been driven by just such a desire to bring together the sparks in people of different faiths and races. That is why very early in my rabbinate I established a bond with the Black Jewish community in Harlem, why our congregation took a leadership role in the efforts to rescue Ethiopian Jewry, why we have sought to communicate with our Christian and Islamic brethren, why we seized the opportunity to teach seminarians from the General Theological Seminary to see the world through Jewish eyes.

I have also been guided by the rabbinic philosophy of *gam zu l'tovah* (this, too, is for the good), analogous to the Emersonian law of compensation that it is possible to derive an advantage from what is seemingly a disadvantage. I try to see the bright side of whatever happens and benefit from each encounter with life; I believe there are events in life that are *bashert* (providential), that we have to leave a little for God to do and that *Ha-Shem* will provide answers. And how often I have understood the wisdom of the saying that what the mind cannot resolve, time eventually does.

I believe that the Torah and our liturgy belong to all generations, past, present and future, and I painfully question the widespread practice of congregations that charge for worship at the High Holyday season. The right to pray is an inheritance which belongs to the rich and poor alike. At The Brotherhood Synagogue our doors are open to all. As the Psalmist joyfully acclaimed, "In the midst of the congregation, I will bless God."

I believe it is better to be a shepherd than a *nach-shlepper*, a leader rather than a follower, to pioneer new areas of congregational activity rather than constantly borrow ideas from other congregations whose membership and needs may be different.

I believe in harmonizing diverse and even conflicting viewpoints rather than adamantly holding to a fixed position and refusing to discuss the matter further. I feel that we must not only fulfill our obligations to the letter of the law, but go beyond to the very spirit of the law, for therein we will find the paths to peace. When perplexed about resolving a problem for which there are various valid solutions, I would choose the one that provides a long-term advantage over a short-term response and that most expresses confidence in God's faithfulness.

I believe that the House of God must be a sanctuary of warmth, of friendship, and of love, where the holy must never be profaned nor any wrong sanctified. It has been observed that a community's greatest joy is to erect a synagogue, because historically the generations of Israel are renewed by their congregations. The important question is, "What is the nature of an ideal synagogue?"

I believe that every synagogue should be maintained as beautifully as if it were a king's palace—it is after all, God's house. In planning the new Ark to commemorate our congregation's 40th anniversary in 1994, the designer, Ismar David, selected the finest craftsmen and beautiful rare woods. While giving emphasis to the holiness of the Torah, the Ark embodies spirituality and enhances not only the sanctuary, but every aspect of religious life for our congregation.

I believe it is the obligation of the rabbi to develop the art of listening and to distinguish between what people want and what they really need. A rabbi must also assume the mantle of a prophet, challenging and exhorting in the name of the Lord. I was always cognizant that the preacher does not speak *for* the congregation but rather *to* the congregation.

I believe that a synagogue must be deeply committed to the neighborhood of which it is a part, and that The Brotherhood Synagogue came to Gramercy Park by the hand of God, destined to play an important role in the life of our community and city. I have always believed that the Jewish people have made and will continue to make remarkable contributions to their communities and that the world desperately needs us to set the standards for life. Therefore, I implore all members of the Jewish community to support the synagogue in their neighborhood so that our children will be steeped in the teachings of the Torah to ensure the future of Judaism for generations to come.

While people may often be impressed by the size of a synagogue's membership, attendance at services, and the number of children in the religious school—and rabbis like to state with pride that they serve a large congregation—after more than four decades I know deep down that size makes no difference as long as the hearts of the congregants are directed toward heaven.

Yes, houses of worship need funds to maintain their buildings and carry out their programs, and we should respect all efforts by the committees that work gladly and ardently to raise funds. However, what is more important is the members' sense of commitment to Judaism. People affiliate with a synagogue not because it has a balanced budget but because of its compassion and concern for congregants and the community alike, and its commitment to the survival of the Jewish people. I have always been proud of the members of our congregation for their loyal support of our pioneering programs.

A synagogue should strike a balance between the traditions of the past and a modern outlook. It should hear the plaintive cry of the disabled, assist them in every possible way, and be a place to find the inspiration to cope with the vicissitudes of daily living.

A synagogue should be a place where friendships are formed and where people truly feel at home, "a place where the doors will be open wide for anyone who has no one," as one of our members commented, reflecting on her own life.

A synagogue should reflect and exemplify the qualities of individuals who speak quietly and walk humbly with the Lord, and who stretch out a hand to the less fortunate among us. The Brotherhood Synagogue has been and, God willing, will forever be, such a sanctuary.

The physical esthetics of a synagogue reflect the approach of its architect. The spiritual strength of the congregation comes from its rabbi, who sets the tone for the congregation and whose task it is to ensure that God's house is worthy of its position of centrality in the community and that it responds to issues in the broader Jewish community and in the world beyond.

Synagogue leaders must be committed to the furtherance of Jewish education, for in learning we find the secret to the survival of the Jewish people. They must also be committed to the State of Israel, both by personal involvement and by a sense of history.

The question is often asked: Why join a synagogue? For one thing, the synagogue is the institution around which everything else revolves. You join because the synagogue gives emphasis to the importance of prayer, study, and community, each of which maintains the integrity of our people and ensures our survival.

Many have called our congregation their home away from home, and through their affiliation they have become aware that Judaism is a glorious heritage.

You also join because of a need for fellowship, *chavruso*. It is in the synagogue where new friendships are made and old ones strengthened, where you can find opportunities to perform many *mitzvot*. Where else can you find men and women who were strangers a short time ago now filling a void in the lives of others? It is a fellowship that brings forth sacrifices such as taking someone who is alone to the hospital at 5:30 in the morning, and helping others ease pain and loneliness by visiting, preparing meals, shopping, and even arranging for medical care. I am proud that we have been called the friendliest synagogue in town.

Could I have done things better and accomplished more? Assuredly. Many aspire to reach new heights, but few attain their ultimate goals. The men and women who joined with me in establishing our Synagogue were pioneers, and I am grateful for their confidence in me. I am exceedingly proud to have had the opportunity to represent Judaism and the Jewish people on radio and nationwide television and in my travels with the Reverend Dr. Stitt, as we sought to explain the dimensions of our venture. Many have said that the bond between us, and particularly the example of the lay leaders and members of our two congregations working together in the community, inspired major changes in Christian–Jewish relationships and attitudes.

Throughout the years I have been asked to perform interfaith marriages, and I know full well that for many couples Cupid overrides conviction. But from the onset of my rabbinate, I elected to perform only weddings that were in accordance with Jewish law, and I did not make referrals to colleagues whose practice was different. Although I understand their reasoning, their decision contravenes my own approach.

We live in a democracy where every adult is free to make decisions about religious affiliation. While some in the Jewish community have embraced other faiths, there have been an increasing number of conversions *to* Judaism. I have been privileged to convert approximately five to seven new adherents to Judaism each year; when that number is multiplied by 40 years in the rabbinate, that is a sizable number. Our losses have been more than offset by our gains.

In a long career there are bound to be regrets for goals not attained. In spite of the fine education offered by synagogues in after-school programs, I believe that many of our children should have the advantage of a more intensive Hebrew education. I regret that I was unable to establish a Hebrew day school in our community.

Time has brought about many changes and new directions in religious communities everywhere. The walls of isolation and separation among the faiths have been tumbling down, and in the past half century religious leaders have developed a compelling urge to work with one another. Call it brotherhood, interfaith, ecumenism, whatever name you choose; it reflects the growing awareness on the part of clergy that God wants us to live together in harmony. I regret that I never had the opportunity to establish a formal consultation center for clergy and others to work together in an ecumenical setting.

There has also been a metamorphosis in the Jewish community that has considerably affected the role and functions of the rabbi. For centuries the rabbi had been the judge and arbiter, the prominent voice of the community. Recognizable by his distinguished appearance and distinctive attire, he was the teacher and spiritual overseer, friend and confidant. In the United States added duties were thrust upon the rabbi: administrator, public relations expert, fund-raiser and envoy to the non-Jewish world. In the last 25 years scores of women have been ordained by the Reform, Conservative, and Reconstructionist movements. They are knowledgeable, sincere, and committed rabbis who have certainly been bringing changes to the landscape of Jewish life.

Regrettably, however, too much attention is being given to the divisions of Judaism—Orthodox, Conservative, Reform, Reconstructionist—to such an extent that the focus seems to be more on the categories than on the unity of the Jewish people. I am never at ease with emphasis on divisions; to me a Jew is a Jew regardless of the traditions and rites he or she practices. I have never seen a cemetery monument bearing the inscription, "Here lies a true Reform Jew," "Conservative Jew," or "Orthodox Jew," but I have seen inscriptions reading, "Here lies one who loved humanity."

Over the years I have been blessed by friendships I have made with rabbis, priests, and ministers—trailblazers in ecumenism—with whom I worked, as together we sought new frontiers in faith. Because we stressed brotherhood among religions, I never heard anti-Christian remarks from students in The Brotherhood Synagogue Religious School, nor anti-Jewish remarks from other children who saw the example of our Synagogue and churches working together. On the contrary, in their Bar and Bat Mitzvah speeches many young people have cited the activities of our Synagogue in the community, even the slogan on our stationery: "Brotherhood—Still the Hope of the World."

I love Israel, and I am also a proud American. I volunteered for military service in World War II, have gladly served veterans' organizations, and always urged my congregants to participate in the electoral process. It was a thrill to be invited to offer the opening prayer at a session of the House of Representatives and to stand at the same rostrum where Presidents and world leaders address the nation.

Although I had served in the United States Army during World War II, I still regret that I did not accept an offer to serve as chaplain in the U.S. Naval Reserve. My high school yearbook records that I hoped to have a career as a naval officer. The invitation to become a chaplain in the Naval Reserve came at a time when I was already fully engaged in building our Synagogue. When I finally felt ready to take on this added assignment, I no longer qualified because of the age restriction. (I was "too old!")

Forty-five years in the rabbinate have come and gone, years filled with wonderful events, not only major projects but small, unnumbered acts of kindness and friendship, which ultimately are the true measurement of love. One of the great joys of serving a congregation over a long period of time has been the warm relationships I developed with many families. As their rabbi, I have shared in the joys of the birth of their offspring, rejoiced at the celebration of the Bar and Bat Mitzvah of their sons and daughters, and solemnized the weddings of their children, and even their grandchildren, and consoled them in times of illness and sorrow. I have had the privilege of naming grandchildren, and officiating at the Bar Mitzvah of the son of a member whose own Bar Mitzvah I had conducted many years earlier. So attached have my wife and I become to some families, and they to us (even for three, and in a few instances four generations), that there is hardly a life-cycle occasion that we have not shared.

The most joyful moment of my life was undoubtedly my marriage in 1964 to Phyllis Susan Robinove, whose family I had known from my days as a rabbinical student. Our wedding ceremony brought together literally hundreds of members, family, friends, community leaders, and colleagues of all backgrounds. I have been blessed with a wife of outstanding qualities, in whom character and intellect blend beautifully. She holds a Ph.D. from Columbia University and is a member of Phi Beta Kappa. In addition to all her attributes, she possesses excellent writing and editorial skills (she was a senior editor in a large publishing house), which she graciously contributed to the congregation for more than 30 years as editor of our Synagogue bulletin and the annual Memorial Book, bringing professionalism to those publications, and she also chaired the Library Committee. Phyllis is an excellent conversationalist and always befriended newcomers to the Synagogue and made them feel at home. In so many quiet ways her involvement and ideas have contributed to the success of The Brotherhood Synagogue. And I must also admit that many of my best sermons reflect her suggestions and insight. God truly blessed me with an ideal helpmate.

As parents we are immensely proud of our son, Herbert, born during Passover in 1965. His warmth and friendliness toward people of all backgrounds and his community activities reveal his sense of humanity. Although he had not considered entering the rabbinate, his mother often says that he and I are going in the same direction, but by different paths. His passion for politics led to his being appointed as a summer Page in the House of Representatives, and after college he served in high echelons of New York City government. Yet he never hesitated to assist at our Synagogue, rehearsing with Bar and Bat Mitzvah students and serving as *Bal Koreh* (Torah reader) and *Bal T'kiah* (shofar blower)

for ten years. Surely the most unforgettable moment of my retirement years was to co-officiate in the summer of 1996 at Herbert's
wedding to Judith Greenberg, a daughter of Dr. and Mrs. Marshall
Greenberg of New Haven, Connecticut who, by sheer coincidence, have known members of my family for many years.

At the annual meeting of our congregation on April 19, 1994,
my associate, Rabbi Daniel Alder, was joyously and unanimously
confirmed as my successor. A native of California, he is a graduate of Stanford University in biological sciences. After studying in
Israel, he continued his rabbinical training at the Jewish
Theological Seminary, where he was ordained in 1989. But he has
been with The Brotherhood Synagogue since 1988, first as a student rabbi, and he has won the respect of the congregation for
his scholarship, his compassionate manner, and his skills as a
teacher.

In handing to Rabbi Alder the gavel with which to open and
close the annual meetings, I read aloud an "open letter" to him:

> I was your age when I began the congregation, so that puts us on a
> par, but, as I have said so many times, no one individual singularly
> establishes a congregation. It is rather a composite of many voices
> and ideas. You know the verse, "The voice is the voice of Jacob, but
> the hand is the hand of Esau." To many the voice has appeared to be
> my voice in founding the congregation, but the truest efforts which
> fashioned and shaped the congregation were made by many others.
>
> Who ever said being a rabbi is an easy task? Sometimes I feel that
> being a rabbi is like being mayor of a city; there are so many problems
> that test your stamina, your skill, your patience, and your soul. I
> know, as you do, that we are primarily scholars and teachers, expo-
> nents of the Torah and exemplars of Jewish life. So, remember the
> phrase in *Ethics of the Fathers*, "Make God's will your will so that God
> may make your will His will." By your faith in the Almighty you reveal
> your strength.

You will be working very closely with members of the Board of Trustees, who possess enormous talents and a wide variety of experiences, and who will be eager to share their ideas with you—sometimes I feel almost a little too eagerly. It must be a symbiotic relationship. You cannot succeed without them and they will need your guidance. The Board is responsible for the financial strength of the congregation, and without that strength you cannot go forward. A word to the wise: try to cooperate and work well with them, because they have a veto power over all actions.

On the other hand, this is not an industrial corporation, nor a business establishment, but a synagogue. Balancing the budget should not be the ultimate priority. Leading with the heart must be. Therefore, I encourage you to realize that you, too, have veto powers, and when there is a decision or action which is not consonant with the aims of the Synagogue, or with the best in Jewish tradition, speak your mind without hesitancy, because you probably have God on your side.

Remember, our congregation has achieved a national reputation, and it is incumbent upon you to carry on the work and the philosophy of the Synagogue with compassion and love. You have a marvelous homiletic ability with which to teach Judaism. So, let your decisions be guided by the religious way of thinking and strive constantly for peace, because if there is peace in the midst of the congregation, then any error or injustice can easily be rectified.

You may wonder why I have had the honor of presiding at the annual congregational meeting. I am guided by the Religious Corporation laws of the State of New York, which mandate me to do so. But even more than presenting the gavel to you, I transmit to you the most fervent prayers and good wishes of the congregation, and, in the admonition of the prophet Malachi (2:7), "For the priest's lips should keep knowledge, and they should seek the law at his mouth for he is the messenger of the Lord of hosts."

I once visited a member of our congregation in a hospital. "Rabbi," he asked me, "what's new at the Synagogue?" I proceeded to tell him all the details and problems I had been coping with daily. "I don't mean that," he said, "I mean what will be new in the synagogue ten or fifteen years from now." His question made me wonder how I would convey to my colleagues the direction I would like to see houses of worship take. It is not enough to say that I have some thoughts for today. What will be my legacy for tomorrow?

In his retirement sermon Rev. Dr. Stitt said he hoped that the concept of a covenant of brotherhood would serve as an example of what congregations of different faiths can accomplish together. Otherwise, his ministry would have been "in vain."

Leo E. Williams, one of the first Presidents of our Synagogue, stated, "Imagine if you will the great contribution to a better world, a happier world, if we had not one, but hundreds of Brotherhood Synagogues and Brotherhood Councils in the United States." This was the vision we shared as our congregation began its relationship with the Village Presbyterian Church in 1954. We pledged ourselves to a program of brotherhood that we hoped would some day become a model for communities throughout our country.

When we began, our efforts were often brushed aside as a wild adventure or, less harshly, as simply an interesting pilot project. Time, however, proved otherwise. In the almost twenty years I worked with Dr. Stitt, people spoke of our work with admiration and respect, and wherever we shared our story, the response was warm and enthusiastic. Our accomplishments were hailed by a New Jersey rabbi as the "avant-garde of American religious life," and a Christian lay leader commented, "This is truly brotherhood on the grass-roots level of American democracy."

For a long time religious leaders of different faiths ignored one another; then they began talking about one another. Finally, they came to realize they must talk *to* one another. Today dialogues between religious groups are held everywhere, here and abroad, as theologians try to catch up.

Let me underscore one point: Dr. Stitt and I often stated that it was not essential that congregations share the same facilities and physical property in order to emulate our example. What we emphasized was the need to cultivate a profound friendship and collaborative efforts with one another, as set forth in "Our Covenant of Brotherhood":

> We engage ourselves to do whatsoever the hand findeth to do for human welfare, without preference for or prejudice to race, creed or color.
>
> We undertake this endeavor before God to the end that the truth of universal brotherhood may be established in full measure upon the earth, and man's responsibility to man be accepted as the mandate of God.
>
> We moreover pledge that all our activities and programs jointly sponsored and implemented are to be undertaken without compromise to the religious conscience or the established traditions of our respective congregations.

This Covenant was unique in the annals of church and synagogue relations. Someone said about me at the time, "Where does this young rabbi get the *chutzpah* to do something which should have been done by religious leaders long ago?" I am not sure whether it was *chutzpah*. To me it was simply a matter of putting religion into action. I was fortunate to have become friends with a minister who was willing to pioneer a new approach to religious life.

The first seventeen years of our Synagogue represented a rich encounter between two faiths. I still miss the excitement of those years, and I hope and pray that the concept of the Covenant of Brotherhood will inspire and shape religious developments in years to come. I would hope that I have deepened the understanding of what God's house can be so that all who enter the Synagogue can say as did the Psalmist, "I love Thy dwelling place where Thy glory rests."

Have I succeeded? I leave that judgment to others. Heaven will have to decide whether I was a good messenger and a true witness for God. I remember a frail lady dressed in black who, following my talk at a Catholic church, took hold of my hand and gave it a kiss as she would have done for a Cardinal. Another comment touched my heart deeply, from a man who had long isolated himself from Jewish life but enjoyed discussing theology with me: "You made me proud to be a Jew."

I have been enormously moved by the gracious remarks of so many members and friends upon my retirement, among them that our work had brought honor to the Jewish people; that our Synagogue is a "pacesetter"; that I have been an important influence in their lives; and by the words of a young boy of five in our school, who told me, "Rabbi, I'm really, really going to miss you."

Let me sum up by quoting lines from a poem by Ernest Crosby, "The Search":

> *Nobody could tell me*
> *Where my soul might be.*
> *I sought for God,*
> *But God eluded me.*
> *I sought my brother out,*
> *And found all three.*

Addendum

PRESIDENTS OF THE BROTHERHOOD SYNAGOGUE
1954–1998

Prof. Leon Brody
William Cohen
Malcolm Davis (1997-)
Inge Dobelis
Dr. Bernard Esrig
Gerald J. Friedman, M.D.
Vertella Gadsden
Ben Hanft
Mortimer Kane
David S. Lande
Marvin Levy
Irwin Magerfield
Prof. Julius J. Marke
Herbert Plaut
Hinda Potenz
Louis Rivkin
Louis H. Solomon
Irving Statsinger
Howard D. Westrich
Leo E. Williams

RABBIS AND CANTORS
1954–1998

Rabbi Irving J. Block, Founding Rabbi (Emeritus 1994)

Assistant and Associate Rabbis
Rabbi Leo Storozum
Rabbi A. Allen Block
Rabbi Leonard Bronstein
Rabbi S. Daniel Breslauer
Rabbi Alvin Wainhaus
Rabbi Daniel Alder
(named successor in 1994)

Cantor Leib Mirkovic (Emeritus 1974)
Cantor Jay Corn
Cantor Ira Fein
Cantor Stephen Cassell
Cantor Herman Diamond (Emeritus 1994)
Cantor Shiya Ribowsky (1994-)

Executive Directors
Martin Warmbrand
Sol Schulman
Phillip Rothman (1981-)